CONSTITUTING
CENTRAL AMERICAN–AMERICANS

Latinidad

Transnational Cultures in the United States

Matt Garcia, Series Editor, Professor of Latin American,
Latino and Caribbean Studies, and History, Dartmouth College

This series publishes books that deepen and expand our understanding of Latina/o populations, especially in the context of their transnational relationships within the Americas. Focusing on borders and boundary-crossings, broadly conceived, the series is committed to publishing scholarship in history, film and media, literary and cultural studies, public policy, economics, sociology, and anthropology. Inspired by interdisciplinary approaches, methods, and theories developed out of the study of transborder lives, cultures, and experiences, these titles enrich our understanding of transnational dynamics.

For a list of titles in the series, see the last section of the book.

CONSTITUTING CENTRAL AMERICAN– AMERICANS

Transnational Identities and the Politics of Dislocation

MARITZA E. CÁRDENAS

RUTGERS UNIVERSITY PRESS

New Brunswick, Camden, and Newark, New Jersey, and London

Library of Congress Cataloging-in-Publication Data

Names: Cardenas, Maritza E., author.
Title: Constituting Central American-Americans : transnational identities and the
   politics of dislocation / Maritza E. Cardenas.
Description: New Brunswick, New Jersey : Rutgers University Press, [2018] | Series:
   Latinidad: transnational cultures in the United States | Includes bibliographical
   references and index.
Identifiers: LCCN 2017035055 | ISBN 9780813592831 (cloth : alk. paper) | ISBN
   9780813592824 (pbk. : alk. paper) | ISBN 9780813592848 (epub) | ISBN
   9780813592862 (Web PDF) | ISBN 9780813592855 (mobi)
Subjects: LCSH: Central American Americans—Ethnic identity. | Central
   Americans—United States—Social life and customs. | Hispanic Americans—
   Ethnic identity.
Classification: LCC E184.C34 C37 2018 | DDC 305.868/073—dc23
LC record available at https://lccn.loc.gov/2017035055

A British Cataloging-in-Publication record for this book is available from the British
Library.

∞ The paper used in this publication meets the requirements of the American
National Standard for Information Sciences—Permanence of Paper for Printed
Library Materials, ANSI Z39.48-1992.

www.rutgersuniversitypress.org

Manufactured in the United States of America

For Jude, Winnie, and my abuelita Cruz

CONTENTS

CONSTITUTING
CENTRAL AMERICAN–AMERICANS

INTRODUCTION

Today, some of us of Central American background are becoming scholars. With more Central American programs we will be writing our own
literature, form our own discourse, shape our own culture, and forge our
own identity.

> —Nora Hamilton and Norma Stoltz Chinchilla,
> "Identity Formation among Central American Americans"

We are often asked why we want to distinguish ourselves as Central Americans. Why not just join or blend into other cultural and political movements
that have more established visibility and community support? Many of us
are a part of community spaces where we work as a part of or in solidarity
with communities of color, queer folks, immigrants and educators. But we
feel the need to create a space of our own U.S. Central American voices,
which are still rarely heard.

> —Maya Chinchilla, "Welcome to Epicentroamerica: An Anthology"

In her seminal work, *Ethnic Labels, Latino Lives* (1995), Suzanne
Oboler explores the complex ways in which individuals of Latin American
descent (dis)identify with ethnoracial categories in the United States. Oboler's
work is of particular importance for Central American scholars, as it was one
of the first to feature the perspectives of three different Central Americans living in New York: Charles, a self-identified Garifuna from Honduras; Dolores
from Guatemala; and Rosa from El Salvador. Oboler notes that these "new"
immigrants, along with others, tend to reject the label Hispanic (and perhaps,
by extension, Latina/o).[1] Among some of the reasons provided for the rejection
of this term are the respondents' socioeconomic backgrounds and racial preju-
dices, as well as the social value and negative connotations Anglo-American
culture has imposed on the label Hispanic. While these factors certainly contributed to the respondents' refusal to employ "Hispanic" as an ethnic designation,
Oboler's possible explanations do not acknowledge the fact that some subjects

in the isthmus had already adopted an alternative supraethnic mode of identification. Rosa's response exemplifies this phenomenon: when asked whether she sees herself as "Hispanic," she answered, "No, I don't. I'm Central American . . . So when someone asks me what I am, I say I'm Salvadorean. I'm Central American from El Salvador."[2] Rosa's response is noteworthy for its rejection of the pan-ethnic category "Hispanic" in favor of a (trans)regional identity, "Central American," and a (trans)national one, "Salvadorean." Here, regional identity refers to a place-based mode of identification—one that emerges from discourses about the geography, nature, and culture of a particular space.[3] Though regional and national identities share some similar attributes, the latter is usually (though not always) connected to a nation-state whereby subjects identify with a political and cultural community within a bounded territory. Given Rosa's multiple loci of enunciation, we might view both identity labels as operating on a transnational scale as well, since as Linda Basch et al. argue, migrants who develop subjectivities embedded in "networks of relationships that connect them simultaneously to two or more nation-states" have transnational identities even if they "rarely identify themselves as transnational."[4] In this example, we see that Rosa oscillates between using regional and national terms as a primary axis of identification. She initially positions herself within a broader collective, "Central American," then later proclaims that she is "Salvadorean," and finally concludes by stating that she is a "Central American from El Salvador." Such ordering suggests that Rosa might equally value her Central American identity as she does her national one. Her answer therefore reveals not only the ways in which some subjects from the isthmus adopt multiscalar forms of identification but also how they often disidentify with other categories such as "Latina/o," or in this case, "Hispanic."

While Rosa in New York asserted her Central American–Salvadoran identity, on the West Coast of the United States, a flourishing of institutions, community organizations, university student groups, and everyday individuals had already begun to use "Central American" as an ethnic organizing principle and mode of identification.[5] Perhaps the most visible assertion of this phenomenon emerged from the Central American United Student Association (CAUSA), a student group at the California State University, Northridge (CSUN). Formed in 1990 with the objective of producing social and institutional spaces that catered to Central American students on the CSUN campus, in 1993, CAUSA began lobbying for a Central American Studies program (CAS), and they finally achieved that goal in 2000 with the help of Movimiento Estudiantil Chicano de Aztlán (MEChA) and Chicana/o Studies faculty. In many ways, the formation of CAS was a watershed moment since cultural entities like CAS and CAUSA are integral to creating and fostering the notion of a common Central American identity.[6] The fact that a group of disparate students from various national backgrounds came together and not only created their own student group under the rubric "Central American" but, in addition, lobbied to create an academic program under that name highlights the usage of a new type of diasporic ethnic sociocultural subject that has entered the U.S. American lexicon of identity politics and is the focus of this book: Central American.

Indeed, the development of spaces like CAS by students self-identifying as Central American challenged the then prevalent notion of a "lack of [Central American] identity politics," as well as dichotomies often promulgated in Latina/o discourse.[7] Within Latinidad, modes of identification have been presented in a dyadic form and within a hierarchal system of preference. It is generally presumed that subjects who rely on a particular ethnocultural identification will choose the local-national (e.g., Puerto Rican or Chicana/o) or the larger pan-ethnic category of Latina/o.[8] Juan Flores succinctly articulates this notion when he proclaims that there is an "important stake in upholding the specifics of one's own nationality and a strong sense that 'if I'm Latino or Hispanic, then I am Dominican, or Puerto Rican, or Mexican American first,'" and "consciously and intuitively, personally and collectively, Puerto Ricans, Mexicans, Cubans and Dominicans, and each of the other groups most often project their own respective national backgrounds as a first and primary axis of identity."[9] Consequently, one either chooses their particular national community or, when in need of political visibility, usurps the pan-ethnic identity of Latina/o.

With this in mind, we can see how the self-designation of "Central American" by subjects throughout the United States can be read as a rejection of this Latina/o dyad. In the case of CAUSA, for instance, rather than opting to imagine themselves as part of a larger community formation by unifying under the term *Latina/o*, or positioning themselves within a more specific national subgroup like Guatemalan or Honduran, they asserted an alternative option. The construction of a Central American identity in the U.S. diaspora problematizes this dichotomy between the national and pan-ethnic and also undermines the notion that the category of Latina/o encapsulates the social experiences of U.S. Central Americans. William Flores and Rina Benmayor have suggested that Latinidad as a rubric can provide a type of "cultural citizenship," which functions as an alternative form of belonging for subjects who are usually excluded from U.S. American discourses of culture and citizenship.[10] The use of "Central American" as an identity marker then takes on greater magnitude since one must also consider the fact that it emerged after the category of Hispanic or Latina/o came into prominence.[11]

The examples of Rosa, CAS, and CAUSA therefore reveal that for some subjects within the temporal demarcation designated as the "Hispanic era" (post 1980s), the shift toward using "Hispanic" or "Latina/o" as labels did not usher an immediate mode of identification but instead enabled the production of another mode. An isthmus-based identity seems to offer these subjects a tactical speaking position, a means to claim political and cultural visibility that other signifiers like "Latina/o" or "Nicaraguan" cannot provide on their own. This is not to suggest that some U.S. Central American subjects do not identify with a larger Latina/o community and/or with their own respective national groups.[12] Nor does it mean to imply the absence of tensions among various subgroups since this too has been well documented within Central American scholarship.[13] Still, what is becoming increasingly evident is that there is a faction of individuals who see themselves outside of traditionally established categories and are using a more isthmus-based notion. As Yajaira Padilla notes, many diasporic subjects are conceiving of Central America as a "transnational imaginary," a unifying space where strategies of selfhood are claimed.[14] Such a view of Central America as a site of belonging is demonstrated by the following response provided in Nora Hamilton and Norma Stoltz Chinchilla's recent work (2013), where one of their interviewees named "Mario" explains what it means to be Central American:

> I feel like we are all Central Americans and that Central America is really one country . . . We are mixed, historically, racially etc. but we are united too. We share a common history with [in terms of relations with] the United States, for example, and of war and repression. We share a certain collective experience. Within the U.S. context, I think Central Americans are an ethnicity. The Central American experience is unique and distinctive within the Latino-Latin American context.[15]

> [. . .]

> [T]he *vieja vanguardia* [earlier generation of Central American immigrants] homogenizes the different identities in our community—indigenous, gays and lesbians, women etc. We on the other hand, take seriously the multiple identities within us and among us. We know we are very multi-dimensional. We know that there are differences among us—linguistic differences, differences in our views of nationalism, etc.—but we emphasize that which binds us.[16]

There is an inherent ambivalence regarding Central American identity in these two statements. Initially, Central Americanness is positioned within a nationalist framework of common origins, as indicated by the declaration that they "are an ethnicity"—one that shares a "common history" and a "certain collective experience." Such assertions, in conjunction with proclaiming a singular "Central American experience," come dangerously close to marking this identity within an essentialist realm. However, Mario's second statement potentially undermines the first as he displaces the centrality of "Central American," viewing it as just another subject position available to this collectivity, already composed of multiple racialized, gendered, and sexual subjectivities. The second statement emphasizes the vicissitudes of Central American experiences, as Central Americanness is linked with fragmentation and plurality, featuring the "differences among us" and their "multidimensional" interrelations with one another. Central America in this context is viewed as diasporic—a geocultural formation of diverse histories connected by overlapping modes of political, economic, and cultural oppression.[17] Analogously, Central Americanness is framed as a mere fiction of identity in which these subjects acknowledge no common origins but choose to "emphasize that which binds [them]." Asserting this temporary unity is tied to other forms of collective identities, as it is only in relation to and within a Latino-Latin American context that "Central American" appears "unique" and "distinctive." Perhaps, then, the (re)emergence of Central American as a mode of identification in the diaspora, particularly in the United States, should be read as a subject-effect of Latinidad and its failure to interpellate all its presumptive constituents.

As such, *Constituting Central American–Americans* explores the historical and disciplinary conditions that have structured U.S. Central American identity as well as the ways in which this identity challenges current discussions of Latina/o American ethnic and diasporic positionalities. In focusing on the formation of Central American identity in the United States, this book challenges us to think about Central America and its diaspora in relation to other U.S. ethnoracial identities. By calling attention to Central America(n) as an important discursive category of analysis, this work, as well as that of the field of Central American studies in general, unsettles not only the scholarship that promotes the aforementioned Latina/o dyad but also the binary nature of hemispheric studies that parcels the world into east/west and north/south, thereby excluding the important role the isthmus has played in global events. In addition, studying Central America and U.S. Central Americans further disrupts U.S. constructions of this geopolitical space as America's "backyard" (a space constructed as proximal but still subordinate to and outside of the confines of the U.S. political landscape) and of Central Americans as peripheral and external to the American body politic.[18] This book decenters this myopic vision by making Central America(ns) a primary site of investigation, underscoring how the borders between these geopolitical spaces (the United States and Central America) are being eroded by its U.S. diaspora. It also redirects the conversation within academic discourse, which tends to be unidirectional (mostly focusing on how U.S. political and economic processes have impacted Central America), to one that highlights the way textual productions from that region actively shape the sociocultural life of the United States.

Due to its transregional and transnational focus, this book does not exclusively examine one particular national community from Central America nor does it limit its scope to a single methodological lens. Instead, I employ an interdisciplinary framework—combining discourse analysis, textual analysis, ethnography, and queer theory—to analyze works, structuring logics, and socially symbolic gestures by (U.S.) Central Americans. My aim is to provide some of the sociohistorical contexts that account for how and why a transnational cultural identity—U.S. Central American—emerged in the diaspora, specifically in urban cities like Los Angeles. I also explore how some individuals become interpellated into seeing themselves as Central American. Recall here Mario's words from the interview quoted previously that a Central American identity is a strategic one that "emphasizes that which binds us," for that is among one of the central questions explored: What binds Central Americans? What cultural practices and discursive formations have contributed to fostering this isthmian form of identification? While clearly there can be many social and political forces attributed to this binding process, including imperialism, migration, globalization, neoliberalism, and the racialization immigrants encounter in the United States, some of these dynamics have already been explored in other works.[19] *Constituting Central American–Americans* examines other possible sites and suggests that U.S. Central American identity is produced via the articulations of three textual spaces: the Central American national imaginary, the translocal landscape of the U.S. diaspora (particularly Los Angeles), and the, at times, "nonspace" that Central Americans occupy within Latinidad.[20] I contend that these three discursive spaces have together produced a particular kind of U.S. Central American subjectivity, one that is connected to and yet simultaneously disconnected from the primary tropes that define these spaces. Indeed, the chapters assembled in this book demonstrate the multiscalar forms of displacement that occur within these three textual spaces, revealing how a notion of Central America(n) is often defined via the expunging of other geopolitical spaces and ethnoracial communities (e.g., indigenous and Afro-populations) as well as the way Central American experiences are frequently abjected within the category of Latina/o itself.

We must therefore understand that the term *Central American* always already emerges from a series of erasures by subsuming different national cultures and identities (e.g., Salvadoran, Nicaraguan), which have also emerged from the often violent homogenization of diverse subjectivities into one singular national culture. Thus the subtitle of this book, "the politics of dislocation," indexes the myriad forms of effacement and displacement of Central America(ns) within various geographies and imaginaries while also describing the internal forms of expunction that transpire within articulations of Central America(n) both on and off the isthmus. The subtitle also not only serves as a reminder that "politics" (e.g., political ideologies, policies, and practices, both internally and externally imposed) continues to be a catalyst for the dislocation of peoples from the isthmus but also emphasizes how the U.S. diaspora views this particular spatial construct—Central America—as a site from which to assert their own sociopolitical claims. As such, the phrase "a politics of dislocation" builds from and is an extension of other idioms produced within feminism, women of color feminism, and Latina/o studies such as "a politics of location" and "a politics of translocation," which call upon scholars to be attentive to how "geographies of power at various scales (local, regional, national, global)" are linked with subject positions and "diverse modes of domination."[21]

Before moving forward, a few points require some clarification. Rather than making the claim that a Central American identity has emerged and operates in the same manner throughout the United States, I argue that it is a tactical and often translocal cultural identity that shifts in form and content depending on the rural and urban locations in which diasporic subjects find themselves. Following Ana Patricia Rodríguez's call for Central American studies scholars to read Central American textualities within their "local specificities,"[22] this project emphasizes the importance of examining representations of Central Americanness based on translocal community formations, since practices of transnationalism are often situated in specific local contexts. Translocality, as Katherine Brickell and Ayona Datta posit, underscores the importance of examining "locally specific configurations of identity" and elucidates the ways in which social actors experience deterritorialized networks of transnational social relations.[23] In focusing on a particular manifestation of Central America that is both transnational and translocal, this book asserts that there is nothing inherently stable or essentially "Central American," for as Stuart Hall reminds us, identities are strategic points of identification "constructed within, not outside, discourse," which emerge "within the play of specific modalities of power."[24] To insinuate that modes of identification are strategies does not necessarily amount to viewing Central American identity purely as an agentic act and thereby disavowing the way structures determine and produce subjects. On the contrary, we must acknowledge that external categorizations limit the types of social locations and speaking positions available to subjects. Consequently, a key task of intellectual inquiry is noting the particular discourses and politics that have limited the ways in which some subjects from the isthmus can make claims to power and representation. As I later explain, in the norms they define and circulate, these discourses and politics constitute "regimes of recognition." Joane Nagel articulates my position best when she states that "ethnic identity is both optional and mandatory, as individual choices are circumscribed by the ethnic categories available at a particular time and place . . . limited to socially and politically defined ethnic categories with varying degrees of stigma or advantage attached to them."[25] Accordingly, we must read the deployment of a Central American identity as both an option and imposition: it functions as a tactical speaking position that marginalized subjects are forced to occupy in order to participate within the terrain of U.S. American cultural politics.

My use of the term *Central America(n)* then does not refer to some knowable stabilized ontological entity. On the contrary, this book questions the assumptions behind the construction and deployment of this signifier and focuses on broader questions: How have geographical, sociocultural, and historical discourses constructed the notion of Central America and by extension Central American identity? What is excluded from a term like Central America(n)? What kinds of bodies are privileged in representations of Central Americanness? What racial, class, gender, and sexual subjectivities have been fused with Central American experience(s)? How is the category of Central American deployed in daily lived experiences? How do these social actors come to see themselves as Central American? How do U.S. Central Americans as critical cultural producers reify and/or problematize the idea of Central America(n)? What spatial (dis)locations have produced Central American(–American) subjects? And finally, what is the relationship between Central American and other pan-ethnoracial categories like Latina/o? In beginning to address some of these questions, *Constituting Central American–Americans* foregrounds how we can view Central American identity as a "temporary attachment to the subject positions which discursive practices construct for us."[26] In doing so, this project highlights the conflicting dynamics and discursive locations that produce Central American–American subjects.

CENTRAL AMERICANS? U.S. CENTRAL AMERICANS? CENTRAL AMERICAN–AMERICANS? ON TERMINOLOGY AND THE MAKING OF THIRD WOR(L)D SUBJECTS

By now, the attentive reader has no doubt noticed an inconsistency in my terminology as to how the words *Central American*, *U.S. Central American*, and *Central American–American* have been deployed. While these terms are all fluid, and there are indeed several slippages throughout this book, for the sake of clarity, it is helpful to delineate briefly how each functions and what some of the important differences are. First, the most popular term employed, Central American, signals a diasporic mode of identification since both peoples on the isthmus and their multiple diasporas will sometimes refer to themselves as Central American. This is an embodied term for, in the practices of everyday life and in the language of common idioms, Central American appears to be the most utilized category both on and off the isthmus. Moreover, in the terrain of identity politics, organizations, clubs, and groups unite under the rubric "Central American," as opposed to something like "Isthmian American," if they are trying to invoke a regional or pan-ethnic identity. Often, it is within these identitarian movements that the term relies on a static notion of Central America as a way to forge a type of belonging for certain subjects.

U.S. Central American and Central American–American are less embodied terms, meaning that it is rare to find someone refer to themselves as a "U.S. Central American" or "Central American–American." These labels have obtained a type of currency mostly within the academic fields of Latina/o and Central American studies to refer to a particular population. Within these fields, such terms have distinct sociological connotations, often specifying "Central Americans who are part of the second generation or the 1.5 generation" and/or someone "born in the United States with ancestry from Central America."[27] Defined in this manner, both U.S. Central American and Central American–American are therefore limited to a particular generation and a very specific geopolitical location (the United States). Although the necessity of using such stabilizing concepts is clear, it is equally important to note how the theoretical possibilities that are encompassed in the term *Central American–American* become minimized when the term is seen solely within this sociological frame.

Central American–American names both a form of subjectivity and an analytic. Central American–Americanness as a subject position is a discursive lacuna; it is the constitutive excess of other marginal identity categories like U.S. American, Latin American, and Latina/o. As explained in greater detail in chapter 4, articulations of Latinidad have often excluded the experiences of U.S. Central Americans. There has been an unspoken Latina/o normativity or Latina/o "grid of intelligibility" that has fused this category with some national, cultural, and racial signifiers at the expense of others. Hence Central American–American subjectivity is not produced from a center-margin dichotomy that has been linked with ethnoracial subjects within the Latino/a category like Puerto Ricans or Chicana/os. Instead, it emerges from being rendered invisible by two U.S. peripheral locations: the Latina/o world and the Latin American discursive community. This expunction ironically writes the absence of Central America within a North (Latina/o)-South (Latin American) divide. Being imperceptible and/or unintelligible to Latina/o and Latin American marginal identity formations produces Central American–American subjectivity. Central American–American operates in a similar fashion to Gayatri Spivak's "female subaltern"—a figure that delineates a type of "effective subject," one that exposes the limitations of discourses that attempt to account or to "speak for all," and in the process efface the subjects for whom they claim to speak.[28] It also functions in a way similar to David Halperin's description of "queer," not as a "positivity but a positionality" defined by "*where* it is and *how* it operates."[29]

Central American–American identity is therefore fundamentally dialectical and relational to the Latina/o subject.

Central American–American challenges us to think about what modes of selfhood may or may not be inscribed within the field of Latino/a studies.[30] It exposes how regimes of recognition—the discursive matrices that delineate and enforce particular norms that determine which types of subjects are culturally legible—function within Latinidad. As Antonio Viego has keenly pointed out, the field of Latina/o studies scholarship is mostly governed by conversations around "Latino hybridity, mestizaje, border subjectivity"[31] and thereby places the "subject imagined to sit at the center of academic oriented discourse" as not only "oppositional and resistant" but also synonymous with the "border subject."[32] With this in mind, we will return to the Central American–American subject to interrogate if it too can be described within these tropes of hybridity and discern if the Central American–American subject is a border subject. In posing this question, we must not look for a definitive answer but, rather, note the limitations of mapping this paradigm on other subgroups, as well as open up the possibility that there might be other modes of selfhood that are not always already border subjectivities.[33]

A cursory glance at the etymological and discursive history of Central American–American reveals that since the term's inception it has resisted being viewed as an inherently hybrid or border subject. Guatemalan American poet, Maya Chinchilla, who coined the neologism Central American–American in her poem "Central American American" (1999), begins that text by asking,

> Centralamerican American
> does that come with a hyphen?
> a space?[34]

Though the remainder of the poem keeps the question open, the visual representation of the query denotes that "Centralamerican American" does not come with the traditional "hyphen" often included in the naming of hybrid and/or border subjects. In fact, in asking if "Centralamerican American" comes "with a space," the speaker in Chinchilla's poem suggests that subjectivity is engendered via absence and silence rather than emanating from the fusion of other identity categories. Although later that same year the neologism would appear with a hyphen in an essay by Arturo Arias (1999), it denies us the possibility of viewing it as a border subject position. In it, Arias claims that Central American–Americans live "life on the margins of those marginal hyphenated others (Cuban-Americans, Mexican-Americans)."[35] He advances the notion that Central American–American subject formation is the effect of a silence, of a double effacement, of living on the "murky margins," on the "margins of those hyphenated others."[36] In a subsequent essay, Arias would further add that despite the hyphen in the sign Central American–American, he viewed those subjects as living "life off the hyphen . . . [not] because these people already inhabit a world that is a montage of cultures, a hybridity so advanced that it has already conformed to a new subjectivity . . . It is a population that has not yet earned the hyphen to mark its recognition, its level of assimilation and integration, within the multicultural landscape of the United States."[37] Arias's conceptualization of Central American–American explicitly frames it as dissimilar to a Latina/o (border) subjectivity and instead positions it as a form of abjection within Latinidad.[38] Rather than arising from spaces of "hybridity," "mestizaje," or "resistance," Central American–American subjectivity as described by both Chinchilla and Arias, is produced in spaces of silence, perhaps in those moments and processes that, as Arias argues, "doubly marginalize and invisibilize them."[39]

The Central American–American subject should therefore be read as belonging to a new constellation of ethnoracial subjectivities that this book refers to as "Third Wor(l)d subjects." Third Wor(l)d subjectivities speak to a type of excess, one with new phonetic and visual signifiers that code pan-ethnic identities that have emerged in the U.S. landscape and that previous categories have not taken into account, such as South Asian Americans and Other African Americans. These terms, and the groups they represent, are linked in multiple ways, including their emergence at a particular historical moment: the post–civil rights, transnational, and highly globalized present. They are also connected by their shared refusal to adhere exclusively to current classification systems for ethnic American subjectivities that were produced during the previous era (the 1960s). They are subject-effects of civil rights identity politics, engendered via their exclusion from the categories of "Asian American," "African American," and "Hispanic or Latina/o." As Lavina Shankar and Rajini Srikanth claim in *A Part, Yet Apart* (1998), South Asian American experiences have been excluded from Asian American identity—an identity that has traditionally been viewed as exclusively synonymous with East Asia.[40] Akin to the relationship Central American–Americans share with the category of Latina/o, Shankar and Srikanth assert that South Asian Americans "find themselves so unnoticed as an entity that they feel as if they are merely a crypto-group, often included but easily marginalized within the house of Asian America."[41] Similarly, the anthologies *Problematizing Blackness* (2003), *Other African Americans* (2007), and *African and American* (2014) all document the "absence of black immigrants from popular and scholarly representations of blackness" in the United States.[42] Such invisibilities spur the rise of new identity terms like "native-born blacks," "non-American blacks," "American Africans," and "Other African Americans."

Finally, within their respective larger pan-ethnic communities, Third Wor(l)d subjects share the same type of discursive framing in which they are seen as "third world"—as the "new" or "recent" iteration of immigrants. For instance, the term *newly minted blacks* (coined by Olúfémi Táíwò), addresses the way black immigrants are not only depicted as constantly foreign or "new" but also viewed as doubly "inauthentic" by both Anglo and African Americans.[43] Within Latina/o discourse, distinctions are also made among "historical minorities" (e.g., Chicana/os and Puerto Ricans) and subgroups like Central Americans that are constantly characterized as "new" or "recent" immigrants. This sort of division, as María Elena Cepeda writes, "tends to mask not only the longstanding presence but also the multiple society contributions of Central, South American and certain Caribbean immigrant communities."[44] Likewise, South Asian American scholar Sucheta Mazumdar questions the terminology deployed of "old versus new" immigrants when she asks, "Do 'old' immigrants and their histories have greater legitimacy than the histories of 'newer' Americans?"[45] The construction of these alternative pan-ethnic terms reveal the limitations present in contemporary ethnoracial categories (e.g., Latina/o, African American, and Asian American) that cannot account for the demographic and cultural changes occurring in the U.S. multicultural landscape, as well as the ways in which identity politics often recreates the invisibilities it seeks to contest.

But if the Central American–American, as a Third Wor(l)d subject, is produced from the failure of unifying projects, then how can we avoid the potential erasures caused by a Central American identity? The next section delineates how we can use Central American–American as a hermeneutic in our reading of Central American identity and cultural texts; one that allows us to engage in what Carla Kaplan calls a "progressive identity politics," which acknowledges the continuous need for identity politics among marginalized communities who seek cultural recognition while still addressing the theoretical and political limitations of identity politics.[46]

READING/QUEERING
CENTRAL AMERICAN–AMERICAN SIGNS

Central American–American, in both its etymology and its epistemological undertakings, is a queer sign. Yielded from the mind and thoughts of a queer Central American (Maya Chinchilla), this signifier materializes from an embodied location and belongs to a critical genealogy of queer women of color who often theorize via poetry and narrative.[47] But Central American–American is a queer sign not because of some facile notions of essentialism where nonheteronormative subjects produce queer works but precisely because the text that generated this term is fundamentally linked with a queer practice—the process of exposing and critiquing (Latina/o and sexual) normativity and the ontological stability of Central America(n) itself.[48] Chinchilla's poem, after all, begins by halting the chain of signification, as it does not allow the signifier "Centralam-erican American" to be connected to a stable signified. Instead, it resists foreclos-ing the possibilities of that very term and leaves that signifier open by having the speaker ask if it comes "with a hyphen or space." By also asking, "Where is the Center of America anyway?," an inquiry that challenges the assumed con-ventional demarcations of both America and Central America, the text further questions what, where, and who is Central America(n).

I contend that as both an identity paradigm and a hermeneutic, Central American–American enables a similar destabilizing practice toward the appara-tus of recognition, which only validates certain kinds of subjects epistemologi-cally and/or politically. It does so by engaging in a politics of de-recognition. The addition of the prefix "de-," as opposed to "un-" or "mis-," to this term is delib-erate because while "misrecognition" implies a presumed subject that is falsely recognized as something else and "unrecognition" suggests that a subject is not recognized at all, "de-recognition" acknowledges not only the need to be rec-ognized but also the equally important political task of "undoing and reversal," even if it is only ephemeral. De-recognition marks those moments that simulta-neously participate in and are critical of the ideological matrices that normalize and proscribe subjects. As a radically unstable sign, Central American–American encourages de-recognition within the particular discourses that constitutes its own subjectivity.

One manner of deploying Central American–American as a hermeneu-tic is by viewing its sign as a trope—as a form of catachresis and antanaclasis. A traditional notion of catachresis defines it as an "application of a term to a thing which it does not properly denote"[49] and as the "use of a borrowed word for something that does not have a name of its own," which emerges when "a 'proper' name is lacking."[50] One witnesses this catachrestic quality in the sign "Central American–American," which improperly uses the hyphen. The hyphen has become a political signifier for ethnic and racial identities within the United States, it is symbolically wielded to both link and sever with whatever domi-nant articulations of (Anglo) Americanness are circulated in that given histori-cal moment. Early twentieth-century ethnic communities like Italians, Irish, and Germans were often viewed in a derogatory manner, as "hyphenated," due to their linguistic and religious difference from an assumed Anglo-Saxon Protestant–based notion of Americanness. During the civil rights era of the 1960s, ethnoracial groups utilized the hyphen to maintain a "politics of differ-ence" (both racially and ideologically) from Anglo-American assimilationist rhetoric. For ethnoracial subjects, the hyphen has historically connoted the contradictory process of acculturation and conflict within the U.S. multicultural arena. Subsequently, if the hyphen is always explicitly in relation and in dialogue with an Anglo-American identity, then the Central American–American subject is *not* hyphenated, despite the use of the hyphen in its sign. Instead it is what Claudia Milian labels as an "unhyphenated hyphenation."[51] As previously stated, Central American–Americans live life off the hyphen, on the "murky margins," on the "margins of those hyphenated others."[52] The hyphen in the sign of Central American–American is both ironic and catachrestic, since it seeks neither inclusion nor resistance to (Anglo) Americanness but, instead, reveals the impossibility for some subjects of having those dialectical options.

Indeed, catachresis has been an important conceptual tool in elucidating the possibilities and limitations of categories in the process of acquiring signification. Jacques Derrida calls catachresis the process that highlights "the violent, forced abusive inscription of the sign, the imposition of a sign upon a meaning,"[53] while Gayatri Spivak sees it as a "concept—metaphor without an adequate referent" that is utilized to make political claims from a postcolonial space.[54] Both notions of catachresis bring to bear the epistemic violence of recognition, where one is "forced" to acquire a name to delimit certain modes of legibility for oneself and/ or for political visibility. The hyphenated sign of Central American–American reveals this catachrestic "borrowing" of a word (e.g., the hyphenated American) and concept when a "proper" name is lacking, or arguably when subjects are rendered illegible within frames of ontology and identity. In the case of Central Americans, one must also note that the violence is not just epistemic but embodied as well. The forced designation of names such as "communist," "subversive," and "illegal" and the illegibility of these subjects as "workers," "refugees," and "children" effected by various nation-states has translated into physical and social death for countless Central Americans. Catachresis then is the palimpsest for the effects of regimes of recognition, one that momentarily enables de-recognition by exposing the apparatus itself, as well as serves as a reminder of multiple forms of violence enacted by the imposition of labels on subjects.

But catachresis can also be viewed as a type of simulacra. Derrida explains that catachresis is a "sign already affected with a first idea also being affected with a new idea, which itself had no sign at all."[55] Traditional understandings view metaphor and catachresis as distinct because one relies on the substitution of meaning and therefore an assumed "presence," while catachresis acknowledges that there is no presence, that there is no referent prior to the signifier or the sign. As an analogy, we can think of how certain deployments of Central American as an identity category function like metaphor, at times invoking a "presence," as evinced in Mario's first statement about Central American identity, which relies on an assumed "we." Whereas the Central American–American is catachrestic, since it is not based on "presence" or any type of stable meaning (recall here Chinchilla's poem). Rather, its focus is on the constitutive features of language; it is not a prediscursive ontological subject. In its catachrestic form, the sign Central American–American avoids (and reminds us of the perils of) engendering a totalizing, homogenizing subject, since it undermines its own authority by thinking of this subjectivity as a process with no concrete origins.

Furthermore, in viewing the sign Central American–American as a form of antanaclasis we are provided another useful trope for navigating the pitfalls of identity politics. Within the rhetorical tradition, antanaclasis is the name given for the process whereby "the same orthographic or phonological word [is repeated] but in different functional categories or with different or even contrary meanings."[56] The antanaclastic nature of Central American–American can therefore counteract the limitations within identity labels often utilized to obtain cultural and political recognition. In emphasizing the notion that repetition of a word always involves change and variation, as well as contradictory meanings, the use of Central American–American as a hermeneutic resists yielding homogenous renderings of identities. Arias, for example, often uses Central American–American to indicate different functional qualities and even contrary meanings (e.g., he proclaims it "an identity which is not one"). Judith Butler highlights how the performative qualities of identity invite catachresis to occur, as they require repetition. Butler argues that there is a necessity "that the name be reiterated in order to name, to fix its referent"; however, she signals that while this act of repetition is needed, it "fails to repeat loyally."[57] In other words, while identity categories seek to avoid catachresis by stabilizing a signifier with its referent, because the chain of signification relies on the insistent citing of the signifier, there will always be, and as Butler insists, there ought to be, the "risk" of catachresis. It is noteworthy that, from its earliest iterations, the term *Central American–American* has failed to repeat loyally. In Chinchilla's poem, for instance, the sign itself is literally constantly changing (e.g., "Centralamerican American," and "Central American American"). Using the sign of Central American–American as a hermeneutic to read the signifier and identity of Central American, underscores how the need for "citationality," for deploying this name will produce failures and provide moments that open the possibility, albeit only momentarily, for expanding the term itself. Thus despite the delimiting nature of regimes of recognition, which circumscribe subjects into "grids of intelligibility," the type of political exigency that produces the concept of Central American–American provides us with not only a destabilizing subject but also an approach for reading Central American textualities and identity—a "de-recognizing" one that understands that it cannot get out of a form of identity determinism and therefore calls attention to this condition via its (re)iteration. Central American–American, as a hermeneutic, a sign, and a subject-effect, does not obfuscate but, rather, exposes the inherent contradictions within identity politics and apparatuses of recognition. The production and deployment of Central American–American, as both subjectivity and analytic, therefore haunts the signifier Central American, reminding us of its pitfalls and possibilities.

CENTRAL AMERICAN DIASPORIC (RE)IMAGINATIONS

Contemporary U.S. Central American cultural practices and politics emanating from Los Angeles shape the organization, sites of inquiry, and content of this book. Part 1 of *Constituting Central American–Americans* (composed of two chapters) is guided by a locally based form of Central American diasporic nostalgia. My use of the term *diasporic nostalgia* refers to celebratory invocations of particular temporal moments utilized by a community to link the present with a delimited (often romanticized) vision of the past. To date, two of the most visible representations of Central Americanness emerging from Los Angeles have been the annual Central American Independence parade and the construction of the Central American Plaza Francisco Morazán (named after the last president of the Central American federation). The first celebrates colonial independence from Spain (1821–1823), while the second commemorates the period when Central America was briefly a nation and was politically organized as a federation (1824–1838). Both the independence parade and the Central American plaza reveal how this translocal community deems two historical moments as foundational epochs in the making of its diaspora. As a concrete instantiation of diasporic nostalgia, the selection of this historical era (the nineteenth century), by a U.S. Central American community demands a critical interrogation of that period and its key texts.

Part 1 follows the paths of this diasporic memory by concentrating on the independence and federation period. It revisits nineteenth-century texts, such as Central American historiographies and political documents, to provide a counterreading that illustrates how they function not as sources of facts but as mnemotechnical devices. Susannah Radstone and Katharine Hodgkin contend that memory is not personal nor is it merely a transparent ontological phenomenon since "regimes of memory" dictate the "kinds of knowledge and power that are carried in specific times and places by particular discourses of memory."[58] Mnemonic texts (like histories, monuments, etc.), according to John Gillis, are "like any other kind of physical or mental labor, embedded in complex class, gender, and power relations that determine what is remembered (or forgotten) by whom and for what end."[59] Memory practices are space-making endeavors that map the contours and parameters of a given area. As such, part 1 elucidates how cultural productions from and about the nineteenth century become instrumental in naturalizing a particular notion of Central America(n); one defined by the disavowal of blackness and other geopolitical spaces like Mexico, Panama, and Belize from its own imaginary. I therefore begin this section of the book by unmooring Central America from dominant conceptualizations that frequently see it as ontologically stable and/or simply as an "isthmus," since such limited notions of Central America cannot account for the complex ways (U.S.) Central Americans have utilized this spatial concept as a site of belonging.

Chapter 1, "Remembering *La Patria Grande*: Locating the Nation in Central American History," examines isthmian-produced historiographies, colonial ordinances, declarations of independence, and other political documents to reveal how, from its earliest usage, the term *Central America* has conveyed more than just a geographic construct and has often been deployed to invoke a national formation. While there have been multiple configurations of Central America, each serving its own specific function, the one highlighted in this chapter sees it as a national imaginary—containing its own "national fantasy" of images and narratives that circulate collectively and personally.[60] Tracing the discursive history of Central America as a "nation," herein referred to as *patria grande* (a term that emerges in the independence period), is a pivotal focus of this chapter. It begins with a brief discussion noting the limitations present within Central American historiographies that proclaim a type of objective representation of this space but inadvertently serve to police and cement the geographical and social boundaries of the *patria grande*. By focusing on Central America as a national imaginary, I unearth a crypto-nationalism that has been deployed by historians as well as destabilize dominant articulations of Central America that position it as either a geographic or historical construct. The remainder of the chapter, which shifts to the period of Spanish independence (1821–1823), has two objectives: to provide an alternative reading of historical events (colonial independence and Mexican annexation) that are routinely cited as the raison d'être for Central American (comm)unity and to reveal how Central American *criollo* founding fathers were haunted by what I refer to as an *Other Than Mexican* (OTM) logic. Though OTM is an acronym conceived by the U.S. Border Patrol to taxonimize immigrants, as explained in greater detail in chapter 4, I use it to index a cultural logic that frames Mexico(an) as the normative standard for reading other spaces and subjects. Rather than viewing it as a recent phenomenon, this chapter illustrates how an OTM logic was shaped by and during the colonial/independence period.

Chapter 2, "Constructing the Central American National Imaginary," builds upon the previous chapter by analyzing constitutions, national symbols, and print media from the federation period in order to bring to the forefront which spaces, subjects, and peoples were deemed vital to the Central American nation. Focusing on how nationalist memory practices and symbols like flags and coats of arms are imbued with particular racial, class, and gendered ideologies, I illuminate how such texts enabled finite notions of Central America(n) to be circulated within the isthmus and beyond. In doing so, this chapter reveals not only the ways in which Central American nationalism was a top-down project but also how cultural productions from the federation were vital in marking the emerging nation-space as mestiza/o. Such characterizations of the nation as mestiza/o were usually effected via techniques of governmentality that created distinctions about territory, inhabitants, and citizens within the Central American body politic. Despite the fact that the Central American federation ultimately failed as a political project, this chapter also demonstrates how the emotive nationalism produced from this era (and its delimited view of Central America) not only survived but would become symbolically incorporated into the political framework of the future nation-states of the isthmus. Allowing this nationalism to become "banal" during modernity is what would eventually allow many subjects from the isthmus to adopt multiscalar forms of identification, since their individual national identity is viewed as coterminous with a Central American one.

Although the first part of the book is thematically unified by geopolitical location, historical period (the nineteenth century), and the prism of seeing historical works as forms of memory practices, the second part migrates back to where the book began: the contemporary period in the United States. The setting for part 2 is the city of Los Angeles, home to the ethnic enclave known as "Little Central America." The historical scope of this second section corresponds to what some might call a "recognition era," as it focuses on the late twentieth and early twenty-first century, which saw the rise of a very public form of identity politics in this geopolitical setting. The concept of recognition, as Paddy McQueen reminds us, is vital to both political and epistemological undertakings. Not only is it fundamental to understanding how we become subjects, but it is also central to formulating a theory of justice.[61] Part 2 of this book therefore uses "recognition" as its thematic framing to disclose how cultural practices—specifically performances of Central American identity in Los Angeles—are acts generated to obtain sociopolitical validation within the United States. It also exposes how Latina/o discourse has rendered Central American–American subjects unintelligible. That "recognition" is a driving force of this second part of the book does not mean that the role of memory is neglected in it. Cultural works by U.S. Central Americans, especially those living in Los Angeles, elucidate how important collective memory practices have become in the quest for cultural and political visibility. Moreover, as part 1 illustrates, communities rely on mnemonic devices to help define and "imagine" themselves in relation to other groups, as well as to sustain their collectivity across different temporal planes and spaces. As they carefully select certain histories and memories from the isthmus, groups use cultural expressions to re-member—to sustain the process of interpellation where subjects are hailed into that particular community. In the U.S. diaspora, these occasions of re-membrance (e.g., independence day parades, celebrations of national holidays) provide the sites for Central Americans to perform and (re)produce their identities.

Subsequently, chapter 3, "Performing Centralaméricanismo: Heterotopias and Transnational Identities at the COFECA Parade," illustrates how articulations of Central Americanness in Los Angeles are linked with commemorational practices, revealing how cultural traditions that emerged during the Central American nation-building period have been transplanted and translated in the U.S. diaspora. In it, I analyze the visual and material performance of Central American identity via the Central American Independence parade sponsored by the Confederación Centro Americana (COFECA). As an extension of the currently celebrated *fiestas patrias* on the isthmus and through its invocation of a particular historical memory—a time of supposed political unity among Central American countries—this annual celebration allows disparate peoples from different countries, racial groups, genders, and social strata to imagine themselves (albeit unevenly) as Central Americans in public spaces. Because new technology allows Central Americans from around the world to be physical and virtual participants, one of the most important functions of the COFECA civic celebrations is the manner in which it forges a transnational imaginary, as Central Americans on the isthmus create broader social connections with diasporic communities. Since the COFECA parade is an important local cultural institution in Los Angeles, one that has taken place for the last thirty years, this chapter also interrogates the politics of representation within the event, calling attention to how Central Americanness is instantiated through concrete racial, gender, and sexual markers at these public events. One particular point of emphasis showcases how the rather recent phenomenon of incorporating queer performers and organizations in the parade disrupts a Central American national imaginary—which has been conceived within masculinist and heteronormative grand narratives.

Chapter 4, "Subjects in Passing: Central American–Americans, Latinidad and the Politics of Dislocation," explores how a Latina/o matrix of intelligibility has enabled the phenomenon of Central Americans "passing" as Mexican Americans. It examines two texts that focus on the social practice of passing and that highlight the nonrecognition of Central American–American bodies. Beginning with an analysis of Marlon Morales's personal essay "Always Say You're Mexican," I illustrate how this narrative blurs distinctions between active and passive forms of passing as well as how this practice is a byproduct of a Central American unintelligibility propelled by an OTM logic. The chapter then pivots to the discourse generated by the controversy over Honduran American Carlos Mencia and the accusation that he is a "fake Mexican" and a "white man" passing as "Mexican." To date, the Carlos Mencia controversy is the most popular and public example of a Central American narrative of passing. Through an examination of YouTube videos, television interviews, and weblog postings, I read Carlos Mencia as a persona—a text whose physical and discursive body operates not only as a site where relations of power are enacted but also as the effect of dominant narratives of Latinidad that make the signifiers "Honduran" and "Central American" unintelligible. Read together, these narratives of Central American illegibility and passing are important not only because they illuminate how representations of Latinidad often construct the Latina/o experience as synonymous with a Mexican American experience but also because they reveal how power and the parameters of Latinidad are locally enforced in the everyday spaces and social practices that regulate and govern bodies, institutionalize certain discourses, and produce Central American–American subjects. I then conclude the book with an epilogue that discusses how transmigration is reshaping Central American identity and politics.

PART 1

THE ISTHMUS IMAGINARY

La Patria Grande Centroaméricana

1 · REMEMBERING *LA PATRIA GRANDE*

Locating the Nation in Central American History

> An excess of confidence has spread all over the world regarding the ontology of continental divides.
>
> —Walter Mignolo, *The Idea of Latin America*

In 1986, the vice president of Guatemala, Roberto Carpio Nicolle, developed a "credo centroamericano" in which he proclaims in the last line, "Creo en una nación patria de los Centroamericanos. Yo nací guatemalteco de lo cual me siento orgulloso, pero *quiero vivir y morir Centroamericano*" (I believe in a nation of Central Americans. I was born Guatemalan, of which I feel proud, *but I want to live and die Central American*).[1] Carpio Nicolle's statement asserts two cultural identities—one Guatemalan and one Central American—that operate simultaneously although not quite equitably. Despite insisting that he is "proud" of his particular national identity as a Guatemalan, by portraying Guatemala as simply the place of his birth, Carpio Nicolle undermines the importance of such a claim, since his emotive attachment is reserved for another spatial imaginary—Central America. Guatemala becomes an incidental backdrop as he expresses his desire to experience the important milestones of his existence (life and death) as a Central American. By explicitly using the word *patria* (nation) to refer to Central America (and not Guatemala), Carpio Nicolle confers affective dimensions onto Central America. This avowal takes on greater resonance when we consider that he issued it during his time as vice president of Guatemala and did not suffer any negative consequences for his pronouncement. Although it is difficult to imagine an official of one particular nation-state publicly declaring his love for another nation-space and doing so without criticism or accusations of being "unpatriotic," Carpio Nicolle not only avoided such defamations but also was honored by several regional institutions.[2] In fact, some have asserted that it was Carpio Nicolle's view of Central America as a *patria* that made him the perfect choice as the first president of el Parlamento Centroamericano (PARLACEN).[3]

It might seem odd to begin a project about the U.S. Central American diaspora with a political figure like Carpio Nicolle, since the Guatemalan state often enabled a brutal military regime that spurred the diasporic migrations from Guatemala to other countries like the United States.[4] However, Carpio Nicolle's framing of Central America as a nation or *patria* is often shared in the U.S. diaspora as well—perhaps by some of the very same people who were forced to migrate due to state-enforced violence. For instance, twenty-seven years later and more than 2,200 miles away, in September 2013, the Boston, Massachusetts–based cultural nonprofit organization Alianza Cívica Cultural Centroamericana (ACCCA) would share similar sentiments. In a letter inviting Leonel Vásquez Búcaro (then president of PARLACEN) to attend the celebration of Central American independence in the city of Boston, Alfonso Hernández (then president of the ACCCA) reasserted the notion of Central America as a *patria*, stating, "This event is unique in all of the United States, since just like in 2012, we will hoist the Central American flag and play the Central American hymn in the heart of the city of Boston, Massachusetts. . . . We hope that in some way the Central American Parliament will show interest in these initiatives and support our communities, since this project by the Alianza Cívica Cultural Centroamericana is a source of inspiration and a true example for all those who persevere in the dream of constructing the patria grande that Francisco Morazán dreamed of one day."[5] Although such material symbols (flags and anthems) are typically expected at celebrations of national independence, what makes this cultural act noteworthy, as Hernández highlights in his letter, is that the flag and the anthem to be sung at this event do not belong to any currently existing nation-state. Even though the ACCCA celebration showcases flags and national anthems from individual countries of the isthmus, Hernández emphasizes that it is the Central American hymn and flag that will be prominently featured. Hernández's statement discloses how this affective notion of Central America serves as a site of national belonging for peoples both within the United States and on the isthmus when he asserts that he hopes his group's commemoration will inspire those who still preserve "the dream of the patria grande." A defining feature of such "imagined communities" is that individuals will never know or meet most of their fellow community members, "yet in the minds of each lives the image of their communion."[6] Hernández expresses a confidence in the existence of "those" who, like him and his group, believe in and view Central America as more than just a region of the world and see it as their *patria grande* / grand nation.

Carpio Nicolle and the ACCCA's articulations of what Elisabeth Militz and Carolin Schurr label as "affective nationalism"—the quotidian affirmation and feeling of national belonging[7]—toward Central America, as well as contemporary diasporic practices (e.g., the construction of civic groups, parades, and festivals) among U.S. Central Americans, force us to rethink the conventional geopolitical mappings and understandings of this term. Too often the term *Central America* is conceived as a stable ontological and geographical category such as a "region" or an "isthmus." Edward Said reminds us that a region does not originate in specific geophysical characteristics but, rather, its ontological status is confirmed by a history and tradition of ideas and metaphors, "of thought, imagery, and vocabulary that have given it reality and presence."[8] Such is the case with Central America, which, as a signifier, has engendered its own tradition of figurations. Textbooks and epistemological repositories that emerged in the nineteenth century, such as dictionaries and encyclopedias, for instance, have cemented a particular ontological status on Central America by viewing it as a landmass that connects North and South America—one extending from the isthmus of Tehuantepec to the Isthmus of Panama. As part of that geocultural entity known as Middle America,[9] the space is defined within geological discourse as a "tropic zone," whose native inhabitants are "Indian peoples" lacking the ability to achieve the "full development of the human race."[10] This notion of Central America and its indigenous inhabitants as incapable of achieving and reveling in the progress of modernity is mirrored in the U.S. imagination, both in its political rhetoric and especially in the construction and use of the derogatory term "banana republic."[11] As Walter Mignolo's work demonstrates, discursive constructions of geopolitical spaces like "Latin America" often fulfill the sociopolitical function of naturalizing a colonial logic. In this context, these variant ideas of Central America are effects of a longstanding Western imperial gaze that "tropicalizes" a particular Latin American "space, geography, group or nation, with a set of traits, images and values."[12]

Although such representations of Central America are predominant, they fail to account for the emotive and affective qualities that the signifier "Central America" holds for some immigrants living in the United States or for those who still inhabit the isthmus. Cartographic and geographical discourses about a "landmass" and a "tropic zone" in and of themselves usually do not interpellate subjects to want to "live and die" as Central Americans. It is when territory, geography, and cultures become linked and imagined that a sense of belonging emerges in relation to that space. Carpio Nicolle's statement and the emergence of "Central American" as a mode of identification in the United States demands that we inquire how a space that for so many others is viewed as an "isthmus" has come to signify not just a territory or geopolitical space but also a nation—that is, if other iterations of Central America have fulfilled the sociopolitical function of sustaining colonial logic, racialized discourses, and political projects such as U.S. imperialism, capitalism, and neoliberalism, then a different articulation of Central America—one that sees it as a site of belonging—engenders another effect: the production of a cultural identity.

While Central America is itself not a nation-state, between 1824 and 1838 there was a Central American federation—a self-proclaimed sovereign entity with concrete, legislated territorial borders. Attempts to secure some type of statehood for Central America continued well into the twentieth century until the last symbolic attempt was made in 1921. Although it is no longer an official political entity, this does not preclude one from seeing Central America as a nation, as evidenced in the words of Carpio Nicolle and the ACCCA. Central America in this context operates as what Lauren Berlant labels a "National Symbolic"—a space in which its members assume a relationship based on collective practices that generate an affective response to this imaginary.[13] Such national formations fulfill an important social function, since as Craig Calhoun notes, they "produce collective identity, to mobilize people for collective projects."[14] Calhoun therefore echoes Benedict Anderson's position that it is not sufficient to merely accept that nations are invented but, rather, it is the "style" in which they are imagined that should be equally considered.[15]

This chapter focuses on how Central America has been imagined by tracing a particular discursive legacy that views Central America as a nation, which I heretofore refer to as *patria grande*. Conceiving of Central America as a *patria grande* assumes that certain peoples in the isthmus are inheritors of a broader common history and culture and that despite their allegiances to a particular nation-state (sometimes referred to as *patria chica*) they all belong to a larger Central American collectivity.[16] We witness this codetermined relationship in Carpio Nicolle's pronouncement of wishing to live and die as a Central American while still inhabiting the *patria chica* (Guatemala). It is Guatemala that enables him to live (physically and culturally) in the *patria grande* (Central America). There is a symbiotic relationship between the *patria grande* and the *patria chica*, as one does not negate the other; via its histories, mythos, and political rhetoric, the *patria grande* is always spectrally present in the *patria chica*. We also see this type of synecdochical affinity at play in the U.S. Central American diaspora; in the production of independence festivals featuring the Central American flag and hymn alongside the flags and anthems of individual isthmian nations.

I map the contours of the *patria grande* by highlighting how Central America as a national imaginary is forged and sustained by a delimited view of this space—one that sees it as primarily Spanish and mestiza/o. Examining historiographies about the region and political documents from the Spanish independence period (1821–1823), I reveal how Central America gains and maintains an identity of its own via the disavowal of blackness, indigeneity, and other proximal burgeoning nation-spaces such as Mexico. Treating historiographies as space-making endeavors, I illustrate how they unintentionally reproduce a notion of Central America that renders it synonymous with Spanish colonial culture and history. I therefore begin this chapter by briefly discussing the limitations present within historiographies on the region, which proclaim an objective dimension to the study of this space but inadvertently serve to police and cement the geographical and social-racial boundaries of the *patria grande*. I then shift my attention to the nineteenth century in order to provide an alternative reading of historical events (colonial independence and Mexican annexation) that are routinely cited as the raison d'être for diasporic Central American (comm)unity. I illustrate how current understandings of Central American independence are grounded in a systemic form of forgetting. Revisiting this temporal moment not only troubles the accepted narrative that all countries wanted and proclaimed independence simultaneously but also foregrounds how racial logics of that period, specifically fears of indigenous and African political uprisings, played a pivotal role in Spanish independence. I also call attention to the ways that Mexico—as a geopolitical space—became a prominent site from which early representations of Central Americanness would define itself against.

It should be noted that this chapter does not locate a stable meaning for the signifier "Central America," nor does it produce a formal historical treatment of the etymology of that term. Rather, I compose a necessarily selective history of a concept that has been imagined and deployed as a national formation that is Spanish-based and mestiza/o-centric. I therefore outline the predominance of one specific articulation of Central America that emerged during the nineteenth century in order to expose the colonial foundation of that idea and its impact on U.S. Central American identity in the diaspora.

BETWEEN HISTORY AND GEOGRAPHY: REREADING CENTRAL AMERICAN HISTORIOGRAPHIES AS SOCIAL MEMORY

As with other group identities, the collective identity "Central American" is contingent on practices of remembering. Communities need powerful cultural texts not only to continuously interpellate members but also to construct collective memory—one that provides them with an assumed shared notion of space, culture, and history. An important and yet overlooked inadvertent "site of memory" for establishing Central American nationalism are historiographies of the region. Histories are not a neutral form of record keeping, nor are they mimetic texts;

rather, they are forms of narrative production that validate a particular order of things. As Peter Burke asserts, history is a form of social memory that engages in "the complex process of selection and interpretation," as it participates, though not always consciously, in the "social organization of forgetting . . . suppression and repression."[17] A brief examination of historiographies and historical documents on Central America reveals that despite variations in methods and definitions of this geopolitical space, for the most part, they partake in a Eurocentric logic that inscribes this signifier with two ontological features: (1) Central America is an isthmus and (2) five countries in that area share a common history. Ironically, with the exception of Ralph Lee Woodward's *Central America: A Nation Divided* (1985), the title of which explicitly identifies Central America as a "nation," most historians are reluctant to frame the area in this manner. In *A Brief History of Central America* (2007), Lynn Foster warns her readers that "there is, of course, no nation of Central America," claiming instead that Central America is "a tiny region, broken into seven even smaller nations."[18] Almost twenty years prior, historian Hector Perez-Brignoli issued a similar declaration, stating that "there is the need to avoid an abstract idea of a Central American nation."[19] However, Perez-Brignoli does not necessarily share Foster's assumptions, as he proceeds to assert that the problem is the slipperiness of the signifier "Central America" for historians of this area:

> A history of Central America. The topic itself is fraught with problems. On one hand, a shared history forces us to limit consideration to five countries: Guatemala, El Salvador, Honduras, Nicaragua, and Costa Rica. On the other hand, from a geographical viewpoint we might be expected to deal with a larger unit . . . Any of the views mentioned above can be supported by various criteria ranging from physical geography through human and political dimensions and demographics. For us to undertake a valid historical analysis of the region, however, something more than an operational definition of the region's extent and scope is required. It is essential that what we define have common social origins. . . . The first perspective, which we will adopt, leads us to view the region in a restrictive way limiting it those five countries that until 1821 made up the Kingdom of Guatemala and which achieved independence under the name of the United Provinces of Central America.[20]

Perez-Brignoli displays here an acute understanding of the role played by the multiple forms of topography attributed to this area, acknowledging that any definition "can be supported by various criteria." Ultimately, however, he resolves the problem of Central America's limitless significations by advancing a definition that relies on "common social origins," which would restrict the area to "those five countries that until 1821 made up the Kingdom of Guatemala." Perez-Brignoli therefore lobbies for a definition of Central America as a historical construct that includes five countries rather than as a geographical one that would view it as an isthmus consisting of seven countries situated between the two larger continents of North and South America. Perez-Brignoli is not alone in advocating for histories of the region to focus on limited national constituencies, as this appears to be the most pervasive model in Central American historiographies.[21] This "historical" notion of Central America is so prevalent that in his *Manual de historia de Centroamérica* (1996), Rodolfo Cardenal asserts that his work "challenges official histories" by viewing Central America as an isthmus, stating, "Central America is a relatively narrow isthmus that connects the major areas of North and South America. However, despite appearances, this area has no geographic unity. And as we shall see, neither does it have historical unity."[22] Cardenal's isthmus-based notion of Central America is promoted by other historical works,[23] which tend to be critical of Central American historiographical texts that forgo "integrated studies of the isthmus" that would include countries and information not based on Spanish colonial ties.[24] Under these disciplinary parameters, "Central America" becomes synonymous with "isthmus," which in turn is conceived as an ontological reality—a "real," geographic, physical space, usually bounded by Guatemala in the north and Panama in the south.[25]

Although these two modes of representation regarding Central America initially appear to be different, they share overlapping features. They assume, for instance, a stable subject-object relationship whereby the subjects of knowledge (historians) have unmediated access to their object of study (Central America). There appears to be little self-reflexivity about the role historiography has had in perpetuating these ideas about Central America as "truths." Moreover, both unintentionally naturalize Eurocentric criteria in their definitions of Central America, which in turn, reproduce the same type of cultural and national exclusions by neglecting to consider how categories such as "isthmus" and "Central America" rely on discursive formations. The notion that Central America is just an isthmus—a real, physical space—obscures how geographical constructs are enmeshed within colonial discourse. Texts from pre-Columbian cultures, for instance, construct alternative cartographies of the region that do not adhere to isthmian-based criteria or to definitions of the region as a product of colonial history.[26] But even within a Western framework, these ontological claims are difficult to defend. At the time when the Spanish began constructing cartographical representations of the Americas, the territory now known as Central America was not initially configured as an isthmus. When Christopher Columbus encountered this physical terrain in 1502, he did not describe this territory as a land bridge between two continents; to him, it was simply *"tierra firme,"* inhabited by "*gente salvaje* [savage people]."[27] In fact, the idea of a land bridge only began to surface after 1513 when Vasco Nuñez de Balboa journeyed from the Atlantic coastal region and "discovered" the Pacific Ocean.[28]

The representation of Central America as a bridge between two continents would continue by later colonial allocations of power and naming practices in the Americas. Within its colonies, the Spanish empire had created two cultural, political, and economic centers: the Viceroyalty of New Spain and the Viceroyalty of Peru. The Viceroyalty of Spain (Nueva España) was an administrative and political unit through which the viceroy in the capital of Mexico City governed most of North and Central America. Likewise, the Viceroyalty of Peru, housed in the capital city of Lima, governed most of the territory of South America. The territory in between those two spaces, particularly the area we now know as Central America, was not symbolically deemed as important to the Spanish empire. For instance, whereas Mexico was anointed Nueva España, the name attributed to this interoceanic territory in 1542, Audiencia de los Confines, highlights its ability to "confine." Despite providing the Spanish empire with commodities such as silver, cacao, and indigo (to name a few),[29] the name attributed to this region suggests that its perceived significance was related to its strategic location—as the physical space that connected these two larger Spanish colonial territories.[30] According to Ana Patricia Rodríguez, the United States would continue the legacy of defining this space as a geographical bridge: "The isthmus as a whole and the countries located in it would be measured according to their use value as ocean and land-crossing instruments for the United States and other world powers."[31] This idea of measuring space by its strategic value might explain why a dominant definition of Central America as a land bridge has persisted. However, when Central America is portrayed as an isthmus, the shift is merely relative, for the idea of "isthmus" is also a historical construct grounded in its own ensemble of cartographic, geographical, and colonial discourses.[32]

Similarly, the assertion that Central America is defined by "shared history" is its own ontological claim. In naming history as the critical ground that constitutes Central America, these disciplinary accounts privilege a Spanish colonial past over other historical trajectories and dynamics created by indigenous groups like the Maya, or other colonial/imperial networks that enabled the proliferation of diasporic communities such as the Miskito and Garifuna. The assertion that "common" social history is the only "valid" form of analysis neglects to account for the role played by historians' textual production in constructing a confined vision of Central America. As Michel Foucault's work demonstrates, statements about an object are not merely descriptive but constitutive.[33] By choosing a particular language and colonial history as criteria for their study, historians are not studying Central America objectively but are instead part of a discourse that creates a "regime of truth" regarding this category;[34] one that asserts that there is "real" sociohistorical unity between five countries in Central America. In other words, their approach to Central America does more than reinforce the belief that Central America is a historical construct; such scholarship is the vehicle through which that articulation of Central America is produced and naturalized.

In Perez-Brignoli's historical account, for instance, we witness a type of circular reasoning, or what Jean-François Lyotard labels as "metaprescriptive utterances," whereby a historian argues that the only "valid" notion of Central America should rely on history, which is the narrative that the historian constructs.[35] Ironically, despite Perez-Brignoli's warning to avoid reading Central America as a nation, a form of *patria grande* nationalism permeates his own scholarship. Such views are exemplified in the following anecdote he provides in his introduction:

> On a recent trip I had the opportunity to fly on one portion of the journey between Mexico and Costa Rica seated beside a Guatemalan Indian woman who spoke Spanish only haltingly. As we approached Guatemala City I filled out her landing pass (the woman was illiterate). When I asked what her nationality was she seemed not to understand the question. I persevered: "Are you Guatemalan?" "No," she replied with confidence, "I'm from Totonicapán." "Do you live in Totonicapán?" I asked next. "No," she answered, "I live in Guatemala City." To get her correct birthdate and passport number, I needed to see her passport, which declared with all the pomposity and smugness typical of modern bureaucracies, that she indeed was a Guatemalan citizen. This anecdote is more than just quaint. Our conversation cannot be appreciated without understanding our history: a centuries-old past that is alive and breathing today.[36]

Based on the concluding remarks of this anecdote, Perez-Brignoli utilizes this moment of personal encounter to underscore the importance of history in interpersonal isthmian relations when he declares that "our conversation cannot be appreciated without understanding our history." But how does a particular history of the isthmus, which focuses on select nations and Spanish colonial antecedents, allow the reader to appreciate this exchange? What is witnessed here is not a testament to the need for a particular kind of history but instead an empiricist's gaze on the "Guatemalan Indian woman" who is deemed a historical "illiterate." The subject-object dualism that pervades his approach to Central America becomes translated here as Perez-Brignoli is the speaking subject of knowledge—the one who knows "our history"—while the Indian woman is the illiterate subject who has failed to understand her history or subscribe to nationalist modes of identification. Within the context of this narrative, in which Perez-Brignoli is filling out the woman's "landing pass," it is not surprising that he asks her about her nationality. What is more revealing is that he views her answers as a rationale for his insistence on the need to know "our history," assuming that her illiteracy transcends the inability to read or write and that it extends to not knowing who she "really" is. The "our" in this passage clearly does not refer to an indigenous community, as the history he produces does not focus exclusively on indigenous events within the isthmus, nor does it include a broader Latin American community, since his focus is limited to only five countries. Arguably, then, the "our" comes to represent a Spanish colonial-based Central American history, a history the "illiterate Indian" woman clearly has no investment in, nor to which she sees herself belonging. Although the "our" could signify a national-ist Guatemalan collective or refer to the broader isthmus itself, its elusiveness (the fact that it can be both the nation-state of Guatemala and the nation of Central America) is arguably one of the hallmarks of how *patria grande* nation-alism functions. Perez-Brignoli's anecdote therefore demonstrates how the subject-object dualism is troubled when the subject of study (author) turns into the object of study by positioning himself as (albeit unintentionally) "Central American." It also exposes the inherent instability and problematic nature of trying to impose an order and a set of labels on one's object; for the "illiterate" Guatemalan Indian woman in this anecdote troubles those very categories and Perez-Brignoli's broader imperative by not even identifying as Guatemalan at all—a rejection that, according to Perez-Brignoli, she makes "with confidence." Her refusal and her historical "illiteracy" serve therefore to highlight that there are indeed different "memory communities" within a given society that are not invested in the types of institutionalized official histories about Central America, since they are not even interested in individual national ones like Guatemalan and, conversely, whose own memories are not accorded the same value. Her presence serves as metonymic of other communities that are displaced by the assertion that Central America is defined by "shared history" and is a powerful reminder of the way that some ethnoracial subjects actively reject seeing them-selves as Central Americans.[37]

Thus historical accounts that endorse either notion of Central America (as geographical or as primarily historical) inadvertently contain what Paul Gilroy has described as crypto-nationalism: "a quiet cultural nationalism which per-vades the work of some radical thinkers."[38] Even Foster, who emphatically pro-fesses that "there is no Central American nation" and claims that her history will focus on the "seven modern nations that share the isthmus," upholds the histories of only five countries when she states that Panama and Belize "will be discussed insofar as they influenced events in Central America or shared in its history."[39] Panama and Belize are relegated to the outside of Central America and its "shared history," as they are framed as contributing very little to the events of the region. Foster, like Perez-Brignoli, then reinforces the idea that only five countries define Central America, even though she claims that the isthmus contains seven.

But this form of historical silence regarding Panama and Belize and their role within a Central American imaginary is not arbitrary. As Sibylle Fischer notes, ingrained forms of Eurocentric racial hierarchies express themselves in colonialist ways of assessing what matters and is included within a given discourse.[40] Calling on scholars to look for "what is disavowed . . . and for what reason," Fischer encourages us to read the dislocation of Panama and Belize within historiographies as not just a question of "editing" or personal oversight but one that is grounded in colonial racial logics.[41] If we do this, we see that the histories, cultures, and populations of Panama and Belize trouble configurations that view Central America(n) as mestiza/o—a belief stemming from an ideology of *mestizaje*, which views the prototypical ethnoracial subject and culture of this region as a byproduct of mixture between Spanish and indigenous communities with minimal African presence. Mauricio Meléndez Obando observes that "in Central America, even in academic circles, when the presence of Afro-descendants is mentioned the popular imagination refers to the Caribbean," suggesting that the signifier Central America(n) does not index African cultures.[42]

However, thinking of Central America(n) in this way, as "mestiza/o" as opposed to "Caribbean" (which connotes blackness), becomes compromised by the inclusion of Panama and Belize whose African heritage and presence is undeniable. One must recall that the first African slaves brought to the region now known as Central America arrived in Panama, which during the colonial period became a central hub for the import and export of slaves to other parts of the Americas. The development of agricultural industries and regional projects, such as the transisthmian railroad (1856) and later the canal (1907), would ensure a steady stream of African and West Indian black laborers migrating to Panama. In fact, though the census indicates that Afro-Panamanians account for 15 percent of the population, other scholars and organizations have claimed that "up to 50% of the population of Panama has some African ancestry."[43] Likewise, until 1980, the population of Belize was composed of mostly Creole (a mixture of African slaves and British colonizers). Belize, which was primarily colonized by the British, has English as its official language and proudly sees itself as "a Caribbean nation in Central America."[44] Rather than just merely accidental, perhaps the continuous marginalization of Belize and Panama from histories of the region is symptomatic of a broader Latin American anxiety regarding the presence of black cultures within the region.

Now, some might argue that Panama and Belize's displacement within Central American historiographical discourse may have nothing to do with symbolic and embodied associations with blackness, but that it is more a result of the fact that these two geopolitical entities were never a part of the Kingdom of Guatemala. However, if this is the rationale undergirding these choices, they nevertheless remain problematic because they naturalize a Spanish colonial model as the criteria for what is deemed to be Central American. Under a different lens and/or criteria, it would be difficult to easily dismiss perceptions of Belize as irrelevant to the region, since this country houses Maya and Garifuna peoples—diasporic communities that reside in other countries of the isthmus as well.

In bringing attention to the inherent limitations present in engaging with Central American "history" and "historiographies," my aim is to not indict individual historians or their scholarship, which has proven valuable to many of us in this field of study. Instead, I illuminate how the replication of a particular iteration of Central America is not the work of an isolated author, but a testament to how embedded and naturalized a delimited view of Central America (a Spanish-based mestiza/o centric one) has become. It is therefore vital to retrace how this historical construct of Central America is grounded in ideologies produced from nineteenth-century discourses, which continue to permeate and recirculate within twentieth- and twenty-first-century texts.

A COUNTERREADING OF CENTRAL AMERICAN (IN)DEPENDENCE

During the mid-twentieth century when La Organización de Estados Centroamericanos (ODECA) began consolidating important historical documents about Central America, it proclaimed that in order "to reflect in a precise manner on where to aim our historical destiny, the collection begins with our date of baptism, the Declaration of Independence."[45] The invocation of "our" and "historical destiny" makes it clear that one of ODECA's explicit objectives is to promote the idea of a unified Central America—one that is tied by their presumed shared colonial history. Historians of that time period would also issue similar proclamations that viewed colonial independence as a catalyst for the formation of Central American nationalism. Ricardo Gallardo, for instance, states that "September 15, 1821, is the real date of independence from Spain for all of the provinces that at the time comprised the Kingdom of Guatemala . . . Central American nationality began, effectively, on [that] day."[46] The Acta de La Independencia (ADLI) of September 15, 1821, therefore serves as the genesis of the Central American nation, which is officially declared to be born on that day. The belief that September 15, 1821, is the day that ushered in the birth of a new "free" nation (and subsequent nations) is so undisputed that all five states that were former provinces celebrate their independence on this day.[47] However, a critical counterreading of this temporal moment might underscore the way memory practices of the twentieth century, such as ODECA's project of historical recovery, have been crucial in constructing a unifying narrative of "common origins." Indeed, a reexamination of the political documents of this independence period illuminates how another narrative of these events could equally frame the space as sociopolitically and culturally fragmented as opposed to unified, as well as reveal how the desire for a Central American nation was a top-down *criollo* project.

Although the process of transforming an undifferentiated space and endowing it with value to convert it into a type of "place" (e.g., isthmus) began around 1513,[48] at that time, the area we now conceive of as Central America was still not considered to be a distinct political unit. As late as 1530, the Spanish crown had not yet consolidated the region, which was composed of different administrative units such as Comayagua in Honduras and Granada in Nicaragua. A singular geopolitical entity began to emerge in 1542 when the fragmentary, smaller political units in the area became conjoined under the title of la Audiencia de los Confines. The Audiencia's physical parameters began in Tabasco and the Yucatan in the South of Mexico and extended all the way to the southernmost point of what is now Panama. However, the territory and the name of this space would be reorganized in 1568 when it became known as la Audiencia de Guatemala and later el Reino de Guatemala / the Kingdom of Guatemala.[49] In 1785, the area was yet again reorganized via the creation of four intendancies: San Salvador, Comayagua (Honduras), León (Nicaragua and Costa Rica), and Ciduad Real (Chiapas). This arrangement would continue up until 1821 when the Kingdom of Guatemala became "independent" from Spain.

Despite the fact that in 1811 the provinces of San Salvador and Nicaragua would separately stage small-scale acts of resistance toward the Spanish empire,[50] it was not until September 15, 1821, that an official Acta de La Independencia (ADLI) was created and disseminated throughout the region. This title, as several scholars have noted, is a misnomer, since a cultural and juridical split with the Spanish colonial system did not occur.[51] Even though the genre of this document (a declaration of independence) symbolically asserts distance from the crown, the language in the ADLI is laden with a hesitation toward the very action it is intended to complete. In contradistinction to the Declaration of Independence of the United States (1776), which argued for its sovereignty based on "one people" who are innately entitled by God and "the Laws of Nature" and which cast their monarch as the clear antagonist of "the people" who were victims of a tyrannical despot government, Central America's ADLI neither rebukes the crown nor relies on republicanism to assert its secession from Spain. In fact, there is no language in the ADLI disparaging its colonial predecessor. Instead, the need to assert independence is attributed to the effect of external and internal factors; it is at once the result of political events transpiring throughout the region (especially in Mexico), as well as the will of the people:

Given that the desire to be independent from the Spanish government has been public and unwavering, and as written and manifested by the people of this Capital: we received correspondence from the constitutional Ayuntamientos of Ciudad Real, Comitan, and Tuxtla, in which they communicate that they have claimed and sworn independence, exhorting us to do the same in this city: being positive that similar official correspondence has circulated among other Ayuntamientos. . . . Having read these correspondences: having discussed and carefully considered the matter, and having heard the cry of "long live independence" repeated by the people who had congregated in the streets, plaza, the patio, and corridors of this palace, it [the Declaration of Independence] was agreed upon by this Diputación and the individuals of this excellent Ayuntamiento.[52]

In its rationale for independence, the Diputación attributes the news of another's independence, the province of Chiapas (Ciudad Real, Comitan, and Tuxtla) as the catalyst that "*excitan a que se haga lo mismo* [exhorting us to do the same]." But Chiapas's assertion of independence was spurred by Mexican independence and the signing of the Treaty of Córdoba on August 24, 1821, that recognized "the Mexican Empire as a sovereign and independent nation."[53] By framing its rationale in this manner, the Diputación is inadvertently stating that Mexico provided the conditions of possibility for the Kingdom of Guatemala's independence. The notion that the ADLI emerges from the masses is tenuous, as it is presented as an afterthought; it is only toward the end of the opening paragraph that any reference is made to this liberation movement corresponding to the will of "the people," who are described as shouting "*viva la independencia* [long live independence]" throughout the halls of the palace. The adoption of the term *pueblo/people* and its demarcation as a singular entity remains rather ambiguous. It is the nebulous nature of this term and what it can signify that has led many to read this statement of independence to refer to the entire Kingdom of Guatemala, instead of seeing it as circumscribed to the municipality surrounding the palace or the City of Guatemala or the province itself. As mentioned, historically the date of Guatemala's ADLI has been considered the date of independence for all five of the former provinces.

While ODECA's assertion that this document and date are representative of the entire region (a claim to which we will return later), the imagined desired constituents of "el pueblo" amount to a narrow few.[54] In fact, the ADLI itself was never intended to reflect the will of all its inhabitants, as it preserves a Spanish colonial racial and political hierarchy. Miscegenation between Spanish, indigenous, and African peoples in the Americas led the Spanish to develop a racial caste system (*castas*), which mapped out how power and privilege would be distributed among its inhabitants. The *castas* were a form of racial taxonomy that elucidated the hierarchal location of whiteness within racial mixing, as those with a higher proportion of Spanish blood (viewed here as synonymous of white) were not only placed at the top of the racial pyramid but also endowed with political and economic provisions denied to others. According to María Josefina Saldaña-Portillo, while the *casta* system was socially flexible (it encouraged miscegenation) it was less fluid when it came to occupations and class standing. At the very top of this racial order were *peninsulares* (a Spaniard born in Spain) who were eligible for the highest positions of power such as royal offices, followed by *criollos* (a Spaniard born in the Americas) who were eligible for managerial positions and high offices. By contrast, the *castas* (mixed races) tended to occupy low-level occupations and wage labor. Even then, a hierarchy prevailed as *mestizos* could obtain lower administrative positions, while "afromestizos had no legislated positions reserved for them in either offices or in guilds."[55] In fact, "*negros* and *mulatos*, like *indios*, had to pay tribute," a form of tax imposed by the Spanish crown, while mestiza/os did not.[56] Though scholars have pointed out that each of these categories experienced some internal heterogeneity due to the fact that one person could be labeled mulata/o in one context and mestiza/o in another, as well as by colonial edicts like the *cédula de gracias a sacar* (certificates of whiteness), which allowed for some mobility within this racial order, as Ann Twinam notes, these instances of "purchased whitening" seem to be more the exception than the rule.[57]

Such was the racial landscape in the Kingdom of Guatemala when a group of mostly *criollos* convened to decide the political fate of this territory. An examination of the ADLI discloses how maintaining their colonial elite status was a contributing factor for the Diputación's decision whether or not it should secede from Spain. The ADLI's first provision reveals that a central impetus for them to declare independence was to "prevenir las consecuencias que serían temibles en el caso de que la proclamase de hecho el mismo pueblo" (to prevent consequences that would be frightful in the event that the people would take it upon themselves to declare them). In this context, independence is presented as a way of "prevent[ing]" or forestalling mestiza/o, indigenous, and black populations from rebelling and declaring independence on their own terms. Juliet Hooker argues that the specter of the Haitian revolution, which had ended seventeen years prior, loomed large in the minds of *criollos*, who, seeing the emergence of independence movements across the Americas, opted to secure their economic, political, and social dominance by declaring independence themselves before racialized and indigenous communities could do so.[58]

The fear that nonwhite peoples, especially black populations, could mount a political revolution had been a source of concern for Central American elites prior and during the independence period. At the time of independence, African descended communities accounted for a significant portion of the population. For instance, in Antigua (Guatemala), "free people of African ancestry represented perhaps the largest ethnic group,"[59] while in Nicaragua 51 percent of the province's inhabitants were of African descent.[60] According to Justin Wolfe, in 1817, a report from the Audiencia de Guatemala to the King discussed the "risk posed in Nicaragua and El Salvador by 'those who are descended from Africa.' Their exclusion from political citizenship merited immediate amelioration since 'this class [was] the majority of that Province.'"[61] Such documents reveal that while Mexican independence and Chiapas's departure were inciting factors that led to the consideration of Spanish independence, the fear of a black revolt also contributed to this decision. In essence, *criollos* viewed declaring independence as a strategic way to "beat them [black populations] to the punch." Thus if we are to see the ADLI and this historical moment, as ODECA claims we ought to, as "Central America's baptism," then we must understand that the making of this text and space are profoundly intertwined with a fear and disavowal of blackness.

In fact, the ADLI did not constitute an emphatic declarative break from its colonial antecedent (both in its racial logics and its political structure), as it reaffirmed a commitment to a status quo—one that privileged Spanish governance, whiteness, and elitist *criollo* culture. As noted in the ADLI's eighth provision, "Brigadier D. Gabino Gaínza, will continue with the Supreme Political and Military Government, and because he has the character appropriate to these circumstances, a provisional consultative Junta will be formed and will be comprised of members of this Diputación Provincial."[62] This provision empowered Gaínza, who was appointed by the Spanish empire, to continue with his administrative duties, bringing only the modification that he would henceforth be advised by a "Junta consultiva" composed of elite *criollos*. Gaínza, for his part, ensured that Spanish rule would continue and, just two days later, issued a ban in which he asserted that "consequently all of the laws, ordinances, and mandates that were in place will forcefully and vigorously remain in place," adding that "if anyone from any class position or condition directly or indirectly, with speeches or with actions, intends to discredit or dislocate the Spanish government," such people would be labeled as "traitors" and "conspirators."[63]

If rhetorical and juridical assertions of the ADLI undermine the possibility of viewing independence as a complete political rupture from Spain, declarations from some of the other provinces of the Kingdom of Guatemala further challenge this narrative. For, despite being united under colonial rule, the process of independence for the five provinces was anything but unilateral. Leslie Bethell describes the chaotic aftermath and internal wars within each province following independence, stating, "All [provinces] accepted independence from Spain, but there were variations in their approaches to the future. . . . As the national period opened, then, Central America was politically fragmented and caught up in a wave of regional and local acts of separation."[64] Bethell argues that, while "politically fragmented," there was a sense of consensus among the provinces that they "all accepted independence of Spain." His use of "accepted" perhaps underscores the general ambivalence and even reluctance of some provinces regarding Spanish secession. The province of Nicaragua is a case in point: the two largest cities—Granada and León—could not come to a consensus on the matter. The end result was that on September 28, 1821, the Diputación Provincial (a combined government body from the provinces of Nicaragua and Costa Rica) drafted what is now known as el Acta de los Nublados (ADLN; The Decree of the Cloudy Days). A "text of studied ambivalence,"[65] the first three provisions of the ADLN are quite telling of the Diputación's sentiments toward Spanish independence:

1. The absolute and total independence from Guatemala, which appears to have established itself as sovereign
2. Independence from the Spanish government, until the clouds of the day have cleared and when this province can lobby for its own religious endeavors and true interests
3. That, in consequence, all the present authorities continue in the free exercise of their functions according to the constitution and to the laws[66]

Rather than constructing a document that showed support for Guatemala, the ADLN's first order of business was to sever ties and distance itself by proclaiming to be "absolutely and totally independent" from Guatemala. Their position on Spanish emancipation, by contrast, was not absolute. The other provisions not only empowered present authorities to continue their duties; it also stated that independence would be contingent on "the clouds clearing/lifting."[67] In using the metaphor of clouds—a highly uncontrollable entity—independence from Spain is framed as being temporary and arbitrary, since there is never any indication or stated desire to stabilize or "make the clouds part." Moreover, the phrase "clouds of the day" suggests a lack of permanence, since "a day" is a much smaller increment of time than a season or a year. In this sense, the language of the ADLN forms clear parameters: independence from Guatemala would be permanent, but independence from Spain would be temporary.

Considering the rather reluctant tone toward secession from the Spanish in these documents, as well as the rules sanctioned within them that maintained Spanish control, the different decrees issued by various provinces on different days, as well as the fact that some provinces were more willing to declare themselves emancipated from Guatemala than from Spain, why has September 15, 1821, been narrativized and memorialized as an official date of independence for the entire region? The belief that the entire region became independent on the same date is further subverted by the fact that this "tentative independence" was short-lived. On October 19, 1821, Agustín de Iturbide proposed merging the provinces with the newly formed Mexican Empire. In a letter written to Gaínza, Iturbide represents Mexico and Guatemala as similar and in need of one another, when he states that "the actual interests of Mexico and Guatemala are so identical and invariable that they cannot establish themselves as separate, independent nations without jeopardizing their existence and security . . . [it is] as if Nature had specifically destined both portions to form one strong empire."[68] Although proximity of space was never a precondition for the construction of empire, Iturbide reads this spatial relationship between Guatemala and Mexico as a sign of its own form of manifest destiny.

Iturbide's proposal became a subject of debate within the Kingdom of Guatemala as several provinces immediately showed interest in joining Mexico while others again were hesitant. For his part, in a letter to Iturbide dated on November 28, 1821, Gaínza claimed that "Guatemala should not be independent from Mexico, but should form a grand empire . . . [since] Guatemala still finds herself unable to self-govern and can be the object of foreign ambition."[69] Gaínza's words are imbued with gendered and colonial notions of power as he views Guatemala and, in all likelihood, the rest of the provinces that he once administered, as unable to achieve any form of independent status. Guatemala should not, and indeed could not, be an autonomous political body due to "her" inability to self-govern or ward off unwanted foreign advances. Like countless gendered subjects of that time period who were denied access to participation in their own political future in this territory, a feminized Guatemala would suffer the same fate, as her political future would be decided by an elite group of *criollos* who would claim to know what is best for "her."[70] This personification of Central America as a helpless "female" during the independence period was often intertwined with the trope of Central America as an "orphan" or a territory inhabiting an "orphaned condition." Consuelo Cruz posits that in debating reasons why the provinces should join Mexico, "everywhere, creoles decried the 'orphaned' condition of Spanish America, and everywhere allusions were made to the 'orphans' of Central America."[71] Whether perceived as orphans, women, or specifically female orphans, Guatemala and the other provinces were viewed as childlike, feminine, and incapable of self-rule.

The discourse emerging from this potential merger between Guatemala (personified here as female) and Mexico, who is seen as "her" protector (a trait conceived as masculine), reminds us of Doris Sommer's assertion about how nineteenth-century texts often contain a metonymical relationship between politics and *eros*. Though Sommer's focus is on romance novels, her work elucidates how "romance and republic were often connected,"[72] particularly in representations of unions where "the marriage metaphor slips into, or out of, a metonymy of national consolidation."[73] As such, we may want to equally consider how a rhetoric of romance and a logic of *eros* undergird political documents of that era; one that, like romance novels, served as "foundational fictions" utilized to shape the contours of emerging nation-spaces. For instance, in the Acta de Union de las Provincias de Guatemala al Imperio Mexicano (ADU),[74] we can see how distinctions between two proximal spaces began to take shape.

After hearing Iturbide's proposal, the majority of political representatives from the provinces voted in favor of Mexican annexation. On January 5, 1822, the Junta Legislativa Provisional issued their formal response to Mexico via the ADU; in it, they revealed the following:

> It was determined: that the desire clearly expressed for union exceeded the absolute majority of the population convened in this government. And taking into account the Intendency of Nicaragua, which, since its declaration of independence from the Spanish Government, united with that of Mexico, separating itself absolutely from this latter [Guatemala]; of Comayagua, which finds itself in a similar situation; of the city of Chiapas, which united itself with the [Mexican] Empire even before independence was declared in this city; of Quetzaltenango, Sololá and other towns, which in recent days have attached themselves to this union; it was found that the general will was almost absolute. And bearing in mind that the Junta's duty in this case is nothing other than to relay to the Mexican government what the pueblos want.[75]

Citing the "general will" of the people as a reason for forging a union with Mexico, the absence of some major cities, such as Tegucigalpa (Honduras) and Granada (Nicaragua), and of the entire province of San Salvador from the ADU undermines such a claim by revealing how ideologically fractured its constituents were regarding their political aspirations. Moreover, unlike the ADLI, which referred to the people as "el pueblo," in this document the term has been converted to "pueblos." But more important, the ADU represents the provinces of Guatemala as having a familial relation, while Mexico is depicted as "external"—as an outsider to this kinship: "Among the many considerations that the Junta has made in this important and grave matter, in which the people find themselves threatened in their repose, and especially in the union with their brothers and the other provinces with whom they have always lived and bonded through proximity, trade, and other close ties, through a union with Mexico wanted to salvage the integrity of that which had been previously called the Kingdom of Guatemala, and reestablish among themselves the union that had prevailed in the past; nothing else appearing to remedy the division being experienced."[76] Although in their earlier explanation regarding the vote tally in favor of annexation, the Junta declared that this merger was something "the people want," the addition of "no apareciendo otra para remediar la división que se experimenta" (nothing else appearing to remedy the division being experienced) suggests that the Junta itself viewed this option as the lesser of two evils. A union with Mexico appears to be the only way to "save" a type of colonial coherence among the provinces of the former Kingdom of Guatemala. Even those who disagreed with annexation would concede to this union so that they could "reestablish" the same regional community, as it existed under Spanish rule. The ADU, which clearly highlights the division between the provinces, also evidences the labor of constructing a people via metaphors and language that represent the provinces as "brothers" with strong bonds and with whom they have several important "ties." The provinces are instantly transformed from fractured neighbors into fraternal siblings who have been always bound together and who now face a compromising situation in which they must either unite with Mexico or break up the family. Though the Junta claims that the kinship between the provinces emerges from their "proximity, trade, and other close ties," it never fully explains why these characteristics do not apply to Mexico. Mexico, after all, is closer to Guatemala than Costa Rica and became the site of an important trade route for the Kingdom of Guatemala to send their exports to Spain.[77] And yet, while all these attributes apply to Mexico, this proximal space is situated as outside of this fraternal order. Interestingly, the heteronormative nature of the family trope utilized to describe the provinces undergoes a queering of sorts as these "brothers" are also simultaneously portrayed with feminine qualities. Akin to Gaínza's description of Guatemala, the Junta personifies this geopolitical area as having innately female characteristics; the provinces are in constant need of protection from "threats" and are viewed as passive "ladies in waiting" or "reposo/repose" who will not be able to fend off unwanted advances. Mexico is therefore positioned as a viable suitor by the Junta, which constructed an "arranged marriage" to preserve and consolidate their own interests.

Thus while the ADU is significant as an official political document that empowered Mexico to assume control over the territory, it is equally important because it marks the emergence of a discourse that ascribes the provinces of Guatemala with concrete bonds of affinity. In fact, the ADU foreshadows the construction of a Central American nation, not only via its metaphors of kinship but also by hinting that the provinces desired to form an autonomous political entity. A provision in this agreement with Mexico called upon the ability for "estas provincias, las cuales si llegásen a término de poder por sí constituirse en Estado independiente, podrán libremente construirlo" (these provinces, which, if they reached the point where they are able to form an independent state on their own, will be able to freely construct it). The inclusion of this statement in the ADU is significant, as it is one of the first political documents signed on behalf of representatives from most of the provinces (although not all were in favor), declaring their intention to pursue the notion of consolidating the former provinces of the Kingdom of Guatemala into a state. Though the actual name of Central America and the federation that would bear such title did not material-ize until a year later, the ADU contains the discursive trace of that future nation. Ironically, the Central American nation is produced in the same moment in which it is seemingly subjugated to a different imperial entity.

However, not all the provinces accepted Mexican annexation peacefully. San Salvador in particular was so adamant in its refusal that in November 1822, Mexico sent Captain General Vicente Filisola to subdue their armed rebellion. Fearing its impending forced union with Mexico, on December 2, 1822, the San Salvador congress passed a resolution that declared itself a protectorate of the United States, stating, "Being that out of necessity [San Salvador] needs to be incorporated into another nation in the Americas, it has decreed on the date [12/2/1822] to be incorporated into the United States of America."[78] Though a strategic political move, this resolution asserts a contradictory position for the province of San Salvador. On the one hand, the province heretofore had argued for its ability to be independent, yet on the other hand, the resolution concedes that it "needs to be incorporated into another nation." The only feature of the resolution that retains any sense of autonomy for the province is its insistence on the right to decide to which nation they will be subjected; in this case, it willingly opted to join the United States over Mexico.

In fact, whereas in the ADU Mexico had been described as a protector and potential suitor for the provinces, in political documents involving Mexico and San Salvador, those traits are removed and transposed onto the United States. In a letter written by José Matías Delgado (then head of the province of San Salvador) to Vicente Filisola, he warns that to begin a war with San Salva-dor is to declare war on the United States: "This province being united with that Grand Republic of the North [the United States] by her own spontaneous voli-tion, and resisting as a part thereof the invasion of troops under your command, were she to be occupied, even if the [United States] does not endorse this union, it will settle accounts with the Mexican government for its violent occupation and unjust war declared on a province that asserted its union with it [the United States], and placed under its protection and shelter; and then San Salvador will be free, despite the Mexican government."[79] Delgado's letter subverts future his-torical accounts that remember this particular moment as a broader example of isthmian resistance or proof of an innate Salvadoran desire to be independent.[80] In Delgado's words, San Salvador belongs to that "*Gran República del Norte /* Grand Republic of the North," and it is not San Salvador that will seek retribu-tion for this armed invasion; rather, it will be its new suitor and protector: the United States. Feminized like its provincial counterpart Guatemala, San Salva-dor is framed as being incapable of seeking "her" own vengeance or to hold her antagonist accountable, having to wait instead for another imperial father (the

United States) to "settle accounts" with Mexico. Moreover, Mexico is presented as "violent" and "unjust," it is viewed as the singular obstacle that prevents San Salvador from being free. The fact that its own government has willingly asked to become a protectorate of the United States is remarkably not seen as an impediment to autonomy. San Salvador's annexation attempt was serious enough that emissaries were dispatched to the United States to deliver this resolution.[81] This voyage to the United States, along with the resolution and Delgado's letter, suggests that San Salvador was clearly not fighting for its universal political sovereignty—it was simply fighting to be autonomous from Mexico.

But how should we read this moment of inherent contradiction where San Salvador willingly embraces U.S. annexation but resists Mexican annexation? If we read this public political exchange as a metonymy of the way private relationships functioned in that era, San Salvador's decision-making process echoes a colonial logic that endorsed *blanqueamiento*. Social whitening or *blanqueamiento* by way of interracial unions was often encouraged during and after Spanish colonialism, as it not only provided nonwhite individuals a way to improve their social standing but was also seen collectively as a way to "improve the race." Within this racial economy, Mexico, which had just barely removed the yoke of the Spanish crown and shared some of the same characteristics as San Salvador (both were racially heterogeneous with large indigenous and African populations),[82] might not be deemed as the best suitor, since this type of union would not amount to "marrying up" but would instead be viewed as endogamous. By contrast, the United States, which despite its own heterogeneity, was racially coded as "Anglo-Saxon" and ideologically positioned as "modern," might have been viewed as a better "catch." Perhaps it is this racial logic that enables Mexico (as a spatial imaginary) to go from being viewed as a potential suitor by some members of this province to a "violent" invader.

Despite San Salvador's efforts, all these gestures did not dissuade Filisola, who, on January 14, 1823, responded to Delgado by affirming Mexico's dominion over it, saying, "Although that government has declared itself incorporated to the North American federation, that pronouncement is nullified because San Salvador belongs to the Mexican empire."[83] Following this rhetorical annulment, Filisola defeated Salvadoran military forces, and San Salvador became incorporated into the Mexican Empire on February 7, 1823. However, this forced union was short-lived. Iturbide had increasingly alienated the liberal factions within Mexico and after he dissolved the congress in October 1822, several political leaders turned against him. On December 2, 1822, Brigadier Antonio López de Santa Anna issued his *Plan de Veracruz*, which lobbied for the overthrow of Iturbide and the restoration of a Mexican congress. Facing resistance within Mexico, on March 19, 1823, Iturbide abdicated his position as emperor, prompting Filisola to decree that a formal meeting be held on March 29, 1823, gathering representatives from the provinces of the former Kingdom of Guatemala to determine its political future.

On July 1, 1823, a second declaration of independence emerged, known as El Decreto de Independencia Absoluta de las Provincias del Centro de América. Baptized as "Centro de América," this new name claimed a space in the hemisphere by highlighting its location within the Americas. The Decreto proudly announced that the provinces were "libres e independientes de la antigua España, de México y de cualquiera otra potencia asi del antiguo como del nuevo mundo" (free and independent of Spain, Mexico, and every other entity of the old and the new world). The severing of the colony from the crown this time is viewed as "absolute," as part of an entitlement that was not only authorized by the laws of nature but also rightfully earned after years of oppression:

> That nature itself resists dependence of this part of the world to a metropolis separated from it by an immense ocean. . . . That the arbitrariness with which it was governed by the Spanish nation and its conduct since the conquest, impelled the people to have the most ardent desire to recuperate their usurped rights. . . . That driven by these justified sentiments, all of the provinces of America shook off the yoke that oppressed it the for the span of three centuries: that those who inhabit the former Kingdom of Guatemala gloriously proclaimed their independence in the last months of the year of 1821; and that the resolution to conserve and sustain it [the Kingdom of Guatemala] is the general and impartial vote of all of its inhabitants.[84]

In the first portion of the Decreto, colonization stands in direct violation of the natural order of the world, as nature itself resists an imposed relationship between a European metropolis and a territory divided from it by a vast ocean. Such relationships preclude Central America from being happy, since it is reduced to a poor state unable to self-govern and harness the territory's inherent potential greatness. As opposed to the first declaration of independence, which never maligned Spanish governance and, in fact, sanctioned it to continue, this political split is viewed as a consequence of Spain's poor and arbitrary administration of the territory, one that leads "the people" to have the most ardent desire to "recuperate their usurped rights." This second independence document showcases the republican values that the future Central American nation would adopt, framing this movement as the inherent reclamation of rights for colonial subjects. The Decreto also fosters "united" provinces not only by proclaiming that they "are and form a sovereign nation" but also by minimizing vital political divisions in its remembrance of the political events surrounding the first Acta de la Independencia. In advancing the notion that those who "populate the former Kingdom of Guatemala" gloriously asserted their independence in 1821 and that the desire to maintain this autonomy was shared by "all of its inhabitants," this earlier historical moment is recast as one of unity and not division.

Mexican annexation is also reconfigured in the Decreto, for whereas in the Acta de Union (ADU), it was viewed as an agreement between two parties to join forces for mutual benefits, here the power dynamic is not equitable:

> Considering on the other hand that the incorporation of these provinces to the extinguished Mexican empire, verified only at the end of 1821 and the beginning of 1822, was a violent expression taken by vicious and illegal means. . . . It was not agreed upon nor pronounced by either a legitimate entity or by legitimate measures, that because of these principles the national representation of the state of Mexico was never explicitly accepted, nor did it have a right to accept it; and that the provisions regarding this union mandated and issued by D. Agustín de Iturbide were nullified.[85]

While the ADU embodied reluctance toward Mexican annexation, its language interpreted coupling as a compromise rather than as subjugation—that is, it never described the union as a "vicious" or an "illegal" imposition of sorts. The Decreto, on the other hand, disavows any relationship with Mexico. The agreement is deemed illegitimate through the assertion that it was never fully ratified and that it lasted less than a year. The retroactive annulment of the union by stating that the merger went against the party's will suggests that it was also never legally acknowledged. In this sense, the Decreto allows us to see how narratives of divorce, rather than romance and union, can be equally useful in drawing the parameters of national imaginaries. If, as Doris Sommer contends, romance novels served to establish certain unions as "natural" in the forging of the nation-space,[86] texts featuring incompatible suitors can also play a significant role by marking other geopolitical spaces as "unnatural." Like the exchanges between Delgado and Filisola about a Salvadoran and Mexican union, the Decreto dispels the notion that Mexico could ever be a viable suitor. These political documents about (dis)unions depict Mexico and Central America as two radically different geopolitical spaces.

Curiously, then, Mexico, more than Spain, is portrayed here as the primary antagonist, as it becomes the site of otherness needed from which to construct a Central American nation and collective identity against. Homi Bhabha explains that "the 'other' is never outside or beyond us; it emerges forcefully within cultural discourse."[87] In this case, we can see that this idea of Central America emerges from being "other" than Mexico(an). Indeed, in reviewing historical and political discourse, we see how Mexico—both as a political entity and as a phantasm imaginary figure for Central American elites—provides the condition of possibility for the making of a Central American nation. Political autonomy for the provinces is inherently linked with Mexican liberation, as it is both Mexico's war against Spain and Iturbide's abdication that permits this neighboring space to declare its own independence. Such events also provide the opportunity for the emergence of a discourse that renders the provinces as unified and fraternal. For instance, the Decreto claims that Mexican annexation "requires that the provinces of the Kingdom of Guatemala join together and separate themselves from the state of Mexico." In the retelling of this event, the provinces, though completely diverse and heterogeneous in politics and population, become reduced to static *pueblos* bound by their victimization and opposition to Mexico. Mexico ceases to represent that seemingly twin neighboring state that once shared "identical" interests, as it is transformed into a despot government and oppressor. An unintentional "return of the repressed" occurs, since Tlaxcaltecas and other present-day Mexican-affiliated Nahua indigenous groups undertook the battles for the colonization of Central America in 1524. Redramatized in the Decreto, Mexico is once again viewed as an invading, conquering force, but instead of Tlaxcalan warriors and the Spanish, it is the Mexican nation as a new world empire. In constructing Mexico as a foreign enemy and as an empire with differing values, the border and the sociopolitical boundaries of the Central American nation become enacted with Central America defined in opposition to an imaginary figuration of Mexico. However, as Homi Bhabha asserts, such attempts are in vain, since the boundaries that mark the nation's selfhood can threaten this binary division with its difference, as it becomes a space that "is internally marked by cultural difference and the heterogeneous histories of contending peoples, antagonistic authorities and tense cultural locations."[88] The provinces' newly enforced boundary underscores the futility of this imposition, since rather than solidifying a distinction between these two geopolitical spaces, the repetitive assertion of difference manifests a broader anxiety about the long-standing history of intermixing of pre-Columbian cultures in what is presently considered Mexico and the area of Central America.[89] Nonetheless, the annexation emerges as a pivotal moment in the arduous work of nation-making; it provides the opportunity to construct the Central American nation and its constituents as inherently linked via their position as victims/survivors to two distinct subjugating entities: Spain and Mexico.

Yet by interpreting Mexican annexation in this light, which is to say as a hostile, illegal takeover, the emerging Central American nation compounded a prior dilemma that the region had faced—a "peaceful" independence. This geopolitical entity was seen not only as a people who had failed to achieve independence by their own volition but also as a weak nation, one that was so vulnerable that it could not resist being recolonized by a neighboring country. Such events frame the emerging nation as lacking legitimacy that was found in other Latin American republics such as Mexico or Venezuela. The feminization of the nation as "weak," "vulnerable," and lacking masculine heroes would force the Central American nation to find alternative symbolic elements and tropes to construct itself. Continuing the exploration of discursive and symbolic boundaries of the Central American national imaginary, the next chapter examines how the federation period and the postfederation period not only perpetuated this idea of Central America but also further delimited the kinds of subjects recognized as Central Americans.

2 · CONSTRUCTING THE CENTRAL AMERICAN NATIONAL IMAGINARY

By extending the concept of nationalism, the analyst is not safely removed from the scope of investigation ... If the thesis is correct, then nationalism has seeped into the corners of our consciousness; it is present in the very words which we might try to use for analysis. It is naïve to think that a text of exposure can escape from the times and place of its formulation. It can attempt, instead, to do something more modest: it can draw attention to the powers of an ideology which is so familiar that it hardly seems noticeable.
—Michael Billig, *Banal Nationalism*

At the end of the twentieth century, just a few years after the signed *Treaty of Esquipulas* (1987), the government of Costa Rica gauged the temperature of the region, as it was reeling from the aftermath of the civil wars that had spread throughout the middle of the hemisphere. Among its many initiatives was the publication of the *Estado de la región* (1999), "a report from Central America and for Central America" that was meant to provide "a creative balance of diverse points of view rather than those of a specific country."[1] One of the more insightful chapters in this report, titled "The Diverse Visions of the Region," explores the question "what is Central America?" Within the taxonomy provided to account for the ways in which various communities view this geopolitical space, one is labeled "visión Morazánica" after Francisco Morazán, who served as the last president of the now defunct Central American Federation (1824–1838). Those who subscribe to this "visión Morazánica" see Central America as a nation and hold that the principal dream in this vision is to achieve the realization of a full Central Americanness—that is, anyone can be equally Honduran or Nicaraguan without distinction and can declare, "I'm Central American, and I live in Central

America without any internal borders."[2] The fact that this explicit form of Central American nationalism is labeled "Morazánica" invokes Anne McClintock's powerful reminder that all nationalisms are gendered.[3]

While the *Estado*'s assessment of *Morazánicaismo* is useful, one of its shortcomings is that its focus is limited to the realm of consciousness and to those subjects and communities that maintain an overt form of nationalism. Missing from this account is how a view of Central America as *patria grande* has become naturalized in social practices, political discourses, and cultural narratives from the isthmus. The effects of this crypto-nationalism reveal themselves in the ways subjects from the isthmus and beyond see themselves and others as belonging within a Central American imaginary. This point is magnified in the *Estado* report, which contains responses by fifty-three individuals interviewed from the countries of Belize, Costa Rica, El Salvador, Guatemala, Honduras, Nicaragua, and Panama. Below are a few of their answers to the question of what constitutes Central America:

Central America is my country; our common roots are greater than those that separate us.

When I think of Central America I imagine it from Guatemala to Costa Rica. I don't think of Belize or Panama, although they are now participating in *our* system of integration.

There is no Central American identity, there are only Nicaraguans, we see our neighbors speaking the same language but we do not have a regional identity.

As a black woman from Belize, Central America has not had an impact on me like the Caribbean, emotionally I identify myself with the Caribbean, I identify more with Caribbean culture than with Central America.[4]

While initially these answers concerning what Central America is and whether subjects identify with this term appear to be quite varied, a closer look reveals that, even though only one respondent seems to uphold a nationalist "visión Morazánica" (via statements such as "Central America is my country"), there are some overlapping assumptions about what characterizes this space and who belongs within this imaginary. For instance, the respondent who views only five countries from the isthmus as "Central American" maintains distinct boundaries by positioning Belize and Panama as recent newcomers with no historical ties and who do not belong to "our" system. This interviewee literally cannot imagine Belize and Panama as part of a broader Central American collectivity.

However (as we saw in chapter 1), this dislocation of two black racially coded spaces (Panama and Belize) from this isthmus imaginary is not an individual phenomenon but symptomatic of a broader historical discourse about the region. Similarly, the respondent who claims, "There is no Central American identity," implicitly relies on a circumscribed understanding of Central America. The borders of the Central American imaginary here are inherently linked with a Spanish colonial past as this interviewee (who speaks Spanish) sees this geophysical space as synonymous with Spanish-speaking culture in making the assumption that their "neighbors" speak the "same language." Despite the fact that Nicaragua is ethnoracially and linguistically heterogeneous, within the eyes of the interviewee, this state and its neighbors all appear homogenous and monolingual. Moreover, such understandings of Central America excludes a country like Belize, where the official language is English, as well as nonmestiza/o communities within isthmian countries that have African, indigenous, and Afro-indigenous populations that are not primarily Spanish-speaking. Combined, these statements affirm Claudia Milian's observation that blackness, in its recognizable and nuanced forms, is often dwarfed within Central American cultural thought.[5] Not surprisingly, the respondent from Belize expresses her inability to identify as "Central American," since both blackness and Belize have been continuously displaced from this imaginary. In stark contrast to mestizo Roberto Carpio Nicolle's affective declarations for Central America from chapter 1, as well as similar statements by other interviewees in this report, Central America holds no emotional resonance for this respondent.

Such statements disclose how some contemporary peoples and communities from the isthmus view Central America(n) as being constitutive of only certain spaces, peoples, and cultures. Like other community formations that are discursively constructed, the Central American imaginary is fluid and relational, constantly shifting to include or exclude population groups. However, as illustrated in the aforementioned responses, the inclusion and exclusion of who or what qualifies as a part of Central America, and therefore as Central American, often follows a pattern: it is usually limited to five countries (see chapter 1), and it privileges specific ethnoracial populations (like mestiza/os) over others. This delimited view of Central America is arguably guided by a *patria grande* ideology—one that sees Central America as a nation, or what the *Estado* labels as a "visión Morazánica."

This chapter investigates how a Central American imaginary was cultivated during the historical period of Central America's official existence as a nation: the federation period (1824–1838). The choice to label a nationalist ideology as "Morazánica" in conjunction with the fact that in the diaspora there are monuments devoted to this figure, underscores the ways in which this temporal moment has been deemed culturally significant. Indeed, the federation period is an important site of investigation, since it was a time of space-making, of demarcating the Central American nation-space via techniques of governmentality and the production of symbols, which began to make hierarchal distinctions about territories and inhabitants. As Priscilla Wald's groundbreaking work demonstrates, "official stories"—state-authorized narratives that are generated "in the rhetoric of nationalist movements and initiatives," are key sites in the production of a national imaginary.[6] Consequently, in this chapter, I analyze "official stories" such as constitutions and nationalist symbols, as well as cultural productions from this political era like newspapers, in order to highlight the central metaphors and tropes utilized in the construction of a Central American nation. I also illustrate how these texts circumscribe Central Americanness within particular racial, classed, and gendered ideologies that enable finite notions of this term to be circulated within the isthmus and beyond. In this regard, I follow Homi Bhabha's call to outline the "ambivalent margin of the nation-space"[7] as I trace the dislocations in the construction of this national imaginary in order to disrupt totalizing discourses about Central America(n). Moreover, I also disclose how Central American nationalism—as epitomized by the concept of *la patria grande*—later became appropriated by several states. The disintegration of the Central American federation did not foreclose the perception of Central America as a nation but reinforced it in the discursive framing of the subsequent individual nation-states of the isthmus as parcels of a broader collective. Transforming an overt Central American nationalism into a more implicit one enabled a dual nationalism—where one simultaneously belongs to the *patria grande* (Central America) and the *patria chica* (individual nation-state). This type of dual nationalism is one of the unique features of a Central American diasporic identity; as the literature and cultural productions from (U.S.) Central Americans attest to, many subjects view this isthmian form of identity as an extension of their respective national identities.

THE LABOR OF NATION-MAKING: THE BIRTH OF CENTRAL AMERICA

In 1823, when representatives of the Asamblea Nacional Constituyente (ANC) met to discuss the construction of a federation and begin the process of consolidating physical and social spaces that were ethnically, racially, and politically fractured, they were plagued with a series of challenges unique to that territory. Unlike the rest of Latin America, Central American elites were confronted with the daunting task of constructing a national identity in the absence of a mobilized and bellicose independence movement. Wars and treaties are viewed as essential to nation-building, since they create geographical and temporal lines of demarcation between an insurrection/colonial period and the establishment of a new nationality.[8] War is deemed necessary not only in the process of transforming spaces, territories, and peoples into a state but also for its ability to produce "national iconographies"—myths, symbols, and historical narratives that promote a common identity among its citizenry.[9] The art of war holds a special place within the national imaginary, since it allows states to produce historical myths about heroic accomplishment, dedication, and sacrifice.[10] Within a Latin American context, Matthias vom Hau asserts that "the wars of independence were central to official memory work during the oligarchic period," and he proceeds to highlight the central role male figures occupy in historical discourse of both the late nineteenth and early twentieth centuries. In certain countries in South America, independence movements became embodied in the figure of Simón Bolívar who as early as 1819 was being canonized in aesthetic domains as "Liberator and Father of the Nation."[11] Historical texts, like the 1873 *centenario* celebrating Bolívar, would position him as part of a broader male fraternity of nation-builders: "There was one Napoleon I, one Washington, one San Martín, one Bolívar . . . Each of these men have awed the world with their deeds, and each has dignified his respective fatherland with his heroic feats."[12] This personification of the nation not only as white but also in the embodiment of a particular form of masculinity (a revolutionary hero) is utilized to map a particular territorial domain in order to distinguish spaces from one another. However, this was difficult to reproduce in the case of Central America, which lacked this type of male body politic. As the nineteenth-century historian Andrés Dardón explains, "The victories achieved in South America by the liberator Simón Bolívar, that demi-god who paraded the Republic's banner victoriously, and by Hidalgo's heroic struggle in New Spain, were fortuitous for Central America, which was forgotten by her masters while they were engaged in these other ventures, while they were caught in the fire of war. Meanwhile, Central America was able to declare, unopposed, its freedom, thanks to the sacrifices made by its brothers from one end to the other of the Americas and those made by its own men."[13] Dardón's statements link Bolívar and Hidalgo with action verbs, as both figures occupy a metonymic function representing a particular place and space in the Americas. By contrast, Central America lacks any connection to figures or events; it appears as an empty space of signification that finds its fortune due to the ambitions and heroism of others. The "orphan" trope reemerges as Central America is feminized and infantilized yet again; described as "forgotten," she occupies a passive role as mere witness to the war of others, since she is incapable of advocating for self-independence. Any type of autonomy is achieved by the sacrifices of her "brothers" and her "masters" who forget about her. Thus without independence war heroes to memorialize and canonize and without the myth of blood sacrifice, Central American nation-builders would have to depend on other tropes, rituals, and practices to forge the embryonic nation.[14]

To this end, Central American elites relied on the belief that a governmental structure was capable of forging an equally strong communion between heterogeneous peoples. Inspired by the ideals of republicanism, the ANC looked toward the U.S. Constitution and their adoption of a federalist system of government as a successful model to emulate. Not all members of the ANC, however, would be convinced of the applicability of the North American administrative system in Central America. José Maria Castilla, a representative from Guatemala, remarked on November 18, 1823, that "even though the Anglo-Americans are cited as an example of those who have articulated the formation of a big state out of several smaller republics or states, joined by one unifying thread, I don't see them as role models of our particular circumstances, as I see our states as very distinct from the Northern American ones."[15] Though Castilla represents only his province of Guatemala, it is clear that he sees himself and his country as belonging to a larger regional entity that is described as having the same "circumstances" despite being made up of multiple "states." Castilla goes on to assert that Central America's fundamental difference from the United States is its lack of qualified future citizen-subjects:

According to Humboldt's calculation, what was called the Kingdom of Guatemala has 20,920 square maritime leagues . . . and was populated with more than a million inhabitants. From these numbers, two thirds must be subtracted as they are Indians, who, as of today, are incapable of knowing their rights, and will be so for a long time. Also, women, children and the elderly must be subtracted from this number, as well as other inhabitants . . . who are more difficult to civilize than the first ones mentioned . . . Where will we find men suitable to occupy legislative positions as well as municipality ones, such as directors, senators and councilors, magistrates, and so many other civil servants in order to establish the government system.[16]

Castilla's vote illustrates the ways such cultural texts were used to outline who could be seen as Central American even before a proper Central American political entity emerged. Invoking the work of Alexander von Humboldt,[17] he relies on theories emerging from nascent schools of scientific thought—physical geography and demography—to argue for the distinction between "inhabitants" and future citizens. Scarcity of population is not the problem for Castilla; it is the fact that within colonial and scientific discourse only certain kinds of bodies and subjects are recognized as being able to participate civically. In doing so, he demonstrates how the racial economy of the *castas* system was still present during this shift to a "modern" state, as he only views certain racialized gendered subjects capable of occupying positions such as those of "senators, councilors, magistrates." This racial caste system was also inherently class-based, as it usually only allowed *peninsulares, criollos,* and mestizo/as to obtain such legislative positions. Consistent with a racist and patriarchal colonial logic, for Castilla, women are as helpless and in need of care as children. Indigenous communities are unworthy of self-governance, since they do not even know their rights. Black subjects are more marginal still as Castilla makes no mention of the multiple black communities present in the region except by alluding to them as that part of the population "who are more difficult to civilize than the first ones mentioned." Unlike "Indians" who, according to Castilla, will one day (though at a much slower pace than whites and mestiza/os) be cognizant of their rights, black communities are framed as inherently incapable. A racialized hierarchy is presented here not only in the fact that black communities are not provided with a name but also in the way they are distinguished from the other listed ethno-racial, gender subjectivities by their unproven ability to be "civilized."

Sibylle Fischer's argument that political texts are sites of "fantasies of statehood and foundational fictions"[18] allows us to see how Castilla's document contains cultural anxieties that underpin representations of Central Americanness. For instance, if one adheres to Castilla's criteria about who can be Central American, we see that the ideal citizen for this national political community would be a young, white and/or mestizo male. This vision of the ideal citizen-subject is not in itself unusual, since as noted earlier, other Latin American nations were also personifying the nation in a similar fashion. What does make this one distinct, however, is that discursively Central America was being framed as antithetical to this vision: as a female orphan (see chapter 1). Castilla's desire for a particular kind of national subject, then, might be embedded with a larger yearning to undo tropes that depicted Central America as a feminized infantilized space. And yet, the trope of infantilization that Castilla wants to expel from Central America nonetheless surfaces in this cultural text, specifically in his description of indigenous communities as occupying a different stage of human/political development. Here, we again witness a form of historical anxiety manifest. Though Castilla will claim that indigenous communities are "incapable of knowing their rights," recent political events in Guatemala (the province Castilla represents) and nearby indicate that indigenous groups not only knew about their rights but also asserted them. The Tzeltal Rebellion of 1712 in Chiapas and the 1820 rebellion in Totonicapán led by Atanasio Tzul (K'iche' Maya), who refused to pay royal tribute to the Spanish crown and challenged local *criollo* officials, are some examples. This projected fantasy about unpoliticized indigenous subjects paradoxically underscores the fact that while Guatemalan *criollos* rarely physically rebelled against the Spanish, indigenous communities did.[19]

Although Castilla's remarks contain a fantasy for what the constituents of the nation-state ought to be (white males), his text also serves to buttress future totalizing representations about Central America that read it as white and/or a mestiza/o nation. As portrayed by Castilla, Central America is ethnoracially heterogeneous, and that is the precise source of his anxiety, particularly in relation to black communities, which are not mentioned and therefore expunged from this representation of the space. This disavowal in the form of nonnaming, however, only serves to hypervisibilize black subjectivities, as it foregrounds how blackness has been integral to the construction of this imaginary (as a source of racial/cultural anxiety for its nation-builders). As we will see, via imposed silence and absence, blackness will continuously haunt the Central American nation.

Despite Castilla's objections, the ANC would move forward with its federalist project, and in 1824, a formal constitution was issued declaring Central America as politically sovereign and a singular "pueblo." As Jordana Dym notes, the use of the homogenous *pueblo* binds diverse individual groups as they all become part of a single federation common government.[20] The geophysical borders of the Central American nation are delineated in articles 5 and 6, section 2, which hold that "the Republic's territory is the same one as what was known as the old Kingdom of Guatemala, except for the Chiapas province, for now," and claims that the federation "consists of five states, which are: Costa Rica, Nicaragua, Honduras, El Salvador and Guatemala. The Chiapas province will be included as a state once it freely joins the Federation."[21] The Central American federation emerges from a blueprint of empire reproducing the same colonial political cartography first sketched by the Spanish. The province of Chiapas, which was the first to break from the Kingdom of Guatemala to join the newly formed Mexican nation, is still indexed as part of this political community. Its absence from this territory is viewed as temporary, as an exception ("for now") that will become a state of this federation when it decides to return. There is an assumption, if not an expectation, that the colonial configuration of the Kingdom of Guatemala is one that all provinces desire to maintain.

Although its geographic configuration might be entrenched within colonial mappings, in ideological terms, the republic and its nation-builders used constitutional materials to represent themselves as progressive "modern" men (and I use this gender pronoun deliberately). A byproduct of Enlightenment principles of liberalism, in its ideal form, the constitution was an egalitarian measure whereby all were guaranteed civil liberties regardless of religion and race via the state, which viewed them as being all entitled to the same "natural" rights of man. Of course, this political form of equality was often subverted by inherent understandings of social inequality that would hinder laws from fulfilling their promise. For instance, just prior to the dissemination of the official constitution, on April 17, 1824, the ANC issued a decree "abolishing" slavery and bestowing "equal rights" on slaves.[22] Although this fact is often invoked to show how racially progressive Central America was in relationship to the United States and other Latin American nations, it is equally important to note that freedom from slavery was not viewed as tantamount to black subjects being read as "equal" to *criollos* or mestiza/os. This is exemplified by the need to indemnify the slaves' "owners" for their freedom and by the creation of a Junta de Indemnización that would decide based on the slaves' age and gender whether owners were eligible for compensation and, if so, how much they would receive for their "property."[23] But in creating a hierarchy among and between slaves, as well as by providing reimbursement to slave owners for their loss, the slave subject remains an object, as it is relegated to the realm of being someone's property. In other words, while Central American elites viewed slavery as an institution incompatible with the values of liberalism, they did not necessarily view black racialized subjects as their equals.

Analogously, criteria for political citizenship within the constitution disclosed how the republic desired political unity but not equality. Articles 13 through 22, section 2 of the 1824 Central American constitution, for instance, reifies a distinction between citizens and inhabitants by suspending "citizen rights" for "crimes," "immorality," "domestic work," "disability," and "debt," emphasizing that "only lawful citizens can receive services from the Republic."[24] Citizenship is contingent on heteronormative institutions such as marriage and racial caste/class-based ideologies like one's occupation, productivity, and work, which, as previously described, were inherently linked with a racial *castas* system. Even then, the situation was precarious as citizenship would be denied or suspended if one was convicted of a crime, poor (unable to pay debts or rent), a domestic worker, physically disabled, cognitively disabled, or deemed "morally" incapable. In legislating rules whereby citizenship can easily be revoked for failing to pay debts, or for particular types of occupations, the state sanctioned the disenfranchisement of certain social groups and racial populations. The colonial system of *encomiendas* that placed several groups at an economic disadvantage, as well as its reliance on Roman Catholic values (the religion endorsed by the federation in the same constitution) to judge one's "moral" character, enabled the exclusion of certain types of women, sexual, and racialized communities who were innately seen as debtors, barbaric, and/or immoral.

While the constitution failed to construct political cohesion (e.g., the singular "pueblo"), the manufacturing of symbols of this newly formed nation propelled this mission by trying to "hail" these inhabitants to see themselves as "centroamericanos" (Central Americans), even if they could not be citizens or granted the same type of political rights. This arduous process of mythopoeia would begin prior to the enactment of the constitution itself.[25] On August 21, 1823, for instance, the ANC would dictate how the nation would represent itself symbolically via its designation of an official flag and coat of arms.

Historical texts attribute Manuel José Arce as the creator of the Central American federation flag. As told, Arce was inspired by the flag created by the Provincias Unidas del Río de la Plata (1810–1831), which opted during their wars of independence against Spain to abandon the colors of empire (red and yellow) for blue and white. When the province of San Salvador refused annexation to Mexico in 1822, Arce—the general commander of San Salvador's military—asked his wife Felipa Aranzamendi and his sister Antonia Manuela to construct a two-tone blue-and-white flag made out of silk. On February 20, 1822, the flag was blessed in an official ceremony witnessed by townspeople and the military.[26] Interestingly, whereas the flag of the United Provinces of the Río de la Plata (and by extension the current Argentinian flag) emerged from privileging the historical memory of this province's fight against Spain for its independence, Central America's flag is grounded not in a regional war of independence but in a limited battle between San Salvador and its neighboring Mexican empire. The fact that a flag that was used during these military encounters was chosen to represent the Central American republic highlights the inherent dialectical relationship within nationalism between remembering and forgetting: the flag allows the Central American nation to remember the only moment in which one of their provinces engaged in warfare as a form of independence, while simultaneously forgetting that most of the provinces voluntarily accepted Mexican annexation. It also further reentrenches the dialectical relation the Central American nation has with the geopolitical space of Mexico (defining itself as outside of and other than Mexican). In addition, the gendered division of labor associated with the historical narration of the making and use of the flag also inscribed the proper roles one needed to inhabit to be good subjects of the nation: women would be the cultural (re)producers of the nation relegated to the domestic sphere, while men would publicly serve by taking arms to defend and protect the nation.

In adopting this flag and by adding the coat of arms at its center, the Central American nation-state began to forge what Sverker Sörlin calls the "articulation of territory"—a process whereby one area is distinguished from another, "establishing communities of affection and memory" that enable people to feel that "they belong to a place or a nation."[27] The use of geography by state-sanctioned discourses, especially state symbols, is not neutral, as they are summoned and disseminated "for the conscious or unconscious condition of belonging and identity, and for the production and formatting of citizens and their self-understanding as people."[28] The territorial iconography developed to represent the Central American republic featured symbols that presumably transcended localized provincialisms and would help solidify the notion that all the provinces inhabited a shared past, future, and territorial space. To this extent, Central America, as a geographical location, becomes redefined as the excess *other* between North and South America to a strategic geopolitical location. The conflation of Central America with an isthmus gains currency during this historical moment, as it was meant to instill a type of geographical uniqueness to this political space from other nations at that time while simultaneously emphasizing that living in the center of the Americas was a denominator between provinces. When deciding to pick a name for the federation, Central America was chosen with the aim of highlighting "its privileged place among seas and continents."[29] Over time, the isthmus image became the predominant iconic symbol of the Central American republic and figured prominently in all the newly created national symbols like the Central American flag (see fig. 1), the Central American coat of arms, as well as songs composed for Central America. One benefit of adopting the Salvadoran-issued blue and white flag as the "official" flag of the newly created federation was that it visually mimics an isthmus. The blue and white horizontal stripes surround a white panel whose center contains the Central American coat of arms—the only section that features terrestrial images, making the blue portions of the flag analogous to the Pacific and Atlantic oceans that surround Central America and give it its geographic character of an isthmus.

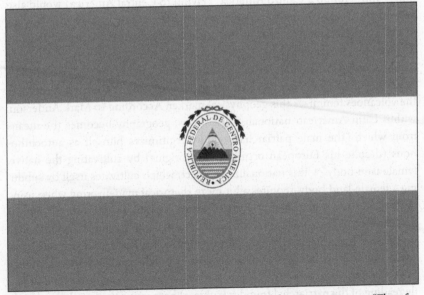

FIGURE 1. Flag of the Federal Republic of Central America. (Guillermo Romero, "Flag of the Federal Republic of Central America," https://commons.wikimedia.org/wiki/File: Flag_of_the_Federal_Republic_of_Central_America.svg, CC BY-SA 2.5.[30])

The coat of arms also reproduces the importance of the isthmus in the national imaginary. Consisting of an equilateral triangle encased by surrounding seas within a broader circular frame, five volcanoes appear inside the triangle, they stand beneath a Phrygian cap, a radiant sun, and a rainbow arc. The image of the isthmus is twice reproduced in the coat of arms, both within the triangle itself, as the five volcanoes are surrounded by water, and in the circular frame that merges the triangle within two bodies of water. The Phrygian red cap, also known as a liberty cap, was a prominent symbol of the French Revolution often used to "cover the head of the goddesses Liberty and Nation, . . . and then the emblem of men and women who wanted to be citizens instead of subjects."[31] In this context, instead of covering female goddesses, it covers "volcanoes," feminizing the Central American landscape and repurposing it as the space of the nation. Unlike previous representations that feminized Central America as a political entity, this gendering of landscape and territory was completely welcomed by nation-building elites. Ella Shohat and Robert Stam explain that tropes that gender the landscape "evoked a quasi-divine process of endowing life and meaning *ex nihilo*, a Promethean production of order from chaos."[32] We witness this conjuring of a "quasi-divine process" in the coat of arms as the sun beaming over the volcanoes and the use of the rainbow invokes a type of divine providence over the land—the rainbow connotes the biblical covenant detailed in Genesis where God promises to protect the land and to allow for new beginnings. The "Himno a Centro América" (Hymn to Central America) would also perpetuate Central American manifest destiny by boldly declaring, "God has placed you [Central America] at the center of the world / and tomorrow its financial center you will be."[33]

The Central American coat of arms also introduces another iconic national symbol: the volcano. As previously mentioned, placing the Phrygian cap over the volcanoes feminizes this geophysical marker. According to Mark Anderson, within Latin American nationalist discourses, geography becomes the means from which "the male patriarchal founder legitimizes himself as autochthonous (despite his European or mixed-race origins) by cultivating the native, female land-body."[34] This nationalized subject, which cultivates itself by subduing a female-land body, requires a bit more rhetorical maneuvering when using the volcano as a trope since it is based on a geophysical entity that is known for its inherent instability. The volcano is a sexually ambiguous symbol, since on the one hand, its activity (eruptions) mimics male physiological processes while, on the other hand, its conical curvature visually parallels female anatomy. Still, while the figure of the volcano may not reproduce the same type of facile reading of the patriarchal founder (subject) harnessing the female-land body (object) since geological discourse prescribes a symbiotic relationship between volcanoes and the land—via its assertion that soil fertility is contingent on the presence (penetration) of volcanic ash—it nevertheless frames the volcano as "patriarchal founder and protector of the fertile female landscape."[35]

If the image of the volcano gendered space and therefore the nation, it also cultivated the notion that its inhabitants shared the same spatial frame. Rather than living in vacant space or territory, the use of this geographical icon conveys the idea that the experience of Central Americanness was rooted in volcanic culture. The volcano naturalizes the notion of simultaneous living conditions, as it was imagined that subjects in Central America were linked by their mutual experiences of existing in the shadows of volcanoes. Under this belief, all Central Americans see the volcano as the prominent feature of their landscape, they all benefit directly or indirectly from the fertile soil produced from volcanic ash, and all are subjected to the volcano's violent wraths and eruptive unpredictability. By endorsing volcanic culture as iconic of the Central American nation, the state encouraged its inhabitants to imagine themselves seeing, feeling, and experiencing their environment as if they were one and the same since it was thought they all shared the broader framework of the isthmus and were exposed to the same geophysical living conditions.

But this attempt to unify inhabitants of Central America by focusing on their shared volcanic culture also highlights which physical spaces the Central American state viewed as representative of the nation. The Central American volcanoes, also known as the Central American Volcanic Arc (CAVA), are mostly situated on the coastal side of the Pacific Ocean.[36] By making the geophysical areas on the Pacific coast a quintessential emblem of the Central American state, nation-builders disclosed which spaces were desired as more representative of the national landscape as well as became a vehicle for the racialization of space. In positioning the volcano(es) as prototypical of the Central American landscape, the state nurtured what Lowell Gudmundson and Justin Wolfe assert as the modern "obsession of Pacific oriented Central America [and/]or its relegation of African-descent peoples to the Caribbean coast, otherness and isolation."[37] Generally, the Pacific side of Central America has been privileged culturally and (as demonstrated here) symbolically within both the federation and the future nation-states that emerged.

Perhaps one reason for this spatial bias is that the Atlantic coastal communities, cultures, and peoples of Central America derail national narratives that frame Spanish culture and mestiza/o racialized subjects as endemic to the territory. The British had for years controlled the Caribbean coastal plains of Central America and forged strong alliances with both the indigenous populations and the black ethnic communities that inhabited the area.[38] For most of the twentieth century, the Atlantic coast of Central America would continue to be heavily populated and controlled by African-descended communities and indigenous subjects who readily spoke English over Spanish, in addition to being conversant in other languages such as Garifuna, Sumo-Mayangna, and Miskito Creole English to name a few. Fusing the volcano with the national iconography enforced a myopic view of Central America that deterred one's eye from seeing black racially coded spaces as equally constituent of the nation. By ignoring and erasing those geopolitical spaces where black cultures, languages, and bodies were at the forefront of everyday life, this prism sanctioned a national conception of itself premised on a definition of "black as other." The volcano trope, however, was one of several textual strategies deployed in the nineteenth century with the aim of minimizing or erasing blackness to pave the way for a mestiza/o nation. Other such strategies included abandoning racial designations such as "negra/o" or "mulata/o" in favor of ladina/o, which connoted "all members of society not identified as Indians"—or rewriting history; as Lara Putnam explains, "Over the course of the nineteenth century Central American elites had rewritten their cities' largely mulatto and *pardo* past with a set of racialized myths that claimed only Spanish and indigenous progenitors for the nation."[39] Via these symbolic representations, a "sleight of hand [occurred] by which blackness and blacks disappeared in the nineteenth century."[40]

This expunging of blackness (by severing specific spaces off) from the larger national body reveals the margins of the nation-space. Despite the nation's desire to make "blackness disappear," it had to contend with the fact that non-Atlantic coastal communities and places had been forged by black subjects and, conversely, that their "manifest destiny" of occupying the "center of the world" was actually limited. For example, the current state of El Salvador, which does not have territory on the Atlantic coast and is viewed as having a "nonexistent" black population by some (its lack of contact with the Atlantic coast is often referenced as proof of its unblackness),[41] at one point had such a large black population that local leaders feared a "racial uprising."[42] Moreover, while it is difficult to quantify racial populations in an area that systemically tried to eradicate Afro-descended groups via structural mechanisms like census-taking,[43] their presence is apparent (albeit problematically) in tourist promotional materials, which promote ideologies of racial democracy by claiming that Salvadorans share "genes of African slaves."[44] The repeated desire to dislocate blackness from this imaginary then only magnifies the anxiety Central American elites had regarding the racial composition of the nation. As Castilla's vote reveals, the inhabitants of the territory (not just on the Atlantic coast) were always ethnoracially heterogeneous. The symbolic representations of Central America as nonblack are therefore constantly undermined by other political documents in this era that spectrally index its blackness. Nevertheless, if the geographical frame of the isthmus symbolically circumscribed its borders and its inhabitants as *centroamericanos* / Central Americans, what these official symbolic gestures foreground is that some spaces, cultures, and races were valued over others.

RETERRITORIALIZING LA PATRIA

By making the national iconography synonymous with geography, national-ist discourse often invoked the superiority of the Central American landscape over others. This ecological "beauty contest" is exemplified in a letter written by José Cecilio del Valle—author of the September 15, 1821, Declaration of Independence and a central figure in Central American politics—to Alexander von Humboldt in 1826:[45]

> Nature has favored my *patria* more than it has Mexico. The latter, like Spain, suf-fers from dry heat and drought throughout most of its highland. Our Central America, on the other hand, is abundantly showered by currents that are easy to navigate. Our vegetation is more exuberant than that of Mexico . . . We have ports on both oceans, and if at some point these two oceans are to be united through a channel in Nicaragua (for which you probably have plenty of docu-ments already), our Republic, placed in the center of America, will connect the West Indies trade with that of China and the East Indies, and thus, it will occupy an important place among all nations.[46]

Del Valle uses the singular possessive pronoun in the phrase "my *patria*" and quickly shifts into using the collective "our Central America" and "our Republic" to suggest that he is speaking for a wider collectivity. Mexico once again emerges as an important space in the Central American imagination, as it occupies a dialectical relation where Central Americanness is constituted by its difference from the country to the North. Conceptualizing the isthmus as a form of divine providence by arguing that "nature" has favored his *patria*, del Valle recirculates the gendered trope of Central America as a plush, fertile Eden at the center of the economic universe and thus destined to be a key player on the world stage. Mexico, on the other hand, has nothing to give to the world, as it is described as barren and arid, perpetually linked to the New World's oppressor: Spain. Although, other representations of these two emerging republics during this historical period would position them as similar,[47] del Valle's insistence on the inherent distinctions in the land and topography between Central America and Mexico asserts not only that these two geopolitical spaces occupy different land-scapes and identities but also that a Central American one is innately superior.

Del Valle's use of the word *patria* is also significant because it highlights how the term becomes resignified during this nation-building period. If the state used the performative function of the constitution and manufacturing of symbols to inoculate its subjects with the notion that they belonged to a broader political entity, other cultural texts played an equally important role in reinforcing this idea by redefining colonial notions of "homeland" or *patria*. It was during the colonial period that Central Americans were first introduced to the idea that smaller political bodies are constituents of a larger family known as *la patria*. Within the Kingdom of Guatemala, *patria* was used to refer to the Spanish monarchy and did not connote a community based on geographic boundaries but one forged via common sociocultural links like religion, king, laws, and traditions.[48] New World political events, however, would alter the scope and meaning of the concept of *patria*. As part of the nation-building process, one of the first acts required by these emerging Latin American states was to sever notions of loyalty attached to the crown and transfer them to their newfound republic. Marta Casaús Arzú and Teresa Giráldez indicate that this notion of transferring one's affective attachments from Spain (i.e., *patria*) to one's new nation-state (in this case, Central America) was burgeoning throughout Latin America.[49] Under this new restructuring, one was not forced to choose to love one's *"patria grande"* (defined as larger confederations like Río de Plata, Gran Colombia, or Central America) more than their own *"patria chica"* (usually seen as a province or state) but, instead, "loyalty should be both to the Central American fatherland, a large entity, and to the other, smaller fatherland [*patria chica*], with which it cohabits and interacts and which is understood as one's place of origin."[50] Unlike previous colonial articulations of *patria*, which were heavily deterritorialized, within this new Latin American, and specifically Central American, context, the term *patria* was reterritorialized to the Americas and became synonymous with the concept of nation on multiple scales.

In Central America, del Valle was at the forefront in reconceptualizing the notion of *patria*, often using the term interchangeably with "nation" when referring to the new Central American federation. As editor of two important newspapers, *Gazeta de Guatemala* (1793–1816) and *El Amigo de La Patria* (1820–1822), he utilized these texts as vehicles to instill in readers the belief that they inhabited the same homogenous empty time and spatial frame. Within this print media, del Valle promoted the notion that the peoples from the Kingdom of Guatemala shared similar political, geographical, and cultural paths. After narrowly losing the bid for presidency of the newly formed Central American republic, del Valle began working at the newspaper *El Redactor General de Guatemala* (1825–1826). Throughout his tenure at *El Redactor*, del Valle presented a synecdochical idea of Central America, one that argued that despite the individual nuances of each province, they were all part of the same whole: "All provinces have united to form one nation. Each one is its own independent state, but all are part of one bigger entity, they are all fractions of a single unit."[51] As a member of the political elite who often deployed the metaphor of the family in Central American political documents like the *Acta de Union* (1822), del Valle also explained the relationship that the provinces had within the larger political entity of the Central American federation, which he also referred to as *"La patria grande Centroaméricana"*:

One brother does not depend upon others, nor is there subordination or superiority between them; but all owe deference and respect to their father . . . Costa
Rica does not depend on Nicaragua, nor Comayagua on San Salvador; Comayagua, Nicaragua, and Costa Rica all have a supreme government that ought to
extend to all its peoples its vigilance and protection. This government is the link
that unites them towards the formation of a singular nation.[52]

We were all born on the same continent; we are all sons of the same mother; we
are all brothers; we all speak the same language; we all fight for the same cause;
we are all called to the same destiny.[53]

Within nationalist discourse, heteronormative tropes of kinship are deployed
to enable individuals to see themselves as belonging to a broader collective.[54]
Del Valle relies on kinship metaphors to describe the internal dynamics of this
nation-state; indeed, it anchors his idea of Central America. Employing the
trope of the family becomes another discursive practice that "transforms individuals into subjects of a collective history" by also concealing what Lauren
Berlant calls the "accident of birth within a geographic/political boundary."[55]
The arbitrariness and "accident" of sharing the same terrestrial and temporal
planes is minimized by establishing the idea that an organic or biogenetic relationship exists between spaces and peoples that are discontinuous and heterogeneous. Like families who may have differences, these differences are subordi-
nated under the belief that a genealogy and common bond exists and that this
source of unity supersedes any cultural and ethnoracial differences.

This kinship trope, as noted by Paul Allatson, situates the nation as "predicated
on faith in the patriarchal structures and heteronormative reproductive logics,
that undergird the ideals of both family and nation."[56] Such logics are manifest
when del Valle asserts that the provinces of Central America must "respect" their
"*padre*" (father), which in turn, establishes a hierarchical relationship between
the provinces and the Central American federation—a hierarchy that is viewed
as natural and logical, similar to the relationship children have with their fathers.
The family metaphor proves useful for del Valle, as it enables him to argue that
the states that compose the federation share a fraternal link that resembles the
relationship between "*hermanos*" (brothers) who do not depend or feel superior
to one another but, instead, understand their role within a patriarchal structure.
Thus while the provinces, like siblings, might have tensions among one another,
they nonetheless must show the highest respect for their "*patria*" (father)—the
one entity that can provide "*vigilancia y protección*" (vigilance and protection) to
all of them.

While del Valle also emphasizes the important role shared government occupies in the construction of national communities by claiming, "This government

is the link that unites them towards the formation of a singular nation," it is clear that the provinces share something greater than just the distinction of being a protectorate under a larger political body. In the second passage, for instance, del Valle reasserts that the provinces of Central America are bound not just by shared government but also by the same culture and territory. Their familial relationship, he argues, emerges from the fact that "we are born of the same continent; we are sons of the same mother," implying that because these provinces share the same physical space of Central America, embodied here in the image of a mother, they share an organic fraternal relationship. The passage also solidifies the notion that culture binds these provinces together, asserting not only that they "speak the same language" but that they are also united for the "same cause" and beholden to the same destiny. Despite del Valle's assertion of familial origins, only certain cultures and racialized subjects belong within this Central American national imaginary—since arguably only *criollos* and mestiza/os would literally and figuratively share the same Spanish "language" and or "mother." Indeed, del Valle's kinship metaphors construct Central Americanness as a form of racial citizenship—one grounded in *mestizaje*, in a Spanish colonial history of sharing the same tongue and desiring the same destinies. This logic of *mestizaje* is embedded in the family structure, as it is a female-gendered America ("the same mother") who is inseminated by Spanish colonialism, making Central America(ns) the offspring of this mixture. In doing so, del Valle's work, as emblematic of a broader discourse that deploys the family metaphor, establishes Central America as a mestiza/o nation.

Lest we think that this type of logic or tropes regarding Central America were limited to this historical period and territory, it is worth noting how contemporary U.S. diasporic organizations, like the Alianza Cívica Cultural Centroamericana (ACCCA) and the Confederacíon Centro Americana (COFECA) reproduce this discourse. On their website, the ACCCA explains that "Central American nations are intimately connected by our origins, by our cultural roots, by our geography and history, and by our own dreams and aspirations. We were conceived by the same fathers and born as independent nations on the same day," while on their website, COFECA proclaims that Central Americans share "roots" and "patrimony."[57] Despite the passing of 150 years during which members of this community were raised within their own nation-states and migrated to another country, ACCCA and COFECA's characterization of Central America(n) echoes del Valle's. In this vision, Central Americans not only share the same cultural roots, geographical territory, historical trajectory, and aspirations but also are a primordial group as they are viewed as "family." The logics of heteronormativity and patriarchy once again undergird this sense of Central Americanness, as both the ACCCA and COFECA view Central Americans as sharing the same cultural seed from their fathers ("patrimony"). Thus consciously or not, these diasporic enunciative acts recirculate long-standing kinship tropes and invoke a historical basis for Central American identity: the *patria grande Centroaméricana.*

Nevertheless, while state-sponsored symbols and other cultural texts like newspapers succeeded at producing an enduring mythopoeia of Central American nationalism, the federation itself was not able to subsist. A combination of factors, including poor infrastructure that hindered interstate communication, jealousies, warfare among the states, and ideological battles between liberals and conservatives, saw the demise of the República Federal de Centroamérica. Interestingly, like the date of its independence, the demise of the Central American republic is hard to determine. Some historians suggest an open time frame and state 1838–1839 as the ending of the federation. Thomas Karnes, on the other hand, decidedly sees it as ending in July 1838, while Noé Pineda Portillo argues that the death of Francisco Morazán in 1842 (Morazán was executed in Costa Rica while attempting to reestablish a Central American republic) marks the symbolic ending of the federation.[58] And yet, the fact that from 1840 to 1940 several efforts were made to reintegrate—the last symbolic attempt at a political union occurred in 1921—as well as the commemoration of Morazán in El Salvador, Guatemala, Honduras, Nicaragua, and Costa Rica,[59] suggest that a Central American national imaginary remained(s) resilient even if the project of producing a Central American federation was a political failure.

THE NATION IS DEAD, LONG LIVE THE NATION!

The eventual formation of individual nation-states from the countries that used to compose the Central American federation did not signify the end of Central America as *la patria grande.* The failure to maintain a Central American federation should not be read as a failure of this nation to "hail" some of its subjects into seeing themselves as *centroamericanos* or to create a form of ethnocultural pan-nationalism. A Central American national imaginary continued to play a great role in the politics and cultural practices on the isthmus, as the demise of the federation did not engender a quick shift into independent nations nor did it quench the desire for a larger supranational political entity. In fact, the dissolution of the Central American republic was not an indictment or a rejection of these states' perception of themselves as interconnected; it was, however, a specific critique of the ways in which federalism was enacted. On April 30, 1838, when Nicaragua releases a *decreto* proclaiming its own sovereignty and independence from the Central American federation, it reasserts that its independence is not entirely based in a desire to be an autonomous republic but is also a means to provide an opportunity to construct a different federal model. Point 1 of the *decreto* states that "the Nicaraguan nation is free and sovereign without any restrictions, other than those agreed upon by any new deal that it may create with other Central American States," while point 10 asserts "that each state should promote on its own the formation of a new federation pact, which corresponds more to the particularities of Central America."[60] Nicaragua's *decreto* perpetuates the notion of a uniqueness inherent to this region in its claim that federalism needs to correspond to "the particularities of Central America," suggesting that the conditions of this political entity are unlike other government models in operation. It also suggests that the dismemberment of the federation is caused not by the lack of a will to form a union, nor by Nicaragua's failure to see itself as a parcel of that broader collective, but rather is the result of poorly employed federalism. In a way that is eerily reminiscent of its trajectory in seeking independence from Spain, Nicaragua claims that it is free and sovereign and without restrictions, with the exception of the ones that a "new" agreement with the other Central American states could impose. This language expresses a certainty about reunification, as the statement places no provisions, nor does it use conjunctions like "if" or "when"; instead, there is an expectation that a new pact will emerge.

Nicaragua's confidence in a future reunification among the neighboring states proves prophetic when, merely four years after separating from the federation, a new political configuration emerged known as *La Confederación Centroamericana*.[61] This political constellation, composed of El Salvador, Nicaragua, and Honduras, was fleeting, lasting only three years. Still, this unifying pledge among these neighboring states signals that most of them continued to view themselves belonging to a larger conglomerate rather than as separate independent republics. It is not until after March 21, 1847, when Guatemala officially declares itself a "República," that the other isthmian states would routinely utilize this term to define themselves politically.[62] Costa Rica would soon follow by changing its title from "state" to "republic" on August 31, 1848.

But other states like El Salvador and Honduras would remain more hesitant. El Salvador, for instance, was pronounced a republic on February 18, 1859, stating that since "the State of El Salvador has done all it can to achieve the reorganization of the old Federal Republic of Central America, without success and, on the contrary, due to this industry it has suffered wars and other catastrophes," it "declares itself a FREE, INDEPENDENT AND SOVEREIGN REPUBLIC." However, "this decree does not preclude El Salvador from engaging in the organization of a Confederate Pact, in union with other Central American States."[63] El Salvador's birth as a republic begins by being represented as a "last resort," one that stemmed from the failure to reorganize the Central American federation. In its rationale for why it became a republic, El Salvador confirms that it always saw the demise of the first federation as temporary, and reasserts that its primary focus was to be a part of a larger cultural and political fraternity of Central American states. This is evidenced by article 2, which like Nicaragua's *decreto*, allows for the suspension of complete state autonomy in favor of joining a federation. In a similar manner, the state of Honduras would also express its reluctance to symbolically secede from the federation by waiting twenty-seven years before officially declaring itself a republic. In noting these delays in adopting and/or infrequently using the term *republic*, I am not suggesting that these aforementioned countries lacked their own political autonomy or cultural identity or that they did not see themselves as independent, rather, I read it as a symbolic expression of a hesitation to appropriate a term that had been reserved for the federation.

Moreover, given the time period, these constitutional clauses in El Salvador and Honduras might be the result of not just a desire for a broader symbolic collective but also a political necessity. The aptly titled *Campaña Nacional* (National Campaign), also referred to as la *Guerra Nacional Centroamericana* (National Central American War; the slippage between "Nacional" and "Centroamericana" again showcases how Central America was conceived as a nation), had just ended in 1857. Spearheaded by Costa Rica, in 1856, the republics of Guatemala, El Salvador, Honduras, and Nicaragua created a coalitional army to fight U.S. filibuster William Walker and his occupation of Nicaragua. A nationalist Central American rhetoric employed to galvanize and motivate the states into action against Walker complimented this military unity. Just after declaring war on Walker, on February 29, 1856, then president of Costa Rica, Juan Rafael Mora, reminded his fellow countrymen that to fight for Nicaragua was to fight for a member of their family, stating, "We march to fight for the liberty of our brothers . . . their cause is our cause . . . no more parties no more fraternal discords . . . God will give us victory, peace and liberty and union of the great Central American family."[64] Downplaying the long-standing violent contentions within and among the neighboring Central American states by labeling them "fraternal discords," Mora frames them as a form of "infighting" and not as external wars. The fact that Nicaraguan liberals invited Walker to the territory and caused this military escalation is omitted in the invocation of nationalist rhetoric proclaiming a Central American manifest destiny where "God" will allow them to maintain their political rights over the isthmian landscape. Mora's political speech, then, not only reveals the emotive currency that Central American nationalism maintained even after the federation period but also demonstrates how textual strategies and political events helped weave this national imaginary into the subsequently created republics.

Indeed, the newly self-fashioned republics never completely undermined the idea of a Central American nation. Ironically, the same period that witnessed the end of the Central American federation and engendered the birth of independent isthmian republics is the same historical moment that would entrench

Central American nationalism within these very states. Official state discourses promoted Central American nationalism by constructing a system that made two nationalisms (*patria chica / patria grande*) complimentary and mutually defining rather than contentious. It is for this reason that even after the states officially became republics and nation-states (as seen in the National Campaign) the identity of a larger *pueblo centroamericano* remained. One need only read the constitutions of the republics of Guatemala, El Salvador, Honduras, Nicaragua, and Costa Rica to witness how political discourses within these countries valued the creation of a larger *patria centroamericana*. For instance, provisions in each of the individual constitutions symbolically made neighboring countries an extension of their own nation-state. Article 28 of Nicaragua's 1858 constitution proclaims that its president needs to be "native from and resident of the Republic . . . [or] can also be the children of the other Central American regions if they have fifteen years of residency and other characteristics mentioned here."[65] Even though such a clause might be a residual effect from the war against Walker—a stopgap measure to prevent other "foreigners" from invading and declaring themselves president of this republic—it nevertheless had an unintended effect. In this context, the former states of the federation are constructed as equally entitled to some of the same privileges as those born in the particular republic of Nicaragua. No other Latin American nations are granted this type of equity or exception in this Nicaraguan constitution.

Furthermore, article 104 of the 1858 Nicaraguan constitution also explicitly creates the juridical and political space needed so that Nicaragua can belong to a broader Central American federation, stating, "This decree does not preclude Nicaragua from forming a National Government with other sections of Central America, or from a federation pact, if the former cannot take place." The other emerging republics would contain similar constitutional provisions. El Salvador, Costa Rica, and Guatemala's constitutions, for example, all included terms that encouraged or allowed for a larger Central American union.[66] Article 2 of the 1879 Guatemalan Constitution claims that "it will foster close familial ties of reciprocity with the other Central American republics. And always promote Central American nationality."[67] We see a mutually defining relationship between the *patria grande / patria chica* operating in this constitution—a political and symbolic entwinement that becomes sanctioned by law with the claim that an important feature of Guatemalan civic duty is not only to cultivate the Central American "family" but also to maintain "Central American nationality." In fact, when one surveys the constitutions of Guatemala, El Salvador, Nicaragua, Honduras, and Costa Rica, a general theme emerges throughout the nineteenth century: these neighboring states were not framed as "foreign" but as fraternal political entities. Within these constitutions, one witnesses the emergence of a form of citizenship that is different from the traditional *jus soli* or *jus sanguinis* paradigm, as some inhabitants could have citizenship and be deemed a "native" national outside of these two options. In other words, one could be born in a neighboring state and still be viewed as a citizen or "native" (as opposed to naturalized) within another isthmian republic. Article 5, section 6 of the Guatemalan 1879 constitution declares that it "will consider as natives from Guatemala those who are native from the other Central American republics, who assert their desire of becoming a Guatemalan in front of a legal authority."[68] Similarly, article 9 of the Honduran 1865 constitution stipulates that "Honduran" indicates "those Central Americans who have earned residency in any province of the Republic," while article 3 of the Costa Rican 1848 constitution asserts that those "who are native from any of the republics of Guatemala, Honduras, El Salvador, and Nicaragua will also be considered native from Costa Rica,"[69] if these individuals meet two minor requirements. These provisions transcend the typical model utilized to grant citizenship, since they position individuals from the other states of the former federation not as *extranjeros*/foreigners but as fraternal *centroamericanos* who are granted the same rights as natives, such as running for president or other government offices reserved for native-born nationals.[70] In defying the typical system of citizenship (*jus soli* and *jus sanguinis*), these constitutions figuratively (and perhaps juridically) maintain the Central American nation, as the *soli* or territorial boundaries of any state belongs to the broader Central American imaginary and its inhabitants are viewed as sharing *sanguinis* and thus belonging to a Central American family.

Though some of these acts might be dismissed as merely symbolic gestures, it is important to note that the language regarding the adherence to and promotion of a Central American nation sanctioned within these constitutions was often invoked during volatile political episodes. A case in point can be seen when Nicaragua signed the Bryan-Chamorro Treaty (1914), which granted the United States territorial rights over parts of Nicaragua. Shortly thereafter, El Salvador and Costa Rica sued their neighboring state in the newly formed Central American Court of Justice.[71] In the complaint filed by the Republic of El Salvador against the Republic of Nicaragua, El Salvador states two primary reasons why this treaty should be nullified: (1) such a treaty violates El Salvador's "undeniable" rights of co-ownership in the Gulf of Fonseca and (2) the treaty also threatens "its most legitimate aspirations for the future of a Central American nation."[72] In presenting evidence for this latter point, El Salvador argued that the inclusion of certain constitutional provisions in the isthmian states indicates a legal and symbolic commitment to seeing these republics as belonging to a broader Central American nation:

The political constitution of El Salvador consecrates the principle that she is a disintegrated part of the Republic of Center of America, and that, as such, the power remains inherent in her to concur with all or any of the Central American States in the organization of a common National Government. This same principle is declared in one form or another in the constitutions of the other States of Central America. It is to be found in the constitution of Nicaragua in Article 2 . . . Alienations of territory by a Central American State to a foreign nation result, therefore, in impairing the transcendental interest that the Salvadorean people have always held, and still hold, constantly in mind as one of their greatest and most legitimate aspirations: that of the reconstitution, undiminished, with the brother peoples of the great country which had been the master of the ancient Central American domain—an aspiration toward which the five states are impelled by their common origin, religion and history. Such alienations would deeply wound that aspiration and detract from the efficiency of the great interests that the Salvadoran people, as a fractional part of the Central American people, hold to be of first importance to its national life in the future. The Nicaraguan people and the peoples of the other three States recognize, maintain and value those interests in the same measure, as is shown by the multitude of historic facts and political acts of their independent lives.[73]

In this deposition, El Salvador represents itself not as an autonomous entity but as a state that belongs to a larger republic of Central America. The federation is rhetorically reconfigured as the term *republic* is specifically reserved for Central America, while the other countries are viewed as "states" or as "peoples." The inexistence of an operative federation does not preclude El Salvador from investing in the idea that it is a part of a "disintegrated" collective of Central American states. To be Salvadoran is to understand oneself as being inherently Central American; both are mutually defining as one enables the other. The reconfiguration of a "great country" (a poor translation for the original Spanish use of *patria grande*) is not just positioned as a goal for the "Salvadoran people" who are a "fractional" part of Central America; it is described as being of "first importance to its national life," it is a sacred or "consecrated principle." As such, what is at the forefront for the *patria chica* (El Salvador) is the sustenance of the *patria grande* (the Central American nation), which is given primary importance and indeed viewed as the bedrock of its own current and future "national life."

Even though the language in this complaint functions as a performative speech act that constitutes a Central American nation, the sociopolitical events that produce the need for such a document threaten the idea of an ontological and unified "Central American people." In fact, the Court of Central American Justice, which reviewed the lawsuits from both El Salvador and Costa Rica, was born out of the lack of political union and "mutual aspirations" present in the region. Its birth emerges from a 1907 peace treaty in which the five signatory states of the former Central American federation vowed to handle disagreements via juridical measures, as opposed to other violent approaches. These internal discords, however, are not noteworthy, for during Central American independence and the federation period, there was never political consensus among the states or nation-building elites. What is significant is that even after becoming republics and engaging in acts of war and violence with one another, such actions were never framed as "national wars." As Luis Roniger notes, "All [Central American] political forces shared the understanding that these were internal, fratricidal wars"[74]—that is, despite constant tensions, these wars did not facilitate a perception of neighboring states as "foreign" nor did they establish concrete boundaries of identity similar to those produced in wars with Mexico produced during the period of Annexation or those that marked the emergence of other Latin American countries (Peru and Ecuador come to mind). Rather, these antagonisms, including the aforementioned lawsuit, are viewed as "fraternal"—typical of a family dynamic where disagreement is not confirmation of inherent differences. One witnesses this logic in the complaint, when El Salvador reminds Nicaragua that "the other states of Central America" not only have the same constitutional provisions but also share "common origins" and the same values, particularly the desire to be reunited and recognized as belonging to the *patria grande*. Consequently, even during some of the most contentious moments of its political history, such as the 1916 lawsuit over territorial rights between El Salvador and Nicaragua, this discourse still cemented their status as "*pueblos hermanos*."

The contents of these isthmian state constitutions, as well as the language in the lawsuit between El Salvador and Nicaragua, are symptomatic of a larger discourse that emerges during the early nation-building period to solidify the belief that these republics are parcels of a larger nation. In doing so, they forge the notion that two national identities can operate simultaneously—the *patria chica/grande*. By the end of the nineteenth century and continuing on in the twentieth and twenty-first centuries, within political discourse, cultural traditions, and national symbols of the former five provinces of the preexisting Central American federation, we find explicit and implicit gestures that position each country as belonging to the larger *patria grande*. This is evinced in that many of the former provinces adopted the symbols and civic ceremonies inherited during the brief period during which Central America was a republic. As discussed in the previous chapter, to date, the five countries continue to celebrate the same independence date, despite the fact that each of the respective countries in Central America became autonomous political entities at different times.

Moreover, all the national flags of the five former countries belonging to the Central American federation continue to index iconic images from the original flag. The Salvadoran and Nicaraguan flags demonstrate the most blatant examples of cannibalizing the former Central American republic into their own individual national mythos. In these two current national flags, the volcanoes, the Phrygian cap, the rainbow, the equilateral triangle, and the blue and white horizontal stripes are virtually identical to that of the former Central American federation. A sense of fraternity and communion is visually displayed as both nations utilize similar symbols to represent themselves. Although the other three former states of the federation would not mimic the exact same iconic images, the symbols of the federation remain in palimpsest form. The Guatemalan flag, for instance, still utilizes the iconic blue and white horizontal stripes, while the Honduran flag, which also has the blue and white horizontal stripes, displays five stars at its center—an homage to the five original provinces/states of the federation. Costa Rica, which within political discourse has often been referred to as the "Central American exception," seems to have a flag that mirrors that "exceptional" status, since it overtly differs from the other isthmian states due to its colors (red, white, and blue as opposed to white and blue) and coat of arms. Yet even in this flag, which admittedly looks very different from the rest, the trace of the *patria grande* remains as the color red is said to represent the blood shed for Costa Rica's liberty (given its "peaceful" independence from Spain this reference most likely refers to the National Campaign against Walker),[75] and the flag itself is composed of five stripes—again invoking the communion with the other former provinces/states. These acts, which preserve Central American national symbols instead of eradicating them, unconsciously link the nations of Guatemala, El Salvador, Honduras, Nicaragua, and Costa Rica to that broader *patria grande* and by extension to each other.

This dual nationalism is what separates Central Americanness from other types of national imaginaries. Usually, national formations designed and enforced by the nation-state operate by creating an artificial unity through the abjection of other competing nationalisms. One only need to look at the policies enacted by the Guatemalan state toward the Mayas or the Nicaraguan government (including the Sandinistas) toward the Miskitos and the Honduran state toward the Garifuna to witness how cultures that threatened a national hegemonic identity are treated with contempt and violence.[76] But Central American nationalism—as *patria grande*—has from the beginning encouraged the idea that two nationalisms can coexist simultaneously. It is for this reason that when the former provinces became nation-states, almost all of them developed their own nationalisms to be coterminous with this notion of Central America. The idea was already in place that one could not belong to their own *patria chica* without belonging to their larger *patria grande Centroaméricana*.

These overt and inferential gestures that link some states with a Central American national imaginary and enable a form of belonging have become "banal" in the twentieth and twenty-first centuries. According to Michael Billig, "banal nationalisms" are located "in the embodied habits of social life" where the "routine and the familiar forms of nationalism have been overlooked" as "our daily nationalism slips from attention."[77] A salient example of this type of "banal" or "unconscious" nationalism is found in Luis Roniger's recent political history of Central America, where he narrates his experience of being in a Guatemalan government office that displays a symbol from the Central American Federation:

> I should stress, however, that recognition of origin of the [federation's] symbols has been lost to many in contemporary society. In December 2006, in the city of Antigua, Guatemala, I entered a municipal office close to the central square of town and saw a wooden shield of the Central American federation hung on the wall. To test the current recognition of the history behind the symbol, I inquired of the two employees occupying that office about the significance, origin, or character of the shield. They looked surprised and, to my own dismay, were unable to articulate a single explanation about what this shield, with the five volcanoes symbolizing the five original countries of the nineteenth-century federation, represented. By the late twentieth century, the process of separation had crystallized and become part of popular representations.[78]

Interestingly, Roniger assumes that all subjects in Central America would know or *should* know federation iconography. This is punctuated by the fact that he is "dismayed" that the employees know nothing about the symbol. His reaction then might reveal the residual power Central American nationalism still holds for some individuals, for why would there be an expectation that these employees would know a symbol that is not Guatemalan? But even then, it would also be misguided to assume that these employees are invested in Guatemalan symbols, since not all subjects who live in Guatemala see themselves or subscribe to those identitarian categories or forms of nationalism. What Roniger's anecdote does, however, reveal is that *la patria grande* (such as its symbolism) has become banal. Though Roniger reads these employees' national illiteracy as proof that the process of "separation had crystallized" between the state of Guatemala and the federation, what is most striking is not that these employees do not know the meaning behind the symbol, but the fact that a wooden shield from a nonexistent nation still presently hangs in a government office of another sovereign state. The fact that this artifact is still prominently displayed and that employees or its patrons have not even noticed it, or do not seem to object to its presence, and that the state itself seemingly endorses it by keeping it in plain view exemplifies how banal nationalism functions. The metonymic image of banal nationalism, Billig argues, is not a flag that is being consciously waved with fervent passion; it is the flag hanging unnoticed on the public building.[79] In this case, the fact that the wooden shield feels so familiar that it goes without notice or without protest suggests that it too has achieved a type of a banal status. As such, Central American nationalism does not remain alive solely because people are aware of it or advocate it (e.g., the *morazánicos*). Its endurance is also sustained by its ability to manifest in texts that both consciously and unconsciously promote a national imaginary contingent on a *patria grande/chica* dynamic, as well as by the idioms of everyday people who see only certain spaces, peoples, and cultures as "Central American."

CONCLUSION

These first two chapters have excavated a discursive history that conceives of Central America not simply as an isthmus but also as a larger national imaginary that I have termed *patria grande*. This configuration of Central America—one that is invoked as a site of belonging for mostly mestiza/o subjects within the isthmus—is a residual effect of a Central American nationalism that emerged postindependence when the provinces of the Kingdom of Guatemala united and created the short-lived Central American federation. Though the idea of *patria* had been in place prior to the nationalist period of the late nineteenth century, it is during this timeframe when Central America as a *patria grande*—limited to five nations that share a supposedly common mestiza/o history, culture, and geographic location—came into prominence. During the postfederation period, this metanarrative of the *patria grande* became naturalized in some Central American cultural texts and maintains itself in the contemporary moment in "banal" forms—in everyday understandings of what constitutes Central America(n). The effects of this construction of a Central American national imaginary have been both productive and ambivalent. On the one hand, Central America as *patria grande* has enabled some subjects from the isthmus to see their national identity with this broader collective identity as coterminous and therefore provides them with a space of belonging. While on the other hand, this national imaginary often excludes viewing Belize, Panama, African-descended, and indigenous communities and their cultural contributions as equally constitutive of Central American culture (as highlighted by the statements of some of the interviewees in the *Estado de la región*). However, the Central American imaginary would be fundamentally altered in the twentieth century, as a series of seismic political events would force millions of its inhabitants to leave the isthmus. In the next chapter, I travel forward to the contemporary moment and illuminate how the U.S. diaspora resignifies Central America(n).

having the same boundaries or extent in space, time, meaning.

PART 2 THE U.S. DIASPORA
Little Central America

3 · PERFORMING CENTRALAMÉRICANISMO

Heterotopias and Transnational Identities at the COFECA Parade

ANGELINO LANDSCAPE

I left my apartment
and walked down Alvarado
without a destination
ignoring the traffic signals
telling me: "Don't Walk"

I saw
the claustrophobia between buildings

the drunken drifters
the cement jungle
the racist grimaces of the police,
in MacArthur Park,
the Third World
"Little Central America"
the eye for an eye of survival
the tooth for a tooth of the next
step forward . . .
my head aches from walking without a destination

I see my face reflected
in the shop window faces
of my Central American brother
who are also walking without a destination, ignoring the nagging
of the traffic signals
that say: "Don't Walk."

—Anonymous[1]

The perception of Central America as a *patria grande* would be challenged in the late twentieth century when more than a million of its inhabitants immigrated to various parts of the Americas. Though Central Americans have had a long history of immigration to other parts of the North American hemisphere—namely, Mexico and the United States—it was not until the 1970s and 1980s that migration from Central America became a large-scale phenomenon. This massive influx of Central American immigrants to the United States, Mexico, and Canada significantly altered that sociopolitical landscape. This is perhaps best represented in the city of Los Angeles, California—often referred to as "the capital of the Central American diaspora"—where the transborder flows of culture and capital intersect in such a way as to blur the lines between the United States and Central America.[2] Central Americans can attend isthmian ceremonies and celebrations, eat from the same franchised restaurants available in their native countries (such as *Pollo Campero*), and can purchase items like furniture in a local store in Los Angeles and have their extended families pick up said item from the same store on the isthmus. Similarly, a resident can have the pay from their job remitted the next day to their extended family in Central America. The circuitry of exchange involving peoples, commodities, and finances from the isthmus and the United States has completely altered the way immigrant communities relate to their homelands. The fact that Los Angeles facilitates deterioration of cultural borders is critical in the development of the construction of a U.S. Central American cultural identity. For Central Americans living in Los Angeles, Central America no longer inhabits (U.S.) America's "backyard" but lives very much within the same physical and cultural limits. By symbolically and culturally inhabiting multiple locations, the boundaries of Central America expand creating a transnation—an imaginary space utilized in the diaspora as a site of belonging and cultural identity.

In this regard, while the Central American diaspora may have scattered to various locations in the United States, the social phenomenon of appropriating the term *Central American* as a form of ethnic identification is one that has emerged most visibly in Los Angeles.[3] Currently this urban space hosts the biggest annual celebration of Central American independence, is the home of the first Central American Studies department (at California State University, Northridge), has an area of the city colloquially labeled as "Little Central America," and contains the first public space in the United States dedicated to Central Americans: the Francisco Morazán Central American Community Square.[4] Commonly referred to as "Plaza Morazán" or "Plaza Centroamericana" by residents, this area was officially inaugurated in April 2013.[5] During that ceremony, community leaders and residents emphasized recurrent themes, such as the notion that this territory "recognizes" the presence of Central Americans living in the United States, and that the commemorative bust of Francisco Morazán—who "died with the dream of Central American union"—signifies that this plaza, like its embodied hero, represents Central American "unity."[6] Plaza Morazán in the diaspora not only functions as a spatial practice that brings visibility to Central Americans but also elucidates how broader sociopolitical forces expand the borders of the Central American imaginary. A public space dedicated to Morazán can be found in every former state of the Central American federation. The production of these acts of commemoration therefore spatially syncs the diaspora symbolically with the isthmus, further blurring the binary divisions of geopolitical spaces and forging a Central American transnation.

The Francisco Morazán bust, the focal point of the plaza, serves as a gendered mnemonic device that codes a historical epoch (the federation period) as formative to Central American culture. The bust sits on plain black marble and appears anachronistic as Morazán gazes south, suggesting that he has always been present in the diaspora and now awaits the arrival of his isthmian compatriots. Significantly, unlike traditional busts that contain a plaque with pertinent information (often biographical) about the figure, there is none provided here, implying that no context is needed because Central Americans know or *should* know about Morazán and his contributions. Ironically, though Morazán's professed dream of a Central American nation was always envisioned on the isthmus, it is in the diaspora that we see glimpses of this national fantasy (re)emerge. The triangular shape of the plaza invokes the iconic symbols of the Central American federation, while the bust is adjacent to a rainbow-colored image of an isthmus stained on a concrete floor. The use of this other "nationalist" trope (isthmus) simultaneously unites, as it divides and excludes, for, on the one hand, the isthmus is colored with spaces that intermingle and bleed into one another, accentuating the porosity of borders and the intertwined nature of cultures from the isthmus. And yet, the use of only five colors in this terrestrial isthmus is a reminder that a Central American imaginary has traditionally been delimited to signify the former five states of the federation, again excluding Belize and Panama from its discursive parameters. In so doing, this urban memorial demonstrates how the diaspora can reproduce problematic notions of Central Americanness while it simultaneously rewrites and remaps its imagined borders, evidenced here in the iconic image of an isthmus that is terrestrial and landlocked, as opposed to surrounded by seas. Moreover, the Central American triangle is increasingly no longer wedded to nation-state symbols, but instead invokes a contemporary moment of violence and migration from the isthmus as most current Central American immigrants are from an area dubbed as the "Northern Triangle."[7]

Plaza Morazán, along with several other public acts that claim textual and physical spaces in the United States as "Central American," reveals the power the term has in the diaspora for both local and national cultural politics. The relevance of these cultural practices forging an autonomous social-physical and discursive space for Central Americans in the United States cannot be understated; they are integral in fostering the notion of a Central American community. For diasporic subjects from the isthmus, the concept of Central America becomes the terrain from which they can inscribe themselves into a larger matrix of discourses that repeatedly position them in an ambivalent sociocultural space as a part of Central America while being physically apart from it. In mobilizing the sign of "Central America(n)" in the diaspora as a grounds for establishing a U.S. sociocultural identity, these diasporic subjects in turn both affirm and alter the Central American imaginary.

This chapter examines how cultural texts in Los Angeles, specifically ethnic festivals known as *las fiestas patrias*, and its most prominent visual spectacle, the Confederación Centro Americana (COFECA)–sponsored Central American Independence parade, enable Centralaméricanismo. The latter encompasses the sociodiscursive processes that foster Central American identification in the diaspora, often (though not exclusively) by promoting the belief that subjects from the isthmus share a common history and social (dis)location within U.S. Latina/o imaginaries. The COFECA parade is shown here to be a vital site of identity-making, becoming a dynamic arena where identities are forged, enacted, and contested.[8] This local-yet-transnational practice (celebrations of independence parades) underscores how on-the-ground exchanges in the diaspora are imperative for narrating Central American identity. Using data collected from attending the COFECA parade in 2006, 2013, 2014, and 2015, I illuminate the ways in which this cultural event becomes a space of interpellation for some subjects from the isthmus—one that shapes ideas of Central American belonging. It is important to stress that this process of interpellation operates unevenly among different subjects. Many mestiza/os, as well as black and indigenous communities, like Garifunas and Mayas, do not necessarily "ascribe to a pan-Central American identity";[9] still, they are often nevertheless read or framed as "Central American."

Though a parade is a multimodal and polyphonic social text, containing myriad interpretations, this chapter focuses mostly on an abbreviated cultural history behind the COFECA event and provides an analysis of the parade and its participants. I highlight how this festive form becomes a prominent space of self-definition where Central American identity is not only constituted and publicly performed but also challenged. As José Esteban Muñoz argues, "Performance functions as socially symbolic acts that serve as powerful theoretical lenses,"[10] which can demonstrate how ethnicity is not a mode of being but performative. Hence the COFECA parade brings to bear how the dual concepts of performativity and performance function within these cultural practices, whereby subjects not only are constructed by such discourse but also position themselves within it.[11] It is in these signifying practices, like parades, that social actors learn to both internalize and display predetermined scripts about (class, gender, nation, race, etc.) in their articulation of Central American identity.

Indeed, the various identity (re)shaping practices that take place in the parade allows us to see how this cultural text functions in the diaspora as a heterotopic space. For Michel Foucault, heterotopias are "counter sites [where] . . . all the other real sites that can be found within the culture are simultaneously represented, contested and inverted."[12] This is witnessed in the COFECA parade, which relies heavily on material corporeality to narrate the nation as the body politic becomes personified in the flesh—predominantly in the form of racialized female bodies and (trans)gender/sexualized bodies. Their presence, in turn, serves as a counterpoint to other sites of memorialization, like Plaza Morazán and Plaza Óscar Romero in Los Angeles, which are highly masculinist, as well as refashions and complicates notions of Central Americanness, which rely on gendered and heteronormative ideologies. Moreover, since representations of Latinidad in Los Angeles often displace (U.S.) Central American experiences, I reveal how this local Central American community uses this public event to visibilize their presence and cultural differences from other Latina/o communities in the area. In doing so, the COFECA parade, as a heterotopia, becomes a key site to contest their social marginalization within U.S. and Latina/o imaginaries.

CENTRAL AMERICAN MIGRATION TO THE UNITED STATES

Transnational migration from Central America to the United States is not a new phenomenon; scholars estimate that it began in the nineteenth century.[13] Settling in such diverse metropolitan centers, such as New York; New Orleans; Washington, DC; San Francisco; and Los Angeles, the reasons for migration from the isthmus were as varied as the immigrants themselves. In that early period of migration, most Central American immigrants were "labor migrants associated with multinational fruit companies, political dissidents, and/or members of the elite class."[14] During this time period, migration from the isthmus was relatively contained. By 1960, there were fewer than fifty thousand Central Americans living in the United States, and the vast majority of these were from Panama, Nicaragua, and Honduras;[15] countries that had historically witnessed an overt U.S. presence either in the form of financial investments by multinational corporations (e.g., United Fruit Company) or via military interventions (e.g., the Panama Canal and the U.S. occupation of Nicaragua between 1927 and 1933). The migration circuits and ethnic enclaves that were established during this early period of the twentieth century would prove to be influential for the subsequent isthmian migrations.

During the latter half of the twentieth century, several economic and political factors encouraged Central Americans to immigrate to countries like the United

States. The creation of the Central American Common Market (1960), for instance, ushered in a new wave of industrialization that promoted the growth of U.S. manufacturing investment in Central America.[16] This economic development in turn had a subtle effect in stimulating Central American migration because it increased the possibilities for workers to learn about opportunities in the United States.[17] The appeal of leaving their Central American homes in the hopes of economic advancement abroad became magnified for some Central Americans during the decades of the 1960s and 1970s. In El Salvador and Guatemala, this time period coincided with one of the worst recessions either country had experienced up to that point. In 1969, the infamous "Soccer War" between El Salvador and Honduras was seen as an ecologically driven conflict, spurred by overpopulation and job scarcity.[18] In 1972, Nicaragua would experience one of the most destructive earthquakes on record, and four years later, Guatemala, a country already in serious economic trouble, found itself in even worse shape after the earthquake of 1976.[19] Though these economic factors (exacerbated by natural disasters) undoubtedly encouraged many Central Americans to seek refuge in places like the United States, the political turmoil spurred by the civil wars in Nicaragua, El Salvador, and Guatemala was an even more weighty factor.

This era of intraregional violence caused a new diaspora to emerge from the isthmus and coalesce. Fleeing the terrors of war, many Central Americans opted to immigrate to such countries like Canada and Mexico, where they often received some benefits that were not provided in the United States.[20] The majority of these immigrants (mostly Guatemalans and Salvadorans), however, sought to relocate to the United States, where many believed that under the newly passed Refugee Act (1980), they would be granted legal entry via political asylum.[21] Thousands relocated to urban centers in the United States that had established small Central American communities from earlier immigration waves, such as New York; Washington, DC; San Francisco; and Los Angeles. In this latest wave, California attracted the greatest numbers of Central American immigrants, especially the cities of San Francisco and Los Angeles. And while San Francisco was the Californian city to which most Central American immigrants initially flocked, by the mid-1980s, 63 percent of Central Americans immigrants had made Los Angeles their primary destination.[22]

CENTRALAMÉRICANISMO

Centralaméricanismo refers to the ways discursive structures, along with micro and macro social-political forces (i.e., migration, racism, imperialism, etc.), enable diasporic subjects from the isthmus to see themselves or be seen as "Central American." Centralaméricanismo is both a conscious and unconscious process. It describes acts that overtly attempt to foster and link Central

American group identification and solidarity via the use of supposed "common" symbols and culture, as well as delineate those larger structural mechanisms and discourses that either "hail" subjects into becoming Central American and/or impose that label. As a form of interpellation, Centralaméricanismo acknowledges the power of discourse in creating a social position for all subjects, including those that may not explicitly identify as "Central American." For even if subjects consciously refuse to see themselves as Central American, it is within institutions and cultural practices that these same subjects become discursively framed as "Central American."

A brief illustration of how subjects from the isthmus both fashion themselves as part of a Central American collectivity and are subject to an external imposition is evinced in the attempted renaming of the Westlake/Pico-Union district (the setting for the COFECA parade) as "Central American Historical District." Filed on May 15, 2007, the proposal was denied by the city later that year due to opposition from the local organization Friends of Pico-Union.[23] Community organizations and local residents disapproved of this renaming in part because they felt that such a name (Central American) singled out *one* social group. Marina, a resident of Pico-Union, stated, "I will not like the idea to change the name of Pico Union . . . an area that lives a lot of Latin American [sic] not only a *single* nationality";[24] a point echoed by other residents who claimed that "the name will just concentrate on *one* ethic [sic] background and Pico Union is made of many backgrounds"[25] and that "it [renaming Pico Union/Westlake area] would be a disappointment to all other nationalities because you are singling one *specific* nationality."[26] While renaming a space discloses how some diasporic subjects from the isthmus willingly self-homogenize in an attempt to obtain social visibility, it also highlights how they are equally rendered invariant by a discourse that denies the internal ethnoracial, national, and cultural differences present in Central America. The constant refrain in the letters questioning why "one," or a "single," "national" group should be privileged over others underscores how homogenization is externally imposed on these diasporic subjects, as it erases the ethnoracial and national heterogeneity present in the mass exodus of immigrants from the isthmus to the United States by labeling them as "Central Americans" and viewing them as a singular ethnicity.

If the above example signals how non-Central American residents of Los Angeles unconsciously create Centralaméricanismo by imposing that label onto all immigrants from the isthmus, in its more conscious manifestation, Centralaméricanismo functions in a way parallel to Felix Padilla's concept of Latinismo—as an ethnic principle of organization that perpetuates a myth of common origins and broader social conditions.[27] In this context, Central American identification develops from the *belief* that people from the isthmus (especially mestiza/os, as discussed in chapters 1 and 2) share a common history and culture. It also stems from the need to create a strategic alliance from which to contest their marginal social location within U.S. American and Latina/o imaginaries. When the mass migrations from Central America took place in the early 1970s and 1980s, more than a million Central Americans who previously lived independently of one another in their respective nation-states found themselves living in closer proximity in the U.S. diaspora. Los Angeles exemplifies this form of cohabitation, as it is currently home to one in five Central Americans in the United States.[28] Living in this new terrain provided immigrants with opportunities to engage with one another in everyday spaces and learn how larger sociopolitical processes like civil wars, displacement, and the homologizing racialization they experienced in the United States similarly affected them.

Spatial proximity proved a vital catalyst in fomenting group identification since Central American immigrants were not only viewed as racial others within the U.S. American imaginary but also invisible within the local Los Angeles landscape. Discourse about the greater metropolitan area of Los Angeles, for instance, has made Latina/o coterminous with Mexican American. Earl Shorris claims that "Los Angeles belongs to Mexicans and Mexican-Americans,"[29] while Rodolfo Acuña has labeled Los Angeles as "Chicano LA" and at times refers to nonwhite people in Los Angeles as "Mexican-looking."[30] In doing so, not only has the cityscape of Los Angeles been discursively marked as Mexican and Mexican American, but, by extension, the bodies—especially racialized "brown" bodies—inhabiting this place have been marked as well. This lack of social recognition within Latinidad in turn propels the conditions for Centralaméricanismo since many subjects believe they share the same space of invisibility. This marks a key difference between Centralaméricanismo and Latinismo since the former feels marginalized from not only within U.S. American symbolic and political practices but also within Latinidad.

The notion that Central Americans are displaced within the broader Latina/o imaginary is one of the components that encourage this explicit form of Centralaméricanismo. The other is the presumption that Central Americans share symbolic attachments like language and history. This ideology of mythic cohesion does not emerge in the diaspora. As outlined in chapters 1 and 2, historical narratives and cultural practices on the isthmus routinely promote a view of Central America as a *patria grande*—composed of five countries that supposedly share a common history and culture. Such articulations contribute to a form of isthmus-based identification by establishing an imaginary that is contingent on notions of shared memory, congruent histories of misery and struggle, and intertwining utopias while ignoring political tensions and fractions within and among various Central American states.[31] As such, it is important to foreground the possibilities and limitations present in Central American identification that relies on a national imaginary. Conceiving of Central America(n) as a *patria grande*—which privileges *mestizaje* via its reliance on Spanish colonialism and language as the grounds from which to assert "common" culture—simultaneously creates bridges and borders among peoples from the isthmus. Relying on mestiza/o based symbols or culture to foster identification excludes other groups, like indigenous and black diasporic populations, that may share the same political concerns, or who are disenfranchised by the same broader sociopolitical forces but may not celebrate Spanish colonial history nor are Spanish-speaking and who experience marginalization by mestiza/o U.S. Central Americans and Latina/os.[32] The characterization of Central America as a *patria grande* obscures the way other forms of identity can emerge for isthmian peoples in the diaspora—one grounded from shared experiences of being displaced and marginalized by colonialism, imperialism, and the sociopolitical order of white supremacy.[33] With this in mind, we return to the COFECA parade, since a primary vehicle for promoting *patria grande* ideology is (re)produced within *las fiestas patrias*, which view colonial independence (September 15, 1821) as a Central American holiday.

COFECA: TRANSPLANTING *LAS FIESTAS PATRIAS*

The first COFECA event took place on September 15, 1983, when thousands of Central American pacifists, along with U.S. Americans, protested for peace and against military intervention in Central America.[34] That this initial protest took place in the early 1980s is not surprising, since as scholars have observed, it is during this era that isthmian immigrants began to forge political coalitions and deploy the term *Central American* to obtain sociocultural visibility.[35] Exemplifying Centralaméricanismo, this first event illuminates how broader social conditions—namely, U.S. intervention and the civil wars occurring on the isthmus, coupled with the assumption of a shared history among certain countries from that geopolitical space—propelled the emergence of a Central American cultural institution like COFECA. According to COFECA, September 15 was selected to "convene the Central American people" due to its historical significance.[36] This public performance of Central American solidarity (in the form of protest) linked the historical memory of a particular past (Central American independence) with then-current events (the civil wars in Central America), which in turn propagates a continuous common history (present and past) among Central American subjects. In fact, a year after this first political manifestation, COFECA was created to unify the local Central American community by preserving its "roots, identity and patrimony."[37] At present, COFECA is responsible for some of the biggest Central American cultural events in Los Angeles, such as the Central American Independence parade, the Central American Independence festival, and the crowning of Miss COFECA. Inspired by festivals on the isthmus known as *las fiestas patrias*, these cultural institutions, attended by many Central American residents in Los Angeles, have proved to be instrumental in constructing Centralaméricanismo.

Las fiestas patrias, which are celebrated throughout Central America, showcase how "invented traditions" rely on symbolic and cultural acts of repetition to naturalize ideologies and create "continuity with a suitable historic past."[38] Emerging in the nineteenth century, *fiestas patrias* create a tradition that privileges the historical period of postindependence when the Kingdom of Guatemala was transformed into a "united" Central America. The annual independence parades in Guatemala, El Salvador, Nicaragua, Honduras, and Costa Rica further promote this notion of a unified Central America, since regardless of the nation-state they inhabit, subjects within these five countries know that every year their fellow compatriots celebrate the same holiday in their own respective countries.

This display of nation and memory, however, is also contingent on forgetting, for only Guatemala declared itself independent on September 15, 1821. As discussed in chapter 1, not only did the other provinces declare themselves independent on a different date, but some opted to separate from Guatemala rather than Spain. Despite the fact that this dominant narrative of unity is undermined by political documents and events that transpired in that historical era, repetition, narrative, and performance allow this idea of shared independence to become generally assumed by many peoples on the isthmus. While manifestations of this civic celebration differ from state to state within Central America, it is important to note how these various performances share particular racial, gendered, and sexualized meanings by positioning whiteness and heteropatriarchy as central to the national narrative. For instance, in several states in Central America speeches are made celebrating *criollo* men of the nineteenth century. In their independence festivities of 2016, Nicaragua honored the memory of José Cecilio del Valle,[39] while in El Salvador, president Salvador Sánchez Cerén mentioned in his celebration speech that Salvadorans should "honor the memory" of independence "heroes" such as "Manuel José Arce and José Matias Delgado,"[40] historical figures who are also commonly referred to as "*padres de la patria /* founding fathers." By presenting *criollo* men as national saviors, such renderings minimize the contributions of other ethnoracial communities to this process and obfuscate how these "liberators" were equally responsible for the construction and enforcement of sociopolitical codes that enabled race, gender, and class stratifications (both Matias Delgado and del Valle were responsible for drafting the exclusionary federation constitution, see chapter 2). Moreover, within parade performances, gender roles are fervently enforced, as men are often represented as active agents of history via their performance of military drills (war heroes), whereas female participants are often relegated to passive roles such as beauty queens—an embodied reminder of how women were the spoils of war.

But these cultural festivities and their respective ideologies of race, class, gender, and sexuality are not limited to the isthmus, as they have been transplanted onto U.S. soil. At present, large metropolitan centers such as the Bronx, Long Island, Chicago, Providence, and Boston also host Central American Independence parades or festivals. The adoption of these festive forms in the U.S. diaspora is significant since it signals how Central Americans are increasingly seeing themselves as a part of a transnational and/or "transisthmus" collective.[41] Consequently, even though the COFECA celebration of *las fiestas patrias* takes place in the Westlake/Pico-Union area of Los Angeles, these *fiestas'* cultural impact exceeds the confines of this urban locale, as it partakes in a larger sphere of Central American (trans)cultural productions.

Large-scale migration from the isthmus to other spaces as well as technological advances in the late twentieth century (e.g., the internet, satellite television, etc.) has created the need and the ability for Central Americans to (re)connect around the world. New media forms allow Central Americans to be virtual participants in events that take place on the isthmus and beyond. Most of the COFECA events, including web video of the parade, as well as the crowning ceremony of Miss COFECA, can be viewed free of charge on websites like YouTube. Twenty-four-hour access enables Central Americans from around the world to partake in festivities and, in doing so, to expand the territorial parameters of the Central American imaginary. In her work on Salvadoran immigrants, Cecilia Rivas argues that media images link emigrants with a "transnational migrant space" as they become reclaimed by their home countries.[42] Arguably, the media dissemination of *las fiestas patrias* operates in like manner as media consumers on the isthmus reclaim Central Americans abroad. COFECA's celebration of cultural nationalism is thus transformed into a larger communal event, where, regardless of their location, subjects of different countries and from different racial, gender, and social strata can conceive of themselves as Central Americans, albeit unevenly. Just as early nineteenth-century technological media such as print capitalism helped create collectivities, these new technological devices have enabled the formation of decentered transnational imagined spaces.

Accordingly, the COFECA parade has been touted as "the largest sociocultural expression of Central America in the world."[43] While this proclamation might read as an overstatement, it is important to note that its cultural importance is continuously affirmed within countries on the isthmus. For instance, in 2015, then presidential candidate of Guatemala, Jimmy Morales, participated in the parade—a month later he would win the election and, at the time of this writing, he is the president of Guatemala. Although Guatemala, unlike El Salvador, does not allow citizens living abroad to vote, the candidate's participation at the parade speaks to the ways the U.S. diaspora and, in this case, the translocal Los Angeles community, continue to play a pivotal role in the isthmus. *Remesas,* or remittances, for example, amount to 10 percent of Guatemala's GDP (7.3 billion dollars).[44] This economic influence is also linked with other sociopolitical types of engagement as many individuals in the United States have retained their Guatemalan citizenship or maintain strong cultural ties to Guatemala via telecommunication networks. Morales's presence at the parade then acknowledges not only the impact that this particular cultural text signifies for the isthmus (as the parade is broadcasted on television via satellite stations such as Centroamérica TV) but also the important role that the U.S. diaspora plays in cultural, political, and economic institutions within Central America.

Within the United States, the annual celebration has attracted crowds as large as 450,000 participants;[45] only the Rose Parade, which attracts 700,000 spectators,[46] and the *Cinco de Mayo* celebrations, which host 500,000 participants,[47] yield larger attendance. The parade's popularity suggests that this isthmian celebration is becoming a mainstream cultural phenomenon. It is estimated that more than a million Central Americans see it worldwide. Transnational television networks like Univisión, Telemundo, Centroamérica TV, as well as emerging technological media like Latinotv.com and CXCA internet, not only assist in the dissemination of transnational Central American culture but also capitalize on the term *Central American*, since as Arlene Dávila argues, "Culture is never free from economic and political determination."[48] Viewing the category of "Central American" as an emerging market and marketable constituency contributes to and shapes current understandings of this term.

In fact, despite COFECA's claim that it is a nonprofit organization, one should be mindful that both international and local corporations are active sponsors that provide the majority of financial support for these *fiestas patrias*. In their marketing materials, COFECA appeals to businesses by telling them that sponsorship of the parade will "turn 450,000 into loyal customers."[49] For those that opt for the "title sponsor package" of $100,000, they promise to "coordinate efforts together with [the] president of COFECA to ensure successful public presentations."[50] Moreover, if we consider that the cost to have a float participate in the parade ranges from $500 to $3,000, it becomes evident that both international and local businesses are key figures in deciding what is deemed as Central American culture, since their financial resources might allow for more participation opportunities.

(EN)GENDERING AND RACIALIZING THE CENTRAL AMERICAN IMAGINARY

While the COFECA parade is an inherited cultural practice, it would be misguided to view it as a pure adaptation or recreation of independence parades and festivities within the isthmus. As Joseph Roach has noted, cultural (re)productions of festivals and parades actually engender new forms of cultural texts.[51] This certainly applies to the Central American diaspora, which uses the COFECA parade as a space to (re)inscribe Central American identity and culture. The COFECA festivities present important distinctions from the cultural tradition they have inherited. Unlike independence parades hosted in the isthmus, which are produced by the nation-state and celebrated on the same day by five countries that are disconnected from each other, in Los Angeles, the parade and festival is not government sponsored (though civic groups and Central American political figures do participate)[52] and takes place in a physical space that enables Central American immigrants to celebrate together. Also, whereas in the isthmus, independence parades emphasize their individual respective national culture, in the diaspora, this cultural event is composed of various nations and cultural identities (e.g., Salvadoran, Honduran, etc.). The structure of the parade itself, which has not changed much in its thirty-three years, further reveals how diasporic subjects have altered this performance.

For instance, the parade always takes place in Little Central America (Westlake/Pico-Union), has an annual theme generally tied to political issues, showcases a grand marshal, and contains floats from seven countries on the isthmus.[53] Usually a banner designating a national country will precede the floats, which are often sponsored by transnational corporations (e.g., Goya Foods), hometown associations (e.g., Belizeans United of Los Angeles), locally based transnational community organizations (e.g., Asociación Adentro Cojutepeque), and local businesses that cater to those populations. The inclusion of themes and a grand marshal are both elements that are uniquely diasporic contributions. The themes in the COFECA parade, such as those chosen in 2006 ("Today We March Tomorrow We Vote") and 2016 ("Our Vote Our Future"), are usually connected to sociopolitical issues salient within the United States. These titles create a teleology for this community's narrative of identity politics: we first have to perform our cultural identity so that we can then have a political one (or political visibility). Therefore, its inclusion (along with that of a grand marshal) indicates the beginnings of a cultural fusion between the signifying practices of the isthmus with those of U.S. culture.

However, the COFECA parade operates similarly to *las fiestas patrias* on the isthmus, in that it often promotes a mythic and utopic vision of cohesion and unity among Central Americans by minimizing the contentious relations that permeate between national and ethnoracial populations. At times, some of the most popular floats (as determined by the spectators' applause and cheers) were those that represented Garifuna and Maya indigenous groups. Ironically, these communities have been physically and culturally marginalized by both individual nation-states and the larger Central American national imaginary, which, in its decision to privilege a particular historical moment, erases other diasporic histories and undermines the political claims of sovereignty enacted by these two groups. Therefore, rather than just reading these moments of celebration by spectators as signs of cultural inclusion and acceptance, we may also view them as an example of how marginalized ethnoracial groups can sometimes be utilized as authenticating measures in articulations of diasporic identity. For example, throughout the years, several floats representing the country of Honduras often played *punta* music—a musical style developed by Garifunas. However, most of these Honduran floats were mostly composed of mestiza/os; only with rare exception were some floats linked with Honduras explicitly devoted to Garifuna culture. Such displays inadvertently reassert the dominant location of *mestizaje* via the visual predominance of brown bodies, which obfuscate blackness within Honduran culture. These representational strategies by some of the local Honduran constituency unintentionally affirm that this arena values commodified unembodied notions of Garifuna culture.[54] Thus every year, for only one day, marginalized ethnoracial populations are symbolically framed as integral to Central American culture, even if their lives and political aspirations are not.

Similarly, several local vendors often use representations of indigenous culture to sell their products as authentically from the region. In 2006, a local business prominently displayed the painted image of an indigenous woman on the side of its float (see fig. 2). An autochthonous and gendered representation emerges of the municipality of Ilobasco in this portrait of a dark-skinned, dark-haired woman holding clay pots and wearing folkloric clothing. The figure of an indigenous woman at the forefront of the image is surrounded by a vast and empty natural landscape devoid of any markers of modern culture. Race, class, and gender ideologies converge in the marketing of this product, for not only is this female figure linked with domesticity (in this case, with a kitchen since the business is a restaurant); it is also deployed to appeal to a mestiza/o class fantasy of having a personal indigenous servant making your food. The float therefore reentrenches class and racial hierarchies, as indigenous women are often utilized as cheap domestic labor within the United States and Central America.

In addition, by framing indigenous subjects as "native" to the land one loves but largely atavistic, the image reifies indigenous culture by situating it outside the current contemporary cityscape. Two problematic tropes are evinced in this float since it presents feminized corporeality as the national archaic located in a permanently anterior time vis-à-vis the modern nation.[55] In this image, both the land and the female body are framed as passive subjects—recipients of the modern gaze, which view them from a distance as "inert, backward-looking and natural," all in the name of consumption.[56] The woman painted here appears to be static and out of time, especially when contrasted with the float's animated physical bodies that are dressed in industrially manufactured

FIGURE 2. Float at the 2006 COFECA parade sponsored by a Los Angeles Salvadoran restaurant.

clothing, like white T-shirts and denim jeans that, ironically, are often manufactured in *maquilas* in Central American countries. Indeed, it is rare to find a float that contains both indigenous (female) participants (not dressed in traditional attire) and mestiza/o participants. Instead, indigenous floats are often solely composed of members from that community, furthering the notion that indigenous peoples belong to the national archaic. In linking a female body with the natural landscape, the float circulates a common national association not only of the landscape as a feminized body (e.g., the motherland) but also about the role of women within the nation, basing their use-value in the ability to biological and culturally (re)produce. Through the display of different racialized female bodies, the parade ascribes and cements gender roles within national identities.

REPRODUCING HETERONORMATIVE
NATIONAL FEMININITY

In its use of racialized, gendered, and classed bodies to sustain certain ideologies about nation, the parade reveals some of its most prevalent contradictions about the role marginalized subjectivities occupy within the Central American imaginary. For instance, mestiza female bodies mostly adorn the COFECA parade floats, regardless of whether they represent local hometown associations, local businesses, or larger transnational corporations. Such bodies are generally circumscribed by scripted roles of acceptable gendered heteronormative national representation: either the past temporal folk roots of the culture, the modern hyperfeminine/sexualized beauty queen, or a hybridized style combining the two. A paradoxical role is endorsed here since notions of femininity defined by the nation delimit female subjects as both traditional and modern. This particular performance of the nation, which relies on autochthonous tropes of indigeneity or folk idioms and costumes, reinscribes the trope of women as bearers/transmitters of national culture, as it frames them as the repositories of national/cultural authenticity.

Within Central American popular culture, folk symbols are often wedded to contemporary discourses of the nation and femininity in the realm of beauty pageants, including the Miss Universe, Miss El Salvador, and the local Miss COFECA pageant, which, as part of the competition process, has its female candidates literally parade in "traditional" folk costumes. According to Sarah Banet-Weiser, beauty queens and beauty pageants "calls up the relationship between discourses of nation and discourses of femininity,"[57] foregrounding such questions as "who counts as part of the nation? What does it mean to be a specifically feminine representative of a nation?"[58] Marcia Ochoa refers to this "specifically feminine" representation within pageants as a "spectacular femininity"—a "form of hyperfeminine corporeality" that becomes "the objec[t] of an imagined masculine gaze."[59] Although Ochoa's work highlights how this form of spectacular femininity transcends cisgendered heterosexual bodies and can be utilized by queer subjects, within the cultural circuit of pageants, it becomes more confined, since it is "highly contingent on patriarchal power and recognition."[60] In this sense, the production of beauty pageants and beauty queens is a site of social signification that syncs embodied displays of nation with acceptable gender norms—specifically, with heteronormative femininity that naturalizes "woman" as feminine and heterosexual.

Beauty pageants and queens, then, have an important symbolic role within nationalism, as they highlight the limited ways gendered subjects can be viewed as good citizens. Whereas male subjects can profess their patriotic duty to the nation by becoming military or sports heroes (e.g., dominant forms of masculinity), one of the few arenas where female subjects can be viewed as tokens of pride to their respective nations is in beauty pageants. Ochoa, for instance, explicates how *misses*—participants in the Miss Venezuela pageant—provides the nation with "a place on the global stage in a way that had eluded that country for centuries."[61] The use of beauty and glamour allows Venezuela, as embodied in its *misses*, to negotiate power and marginality, as the nation becomes "queen for a day," and its place within the order of nations shifts from periphery to center within this global arena.[62] It is at these international events where the nation, embodied as hyperfeminine "woman," takes center stage (literally) and obtains a level of equity with other nations. This is particularly the case for Latin American countries that utilize these events to become global players with nations who

FIGURE 3. Float of Miss El Salvador USA at the 2013 COFECA parade.

in other aspects (e.g., politically and economically) would not be seen on equal footing. Latin American contestants have won the Miss Universe title—the most competitive international beauty pageant—twice as often as those from European countries and three times more than those from the United States.[63] World systems of classification (first world vs. third world, etc.) become inverted and contested in these moments when Latin American countries are temporarily allowed to occupy a type of first-world status. Thus these female contestants, and especially the pageant winners, come to be viewed as "national treasures" and the pride of their nation.[64]

The interconnections between nationhood and womanhood that transpire on a larger scale in these international circuits are manifested in micro and trans-local practices in the U.S. diaspora, as the COFECA parade relies heavily on the presence of this particular archetype of heteronormative femininity. Not only do national beauty queens, such as Miss El Salvador USA, Miss Guatemala USA, and Miss Nicaragua USA, participate in the parade, but locally, every isthmian nation elects their own respective *miss*/queen to participate via local hometown organizations. Like the larger scale beauty pageants, the COFECA parade posits that in order for "women" to be written within the national narrative, they must engage in an embodied performance that views their beauty as a source of pride, which in turn, is always contingent on ideologies of class, race, gender, and sexuality. In high-profile pageants such as Miss Universe, for instance, beauty criteria is rendered synonymous with a "Eurocentric aesthetic" that values markers of whiteness such as "profiled noses, thin lips, straight hair, and small hips."[65] The *misses* (queens) and *señoritas* (pageant participants) that represented the Miss El Salvador USA or Miss Guatemala USA at the COFECA parade often emulated this model, as it seemed as if they had been chosen for their ability to fashion themselves in a way that adhered to Eurocentric standards of beauty like having long straight hair, profiled noses, and a lighter complexion. This embodied performance of race and nation is also conflated with notions of class—as the title "queen" connotes a different and elevated socioeconomic position. Christine Yano notes how beauty queens "borrow commonly recognized idioms of prestige such as the crown, scepter and cape."[66] The use of a particular type of clothing, the evening gown, for instance, is also linked with aspirational class fantasies in which subjects often utilize this type of garment for events catered to particular social strata. More than just a class fantasy, these gowns register these bodies as a performance of both heteronormative and spectacular femininity, since these women are presented as sexually desired objects, often in their form-fitting styles that accentuate their curves and reveal their long legs, suggesting that one's patriotic duty is to be as fecund as the motherland. The queens themselves are always placed on a float or on top of a car where they do little else but sit/stand and wave to the crowds who gaze upon or "catcall" them. The fertile female sexual body, however, is only lauded in this particular nationalist context, for in the quotidian lives of everyday women on the isthmus, juridical policies limit their autonomy over their own bodies.[67]

Although these scripted representations of femininity are problematic, the hypervisibility granted to these female bodies nevertheless serves as a counterpoint to the more permanent masculinization of space occurring locally in the form of statues and street naming that center male icons (Romero, Morazán, etc.). Since the majority of the parade participants are women, witnessing this gendered mass moving within this space becomes an implicit reminder that, initially, Central American migrations were largely composed of women who utilized their labor to establish immigrant networks and enclaves such as Little Central America. As scholars such as Terry Repak posit, "70 percent of Central American migrants in the 1960s and 1970s were women."[68] This gendered migration was largely a result of shifting social and economic conditions and of the growing need in global cities such as Washington, DC, and Los Angeles for domestic workers. Hamilton and Stoltz Chinchilla note that this economic trend took hold in Los Angeles where "networks rapidly developed between the employers of domestic workers and their Salvadoran or Guatemalan employees, which facilitated the subsequent recruitment of domestics from these countries."[69] Paradoxically, the use of beauty queens as a metaphor for the nation—a highly visible manifestation of heteronormative femininity linked to the homeland—mitigates the erasure of Central American women from local symbolic gestures, as it reminds us how women who worked in homes (domestic work) were pivotal in constructing a Central American diaspora.

QUEER FOLK: THE NATION IN DRAG

In many ways, the COFECA parade is not simply a facile articulation of Central American nationalism or nostalgia but also a site of contestation. The participation of the LGBTQ organization Bienestar, for instance, reveals how this event provides a space for marginalized communities to inscribe themselves into a Central American imaginary. The presence of Bienestar elucidates the way non-heteronormative subjectivities and issues of sexuality have largely been absent within a particular strain of Central American identity politics. Bienestar is a Los Angeles–based nonprofit organization founded in 1989 to address the lack of HIV/AIDS services available to the Latina/o community. Over time, Bienestar expanded their objectives to provide not only HIV/AIDS testing but also mental health and counseling services to the local LGBTQ community. As part of their broader mission to contest social marginalization within the Los Angeles Latina/o community, in 2010, Bienestar took their intersectional politics "on the road," becoming the first LGBTQ group to march at the East LA Mexican Bicentennial parade—one of the oldest in the country—and later that year they would also participate in the COFECA parade.

The last time I witnessed Bienestar participate in the COFECA parade was in 2013. That year, this queer contingency fashioned themselves to highlight the heterogeneity present among their members. Though their constituency was small, the structure of their parade unit emulated that of other larger groups: it included two members holding a rainbow banner with the organization's name on it, a float, and members walking in front and behind the float. The Bienestar float consisted of a silver pickup truck decorated with a large rainbow flag at the center of the hood, while the peripheral edge of the hood featured small flags of some of the Central American countries, one of Mexico, and one of the United States. At the back of the truck were speakers blasting music and two larger rainbow flags. The truck was an apt metaphor for Bienestar's larger implicit message: the decentering of all forms of nationalism, a point emphasized by the placement of the flags displayed in horizontal fashion. As all flags inhabited the same spatial plane, the American flag and, in the context of Central Americans in Los Angeles, the Mexican flag were precluded from occupying a space of prominence from any other national group. In this manipulation of signs, the message sent to spectators is that queerness is not a token or an additive component to Central American and other Latina/o groups but is literally placed at the center.

FIGURE 4. Bienestar float at the 2013 COFECA parade.

Behind the truck was a small group of Bienestar participants wearing an array of fashion styles. Some wore everyday clothing, others donned shirts with nationalist logos like the words *El Salvador* on them, some were dressed in "folk" drag, some held rainbow flags and/or national flags (some of non–Central American countries), while others held signs with political slogans (e.g., "Marriage Equality"). By intentionally defying the parade's structure by walking side by side with other national groups, Bienestar rebuffed cultural nationalism as the only means to construct community. Instead, this visual performance of intra/international solidarity emphasizes the manner in which queer Latina/os share affinities not just through their ethnoracial marginalization within Anglo-American culture but also due to their (trans)gender and sexual identities, which are often disavowed in the performance and construction of ethnic identities. Such acts embody José Esteban Muñoz's assertion that "traditional identitarian logics of group formation and social cohesion are giving sway to new models of relationality and interconnectedness"[70]—models based on affective belonging as a result of being dislocated from multiple social spaces. In this fashion, Bienestar's participation at COFECA indexes a type of broader "queer cultural citizenship" where, as Horacio Roque Ramírez argues, queer racial (im)migrants can obtain recognition in contexts of domination and marginalization.[71]

The use of queer symbols such as the rainbow flag and drag performers at the COFECA event is an important spatial tactic that temporarily suspends the function of the parade, as it momentarily transforms it into a mini "Pride parade" asserting the importance of LGBTQ rights. However, unlike Pride parades in Los Angeles, where "white bodies and culture are front and center,"[72] and which have increasingly become corporatized and neoliberal, this micro version at the COFECA parade features no hyperbolic performances to distract from Bienestar's clear objective, which is to increase their visibility within a community that might associate queer issues as non-Latina/o issues. Bienestar's presence in the parade underscores how this festive form has historically endorsed a specific vision of "community" and political issues at the expense of others—that is, while COFECA annually chooses a political theme for its parade, it has seldom explicitly linked its theme with issues salient for the LGBTQ community such as HIV/AIDS, marriage equality, and homo/transphobia.

For instance, up until 1990, homosexuality was utilized as a justification to reject immigration applications, and it was not until 2010 that the United States removed HIV/AIDS testing as a requirement for entry into the country. And yet, these types of "immigrant rights" have tended to receive little attention within COFECA festivities. As illustrated in 2013–2014, many immigration activists throughout the United States responded to the Unaccompanied Children from Central America (UAC) "crisis" by emphasizing the importance of keeping the "traditional" heteronormative family together. This type of activism was apparent in the 2013 COFECA parade, in a sign with the words *No Separación Familiar / No Family Separation*. However, with the exception of Bienestar, no floats or banners explicitly advocated on behalf of queer immigrants. Immigrant rights in this context are therefore premised on heteronormative ideas of biological families and thus marginalize queer subjectivities. But Bienestar's participation contests heteronormative constructions of family (both as the privileged site of immigrant rights and as a metaphor for the nation) by expanding the narrative of Central Americanness and reminding us of other forms of kinship that do not rely on understandings of biology, as they emerge via social and political dislocation. As such, when Bienestar marches with signs that state "Marriage Equality," they challenge COFECA's political efficacy for all Central Americans and indeed question the assumed heterosexual and heteronormative "we," in the parade theme "Tomorrow We Vote," and the "our" in the "Our Voice Our Vote" banners.

Bienestar's public display of queerness at the COFECA parade engages in a politics of denaturalization that illuminates how heterosexist geographies have become normative. As Gill Valentine suggests, "space," particularly public space, is colonized with heterosexual meanings.[73] This is demonstrated in the parade as well as in local Central American identity politics where the nation is remembered via a limited model of the male (Morazán/Romero)/female (beauty queens) binary. For queer Central Americans, symbolic gestures of "claiming" space not only reify a view of sexuality that renders them abject within a Central American national imaginary but also do little to alter the materiality of their everyday existence where, for many, public space continues to be a hostile space. Seemingly agentic acts often rely on a heteronormative reading of space that overlooks the ways heterosexuals benefit from a type of "spatial" privilege where their sexual identities (though perhaps not when they intersect with their gendered and racial subjectivities) are not subjected to the same types of surveillance as queer subjects. In countries on the isthmus, like in Honduras, queer and transgender Central Americans routinely experience harassment not only by their compatriots but also by the state and local police who patrol the streets and gay clubs.[74] Although in the diaspora they may not experience the same level of overt harassment, they still nevertheless encounter regulatory regimes regarding their sexuality in the forms of stares and comments, which their heterosexual counterparts are not forced to endure.[75] Thus their literal "taking it to the streets" at the parade becomes a defiant gesture that moves presumed private and intimate issues, like one's sexuality, out into the public sphere, as well as underscores how acts of recognition that attempt to "claim space" must be tempered by the fact that such lauded acts might occlude how such practices naturalize heterosexism.

But perhaps Bienestar's most powerful statement emerges from some of their members' embodied display of an alternative "spectacular femininity" via their performance of "drag." This manifestation of cross-dressing at the COFECA parade challenges mainstream understandings of drag that have bifurcated the practice as either an act of mimesis of femininity referred to as the "glamour" drag or an intentional hyperbolic performance known as the "clown."[76] At the parade, for instance, one Bienestar participant was wearing a traditional Salvadoran folk outfit of the *azul y blanco*, while the other two were dressed as *muxes* (I use the word *dressed* here because it is unclear whether these two Bienestar members are Zapotec and/or self-identify as muxe or if they are wearing clothing that semiotically indexes muxes).

According to several scholars, within pre-Columbian and contemporary Zapotec indigenous culture, muxes are a separate gender category, or "third gender," because they present "an alternative to the already existing gender identities of hombre versus mujer."[77] Alfredo Mirandé describes muxes as "biological males who also manifest feminine identities in their dress and attire, but they are not transsexual nor are they seeking to become women."[78] Though muxes usually have male anatomy, they are ascribed "traditional" female gender roles such as dating heterosexual men, engage in domestic activities, and often dress as women. Although scholars have also outlined the varied manifestations of being muxe, what Gustavo Subero terms as "Muxeninity," most claim that the "prototypical muxe is a *vestida*."[79] Muxe *vestidas* aspire to "maintain their Zapotec dress, language and customs" and use these cultural symbols and elements to highlight their indigenous heritage and affirm their cultural identity.[80] By insisting that muxe is inherently a part of Zapotec culture, this third gender subject elucidates how "long-standing indigenous conceptualizations of gender and sexuality" can challenge "both sides of the colonial/modern gender system."[81]

In their choice of apparel, the two Bienestar performers invoke this particular manifestation of muxe by dressing like *vestidas* (see fig. 5). This manipulation of

FIGURE 5. Bienestar participants dressed in "folk drag" at the 2013 COFECA parade.

aesthetic codes engages in a form of decolonial practice, as this embodied performance of femininity critiques Western categories of gender and sexuality by
asserting that alternative categorizations exist within non-Western communities.
It also reroutes practices of cross-dressing that are typically linked with Western
and white gay culture by exposing another history of male/female articulation.
For some subjects in Los Angeles, dressing as a muxe *vestida* highlights how culture is a "fundamental part that is aligned with sexuality."[82] In other words, dressing as muxe in the diaspora can be considered a disidentifcatory practice from a
broader white-based, U.S. LGBTQ culture where the notion of "drag queen" is
viewed as showcasing one's sexuality while ignoring race and ethnicity. In this
regard, it is tenuous to even label these two members of Bienestar as "drag," since
muxes themselves do not view their choices of wearing traditional clothing or
makeup as "drag" but as a part of their Zapotec culture. That being said, one must
be mindful that some members of the muxe community view this diasporic
practice as a type of cultural appropriation. In an interview with scholar Alfredo
Mirandé, Biiniza, a member of a muxe organization Las Auténticas Intrépidas
Buscadoras del Peligro in Oaxaca, explained that "being muxe is not something
you put on and then take off like a dress. It's a way of being that includes not only
dressing like a traditional Teca but also maintaining, incorporating, and respect-
ing Zapotec language, customs and traditions."[83] Being muxe here is more than
just a one-time performance or wearing a "dress," since it is linked to a broader
indigenous cultural practice and mode of being. Biiniza's statement thus reveals
the ongoing tensions within attempted displays of queer solidarity, where North
American nonheteronormative subjects may inadvertently further marginalize
indigenous communities, like Zapotecs, by appropriating their cultural symbols while perhaps ignoring this community's struggle for cultural and political
autonomy.[84]

While two Bienestar members attempted to sync their performance within
a pre-Columbian tradition that makes it difficult to label their manipulation of
semiotic codes "drag," the third member's choice to dress in a *traje típico salva-
doreño* / traditional dress from El Salvador, links this gesture to a broader drag
practice. This articulation of drag is notable for a few features, including the
fact that while the choice of dress denotes Salvadoran culture, the invocation
of blue and white connotes a broader Central American mythopoeia in which
national symbols share these same colors. Moreover, unlike broader iterations
of drag, the aesthetic choices of this performance in the parade were quite subdued, utilizing minimal makeup and a simple hairstyle. This public display of
cross-dressing performance does not parody the usual modern idealized notion
of femininity at the parade embodied in the beauty queens but instead opts to
queer an "authentic" symbol of the nation by engaging in folk drag. Folk drag
is a new figure within the broader matrix of drag performances that also evades

the dominant styles of drag (e.g., the clown and the glamour drag). Instead, this practice resembles more closely what José Esteban Muñoz labels as terrorist drag, which functions by "confounding and subverting the social fabric" often by "performing the nation's internal terrors around race, gender, and sexuality."[85] This embodied performance of nonheteronormative femininity terrorizes the Central American nation by becoming a haunting reminder of how that nation-space was discursively gendered and feminized in the colonial period. It also terrorizes the nation by becoming what Marcia Ochoa labels as an "inconvenient body." Inconvenient bodies are those that were abjected in nation-building projects but continue to reappear, disrupting nationalist narratives by "never allowing the nation to be quite as it would like to imagine itself."[86] If the nation likes to imagine itself as modern, Ochoa argues that queer racialized bodies, which are conflated with "the failure to be modern," interrupt this vision.[87] Like "flies in the national ointment," inconvenient bodies trouble and rupture national imaginaries.

As a form of terrorizing "inconvenient body," folk drag becomes a space-making tactic deployed by queer subjects to mitigate their erasure and insist on a type of belonging within a Central American imaginary. In placing a queer body as the symbol of "traditional" Salvadoran culture, and by extension Central American culture, this appropriation of the folk woman figure "terrorizes" the nation by viewing queerness not as a "modern" additive to the Central American imaginary and instead asserts that queer subjects have always been a part of the nation. Folk drag resituates the location of queerness not on the periphery but at the heart of the nation. It engages in an act of world-making by creating a visual icon that creatively imagines the queer body as intertwined with the foundational fictions of the Central American nation. This type of embodiment remaps the Central American imaginary, as the deviant bodies that were once (and that continue to be) excluded from discourses of belonging and citizenship (on the isthmus) become actively present.

Indeed, the aesthetic choices associated with this folk drag performance illuminate how the performance of nation itself is its own type of "drag." There is nothing "natural" about nation and national identities, which, like gender, require citationality to obscure their own conditions of possibility. As noted earlier, the articulation of Central Americanness at this parade privileges the autochthonous female subject or the modern beauty queen, who at this event engages in the hyperbolic use of makeup and a type of camp aesthetics often associated with drag. For instance, the obvious use of fake eyelashes, glitter in the hair, and hair extensions by some of the beauty queens seemed to indicate that there was much more cultural anxiety about performing heteronormative femininity from assumed heterosexual cisgendered bodies than those who were engaging in drag.

Similarly, displays of "traditional" culture (see fig. 6) that were linked with femininity often resorted to utilizing kitsch-style fashion choices to perform national authenticity. In a parade unit, some women dressed in the Salvadoran *azul y blanco* (the same outfit worn by one of the Bienestar drag performers) had their skirts decorated with mini clay pots that acted as a type of fringe to the skirt. Rather than reading these female bodies as symbols of "tradition," decorative objects on the folk dress render a performance of authenticity as anything but that, as it appears kitsch and excessive. The desire to frame oneself as truly "authentic" leads to a type of excess that discloses the artificiality of a concept like authenticity. In other words, if the beauty queens' aesthetic bodily choices reveal an internal anxiety about their performance of femininity, then the type of aesthetic options utilized at this parade by participants performing nation (like the addition of clay pots onto the *azul y blanco*), displays a type of anxiety about performances of national authenticity. Ironically, at this event, some of the most "natural" looking (in makeup, hair, and fashion choices) and least

FIGURE 6. Salvadoran participants at the 2013 COFECA parade.

campy iterations of nation turned out to be the folk drag performers. Thus folk drag in this context discloses that it is not a form of mimesis but rather simulacra, as it seemingly copies other performances of femininity and authenticity, which themselves are copies of a fictive national norm.

COFECA, LATINIDAD, AND HETEROTOPIAS

Ethnoracial, class, gender, and sexual tensions notwithstanding, the COFECA parade occupies an important function in the United States: it offers an opportunity for Central Americans to perform their cultural difference from other Latina/o groups. Despite the fact that the parade often symbolically links "Central American" with mestiza/o, the term *Central American*, like "Latina/o," is not a racial category. Therefore, self-identified Central Americans in the diaspora have no visible markers to differentiate themselves from other racialized groups, and specifically from other Latina/o groups who often also get problematically constructed as mestiza/o and/or "brown." Using this event to self-narrate and perform a particular ethnocultural identity is especially significant given the fact that United States culture tends to read racialized "brown" bodies in Los Angeles as always already Mexican (see chapter 4). The COFECA parade, then, becomes not only a prominent site of self-fashioning but also a vehicle to undermine racist and homogenizing tropes that fail to recognize Latina/o heterogeneity.

One way in which the parade provides a space of self-definition and resignifies dominant understandings of Central Americanness is by including countries that have been discursively marked as falling outside of the Central American imaginary. Central America as a national formation has self-ascribed borders that typically only contain peoples and cultures that were originally part of the Kingdom of Guatemala. However, in the COFECA parade, and in the organization itself, Belize and Panama are framed as Central American.[88] It is then notable that in the U.S. diaspora these two nations, which have no direct relationship to this date of independence, and in the case of Belize has had its own sovereignty constantly threatened by Guatemala, become incorporated into this collectivity. It signals a moment in which diasporic subjects are (re)articulating what they deem as Central American. Silvano Torres, the COFECA Belizean representative, emphasized this point by stating, "We are seven countries, many believe there are just five countries but there are seven, there is Belize, Costa Rica, Panama, Nicaragua, Honduras, Guatemala and El Salvador."[89] Notable is that in his listing of nations, Torres inverts traditional conceptions of Central America(n), particularly in Los Angeles, by placing Belize and Panama first and ending with Guatemala and El Salvador—communities that have obtained the most cultural recognition in this urban locale. Likewise, in the 2012 COFECA parade, Nestor Méndez, the Belizean ambassador to the United States, proudly proclaimed,

"This is one of many parades in which we will be united as a Central American family."[90] Though, as seen in chapter 2, the trope of family and kinship is highly problematic, one must also recall that discursively Panama and Belize have been explicitly tied to blackness, including them in this biological metaphor therefore enables a dislodging of Central America as a mestiza/o space. In doing so, this symbolic inclusion of two black racially coded spaces into the Central American imaginary can relocate blackness from the site of abjection into one viewed as integral to that space.

In delineating how this local community is reconfiguring the Central American imaginary, I do not mean to downplay how the symbolic incorporation of Panama and Belize might inadvertently sustain other dominant ideologies within the isthmus. For instance, their inclusion in the parade might seem to continue the isthmus's racialization of space, where blackness is transposed onto those two nations-spaces and cultures. This mapping of race and space on the isthmus allows the other five Central American countries to perpetuate the myth that African participation in *mestizaje* did not transpire within their own territorial limits.[91] Yet having a visual economy of black bodies linked with "Central American" can also subvert this myth. The presence of black cultures and bodies at this event forces the spectator to revisit the bodies on display within other national constituencies and to see the spectrum of the color line. Claudia Milian's assertion that "side by side brownness and blackness are continuative" becomes embodied in the parade as the "brown" assumed mestiza/o begins to look more like dark brown, and the negated African ancestry becomes visually present. In this regard, Panama and Belize's participation at COFECA is significant on multiple levels. Not only does it demonstrate how this local community (re)defines what and who is Central American, but it also functions as a counterdiscourse to ideologies that dislocate blackness from Central America. In so doing, it provides Afro-Central Americans in the other five nations—which have forged their identity on the basis of mestiza/o nationalism—a space of belonging (even if it is only ephemeral).

While the diaspora has expanded the boundaries of the Central American imaginary, they are not entirely porous, particularly within the COFECA parade. Like the process of identity formation, which is relational and requires a subject to construct itself on the premise of difference from another subject, the parade includes other national communities in order to assert their distance from them. Countries identified as Central American are clearly characterized by blue-and-white banners that contain their name and resemble one another. On the other hand, countries and cultures that are viewed as external to this collectivity are clearly defined by having banners that claim to "salute" Central America (e.g., "Ecuador salutes Central America"), while those that are viewed as Central American are not required to make that distinction. Further, none of the nonisthmian countries are allotted the same privileges that Central American countries receive, like selecting the grand marshal or leading the parade. Their seemingly sole purpose is to display their own individual national cultures, which is then used to highlight their difference from the other Central American countries. Though such gestures of inclusion replicate facile notions of multiculturalism, they can also become a site of critique, especially when one considers how the local urban landscape has been defined as "Chicano LA."

Over the years, representatives from the countries of Bolivia, Colombia, Dominican Republic, Ecuador, and Peru have all participated in the COFECA event. Representing the Caribbean and South America, these groups (with the exception of the Dominican Republic) have often been referred to as "Other Latinos." Developed by José Luis Falconi and José Antonio Mazzotti, "Other Latinos" are groups that occupy "historical marginality or alterity within the Latino community."[92] While in large global cities like Los Angeles diverse Latina/o groups often live side by side, as Falconi and Mazzotti argue, "profound asymmetries remain."[93] In the context of Los Angeles, Mexican and Mexican American culture has obtained cultural predominance within articulations of Latinidad. In fact, while some Mexican cultural groups participate in the COFECA parade (such as mariachis and ballet *folklórico*), their presence has been minimal. This might be due to the fact that many Latina/o festivals in Los Angeles are directly associated with Mexican and Mexican American culture (e.g., Cinco de Mayo). By contrast, "Other Latinos" have fewer opportunities to display their cultural difference and, as the COFECA parade illustrates, either need to create their own events or participate in other national-cultural celebrations. As such, more than just a display of "multiculturalism," the pan-Latinidad present at COFECA is its own form of identity politics, one that allows "Other Latinos" to contest their marginality by highlighting their "other than Mexican" status in Los Angeles.

Indeed, as an act of Central American identity politics—a self-conscious attempt by this community to claim a space and obtain recognition within national and local Latina/o cultural politics—the COFECA parade also provides Central Americans a means to publicly contest dominant U.S. narratives of cultural assimilation, especially for spectators of the performance. Routinely, spectators of the event will wear their respective national colors, which include blue and white, or bring national flags to the parade in order to identify themselves as Central American and perhaps implicitly challenge the idea that immigrants need to or should "melt" into a larger U.S. American culture. At the 2006 COFECA parade, for instance, there was a brown-skinned spectator wearing a dark-blue shirt with white printing that read, "100% Guatemalteco," and a white barcode underneath the printed text. The cultural production and display of the shirt expose an anxiety regarding Central American identity in the diaspora, particularly among mestiza/os—it is an identity that constantly needs to be performed and visibly articulated in order to prevent being collapsed with other Latina/o identities. It also reveals the problematic nature of enacting this identity. To pronounce that there is a 100% Guatemalan subject is a troubling affirmation, especially in light of the fact that the nation-state of Guatemala has engaged in its own violent military campaign to preserve and maintain a national identity that has been defined by the effacement—culturally and physically—of its indigenous and black communities. This spectator then represents an ambivalence that is key for some Central American subjects because it speaks to the ways in which the parade visibly protests the idea of inevitable assimilation by Central Americans, even as it as serves as a powerful reminder of the manner in which nationalism, at both macro (regional) and micro (national) levels, is sustained by a fiction of homogenization (a different melting pot) and ethnoracial erasure. In other words, to privilege a specific implied, racialized citizen-subject as "100% Guatemalan" is to rely on a national identity that was formed via the exclusion of other diverse ethnoracial populations within the nation-state.

Nevertheless, this spectator's choice to wear the shirt must be read within its specific context of an ethnoracial minority subject in the United States visibly asserting a type of resistance toward dominant narratives of assimilation and

FIGURE 7. Shirt worn by one of the parade spectators at the 2006 COFECA parade.

accommodation and ideologies of white supremacy. This is particularly significant, since just four months prior, on May 1, 2006, Los Angeles hosted one of the
largest protests regarding immigrant rights.[94] The political climate in the United
States, and especially in spaces such as Los Angeles and the greater Southwest,
has been hostile toward immigrants, particularly Latina/o immigrants, as evidenced in such political policies like California's Proposition 187 and Arizona's
SB 1070 (to name only a few). Thus this spectator's choice of wearing a shirt that
states he is "100% Guatemalan" with a barcode on it, as if to suggest that his body
and labor are a disposable form of commodity within U.S. culture, must be recognized as a moment of agency, a way of talking back to a dominant consumer
culture that fetishizes and erases not only his own personal labor but also that
of the broader labor force. It also calls attention to the contradictory position of
U.S. American culture toward its immigrants: on the one hand, it resents immigrants like this spectator for their ethnoracial difference and resistance toward
assimilation while, on the other hand, it needs this population as a cheap source
of labor to sustain its economy.[95]

With this in mind, we can see how the COFECA event becomes a site of
radical critique—a manipulation of space in order to cast light on those "other
[discursive] spaces," which continually position Central Americans as racialized
"others" and outsiders. Michel Foucault has labeled such spaces "heterotopias,"
which operate as "countersites" wherein "all other real sites that can be found
within the culture, are simultaneously represented, contested and inverted."[96]
According to Foucault, heterotopias achieve this because they expose those
spaces that produce their own conditions of possibility and act as mirrors where
"I see myself where I am not . . . a sort of shadow that gives my own visibility
to myself, that enables me to see myself there where I am absent."[97] Such *other*
spaces, then, emerge from an act of recognizing one's displacement. Thus we may
need to think about the production of the COFECA parade and of a diasporic
Central American identity itself as heterotopic texts—as remnants discarded
during the constructions of other identities, like "American" or "Latina/o,"
which seldom link those categories with the experiences of Central Americans.[98]

CONCLUSION

The multiple ways in which participants and spectators use the COFECA parade
to enact or contest representations of Central Americanness reveals how this
cultural institution is a complex site where dominant notions of Central American belonging converge with the quotidian lives of diasporic subjects in the
United States. While the parade and *fiestas patrias* are vestiges of isthmian state-
sponsored projects of national cohesion, in the diaspora, they become a critical terrain where Central Americans can contest their marginalization with U.S.

American and Latina/o imaginaries. They also provide subjects from the isthmus with sites from which identities can be articulated and where the notion of a shared culture (one cultivated by social dislocation) can be fostered. The fact that Central Americans have constructed their own celebrations in relation to but as distinct from other Latina/o festivities in California also signals that Latinidad has not been able to interpellate everyone equally. As such, every year that Central Americans march down the streets of Little Central America, they become metaphoric mirrors to a Latina/o discourse that simultaneously speaks for but renders their traditions and social experiences invisible. However, this form of "coming out" is problematized by some participants who bring to bear how this self-fashioning of Central American identity often excludes ethnoracial and nonheteronormative subjectivities. Consequently, the COFECA parade, as catalyst, embodiment, and vehicle of Centralaméricanismo, is a heterotopic space, which not only undermines racist and homogenizing tropes circulating in the United States that fail to recognize Latina/o heterogeneity but also allows marginalized Central Americans subjects to produce, perform, and challenge dominant manifestations of this identity. As a heterotopia, this parade becomes a powerful form of critique; it acts as a mirror from which its mere presence or existence challenges totalizing discourses from the isthmus, the United States, and Latinidad, which claim to be inclusive of all peoples and cultures.

4 · SUBJECTS IN PASSING

Central American–Americans, Latinidad, and the Politics of Dislocation

> In much the same way that you can meet a person and not know if they are gay or straight, you could meet me and not know whether I was of Latin heritage. So I find myself making judgment calls—do I come out of the closet and when?
>
> —Veronica Chambers (Panamanian American),
> "Secret Latina at Large"[1]

In her essay "Negotiating among Invisibilities," Vielka Cecilia Hoy discloses how insular notions of Central Americanness render her black subjectivity marginal within that collectivity. Hoy, who was born in the United States and is half Panamanian and half Nicaraguan, notes that when people think of other racial groups besides mestiza/os in Central America they usually think of indigenous groups, as the idea that "African-descended peoples exist in Nicaragua (estimated as high as 13 percent of the population) and that they speak Spanish . . . is nearly unfathomable."[2] Hoy's assertion is that, within a dominant Central American imaginary, subjects like her are considered unthinkable and therefore occupy a space of nonbelonging. In many ways, the preceding chapters of this book have delineated how this sense of exclusion expressed by Hoy is manifested daily. Iterations of Central American culture that circulate both within and beyond the isthmus often posit it as a mestiza/o phenomenon and commonly consider certain countries within the isthmus (like Panama) as not "traditionally" Central American, leading many Afro-Central Americans to feel marginalized or, as Hoy claims, "invisible." In Hoy's account of her experience, and in the ways in which her black body remains unrecognizable within popular articulations of Central Americanness, she exposes how regimes of recognition—epistemological frames that create the conditions of possibility for one to be seen as a recognizable subject by linking certain characteristics to identity categories—function in the production of Central American identities.

Hoy's personal anecdote also reveals how the signifying economy of the category "Central American" is altered via the process of migration. She adds that, for Central American subjects, modes of identification become "complicated still further once the émigré lands in the 'capitalist backyard.'"[3] Once in the "capitalist backyard," (black) Central Americans "continue to be invisible as Latin@s, because they are separate from the ways Mexican identity is formed. And of course they continue to be invisible as Afro-Latin@s, as this identification hardly exists in the West Coast."[4] Hoy's narrative of invisibility shifts and elucidates how her marginalization is not just due to her black subjectivity but also by virtue of her non-Mexicanness. As she describes it, the hypervisible and easily legible Central American mestiza/o subject becomes reconfigured as invisible within the United States due to its spatial proximity with another identity category: Mexican (American). Central American mestiza/os' racial status (which marked them as a Central American norm) now renders them unintelligible by a new set of regimes of recognition to which they are subjected in the diaspora and on the "West Coast" of the United States in particular. Hoy therefore underscores the ways in which dominant understandings of Latinidad, as enacted within some geocultural spaces, have made this category synonymous with a particular national group: Mexicans and Mexican Americans.[5]

Indeed, for Central Americans in the Southwest and Los Angeles in particular, the category and signification of that very term (Central American) and their cultural identity go into crisis as they inhabit a space where, according to Hoy, "Latinidad is Mexicancentric."[6] Hoy's use of the term *Mexicancentric* echoes Horacio Roque Ramírez's use of "overwhelming *mexicanidad*," which refers to the ways non-Mexicans in Los Angeles become invisible in the "context of the Mexican and Chicano majority."[7] Thus the apt nature of her title, which emphasizes how her multiple subject positions as a black Central American woman all lead to the same path of invisibility due to manifestations of Latinoness in which some national groups occupy a type of "geographic hegemony."[8] As outlined by Hoy, and unlike in the isthmus, being a Central American mestiza/o in the United States does not preclude one from occupying an invisible position within Latinidad (though it might temper those feelings within notions of Central Americanness). Subsequently, while Hoy's testimony is powerful for highlighting the myriad ways in which she is personally marginalized, it also poignantly indexes the ways these local regimes of recognition regarding Latinidad affect U.S. Central Americans. Ironically, in a text that documents her alienation from the category of Central American, she concludes by inadvertently articulating how the "self" of this narrative can indeed be read as a Central American–American subject—a position marked by a relational exclusion and absence from the category "Latina/o."

Hoy's critical personal project of describing the way some ethnoracial categories signify a particular set of experiences, which in turn enables social marginalization for certain subjects, is the focus of this chapter as I expose the discursive effects of a Latina/o matrix of intelligibility. One of those effects is the production of Central American–American subjects. Because Latinidad has constructed its own invisible parameters by repeatedly defining "Latina/o" culture via three national constituencies (Mexican, Puerto Rican, and Cuban)[9] and because in geopolitical spaces like the Southwest "Latina/o" has become a metonym for "Mexican" (as noted by Hoy and Roque Ramírez), a surplus or constitutive outside has been created where subjects like the Central American–American emerge. This subjectivity is an effect of power relations whereby the categories of Latina/o, Latin American, and U.S. American are often maintained through the exclusion of U.S. Central Americans. Echoing Arturo Arias, my articulations of Central American–Americanness position it as a type of abjection, and it is through this abjection from other categories (which can include the category of Central American itself) that the Central American–American subject is constituted. In this sense, Central American–Americanness is more than just a state of marginality, for it is not simply that Central American–American subjects and cultures exist at the periphery of discourses of American and Latina/o cultural citizenship, but rather they are produced in and through those spaces of exclusion.

Another effect of this Latina/o grid of intelligibility is that it renders both Central American–American bodies and the signifier "Central American" unintelligible. Whereas dominant enunciations of Central Americanness within the isthmus delimited which bodies and subjects could be recognized as belonging to that category, as Hoy suggests, the process of migration converts this term into an empty signifier. Central American–American illegibility, in turn, conditions the process of Central Americans "passing" as Mexican Americans, particularly in geographical regions that rely on (what I explain in more detail later) as an *Other Than Mexican* (OTM) logic. Though passing is frequently associated with intentionality, with social actors viewed as "choosing to pass" by playing with semiotic codes (dress, speech, etc.) or via active concealment (not disclosing who "they really are"), it is important to note, as Elaine Ginsberg does, that it includes a much broader spectrum of practices. For Ginsberg, "passing is about identities: their creation or imposition, their adoption or rejection, their accompanying awards or penalties."[11] Key to Ginsberg's description of passing is an acknowledgment that passing is an agentic form, where subjects "adopt or reject" their identities, as well as an act of subjectivization through which identities are created and imposed. My interest is in the latter, in the almost unintentional disciplinary nature of passing, which imposes passing on subjects via a reading that is predicated on a visual economy of the body that relies on discursive and cultural frames that limit the kinds of bodies that can be recognized.

To this end, this chapter examines narratives of U.S. Central Americans passing as Mexican Americans. It includes a critical reading of Salvadoran American Marlon Morales and his personal essay "Always Say You're Mexican," which not only blurs distinctions between active and passive forms of passing but also highlights how this social practice is a byproduct of the unrecognition of Central American–American bodies from an OTM logic. I then pivot to the controversy over Honduran American Carlos Mencia and the accusation that he is a "fake Mexican" and a "white man" passing as "Mexican." To date, the Carlos Mencia controversy is the most popular and public example of a Central American narrative of passing. In it, I read Carlos Mencia as a persona—a text whose physical and discursive body operates not only as a site where relations of power are enacted but also as the effect of dominant narratives of Latinidad that make the signifiers "Honduran" and "Central American" unintelligible. Read together, these narratives of Central American illegibility and passing are important because they reveal how power and the parameters of Latinidad become enforced in everyday spaces and social practices that regulate and govern bodies, institutionalize certain discourses, and produce Central American–American subjects.

PASSING

Passing—the shift from one identity (e.g., race, class, gender, sexuality, etc.) category to another—is a social practice that can encompass a wide spectrum of actions and experiences. However, it is often presented as limited to two forms: active passing and passive passing. Active passing is an intentional act, one where the subject moves from a "stigmatized" location to another that is considered to be "normal" and/or connected to a desirable identity within the given environmental context. Active passing is seen as a deliberative performance of self-manipulation, as "an attempt to control the process of signification itself."[12] Within the context of the United States, active passing historically emerged from racial passing: a movement in racial identity from "black" to "white." Elaine Ginsberg's work, for instance, highlights how some of the earliest examples of individuals who crossed the color/racial line were light "white-looking" escaped slaves fleeing to the north.[13] According to Gayle Wald, the racial binary logic of white supremacy continued to create the conditions of possibility for black individuals to pass as the social and legal implementation of the "one drop rule" and Jim Crow maintained racial asymmetries.[14]

Although passing has been primarily associated with racial passing, this social practice has extended beyond just shifting between white/black racial categories.[15] There are cases of gender, class, sex, disability, religious, and ethnic passing that also transpire. Active passing then is completely linked to social hierarchies whereby within this self-conscious play of material signifiers (speech, clothes, etc.), a subject is able to achieve social, physical, material, and emotional respite from a previous position where those options were denied. In each of these instances, the movement is always spatially configured as vertical (i.e., movement from the less desirable to the more desirable) and the success of that movement is contingent on regimes of recognition. For Jennifer Ann Ho, the fact that active passing is literally and figuratively a form of movement between identity categories makes it a "strategy of resistance" not only for the embodied subjects who via this practice create new social possibilities in their day-to-day lives by passing but also because it upends "rigid definitions and hierarchies of race," as well as class, ethnicity, gender, and sexuality.[16]

Passing is also Janus-faced, requiring simultaneous recognition and misrecognition. For the subject to pass successfully, their performance must be seamless and appear natural. But how this "naturalness" is determined is connected to the way certain behaviors, actions, and cultural codes are linked with particular bodies. For example, for someone with a biological anatomy deemed as female to successfully pass as a "man" requires that their mannerisms, semiotic codes, and behaviors are misrecognized as "feminine" and highly recognized as "masculine." In other words, there needs to be a set of culturally shared understandings of what codes and actions are feminine versus masculine. As such, the same cultural criteria employed for subjects with a male anatomy to be viewed as a "man" applies to subjects biologically labeled as female who want to be seen as a "man." The fact that the ability to pass, like all iterations of identity, relies on external factors not controlled by the subject suggests that one might need to be tentative about the amount of agency recognized in social actors engaged in this practice. While, without question, passing has been vital for shifting the grounds of epistemology in regard to identity categories, disclosing how gender, race, and sexuality, once viewed as immutable, are discursively constructed, it nevertheless, as María Sánchez and Linda Schlossberg note, "generally holds the larger social hierarchies firmly in place."[17] This is not meant to be an indictment of those who pass but a reminder that even active forms of passing are not always voluntary and indeed are enforced by societal institutions and ideologies that deem certain subjects to be more desirable or normative than others.

In contrast to deliberative forms of self-manipulation or concealment, which are viewed as active forms of passing, some scholars have begun to name other moments of identity blurring as examples of "passive passing." According to Kelby Harrison, passive passing is unintentional, since it is "about the assumptions and perceptions of others . . . that one is commonly perceived an identity they don't consider themselves to be, or that the identity they do consider themselves to be isn't recognized by the larger culture at a glance."[18] Passive passing then is linked to unrecognition and unintelligibility whereby the identity the subject sees themselves as inhabiting is not "recognized by the larger culture." While Harrison's definition suggests that what separates passive forms of passing from active forms is that one requires intentionality and the other does not, this notion is subverted when she claims, "Passive passing can be as simple as verbal withdrawal, or a decision not to disclose."[19] In adding these qualities to passive passing, the distinctions become muddled with active forms, since they both ultimately rely on the passer and the "decisions" of the social actor. Subsequently, what at first appears to be an almost binary model between two forms of passing quickly becomes destabilized, indicating the ways in which passing itself is precarious, ephemeral, and, more important, a matter of interpretation. What one reads as passive can easily be viewed as an active form of passing and vice versa.

That being said, a distinction should be made between acts that presuppose a type of consciousness from the subject versus moments where subjects unknowingly are forced into the social practice of passing. For example, if an individual is at a social event with an acquaintance and casually mentions, as an afterthought, that they are Costa Rican or Guatemalan and the acquaintance responds by acting surprised or deceived, perhaps even disappointed, then that exchange begins to mirror a dynamic of "coming out" for that individual. Except that, in this example, the subject "coming out" did not know they were doing so because they were never aware they were in a metaphorical closet to begin with. Yet the listener's reaction and their treatment of the information presented makes the other individual feel as if they had inadvertently engaged in an act of passing, as if they had revealed something about their identity that changes the listener's interpretation of their identity. If passive passing still retains the notion that the subject decides to pass or not, can this scenario be read as passive passing? And what are the material and psychological consequences to such (mis)readings of the body? I label these types of moments, which occur for many Central American–American subjects, as examples of *impassing*. This neologism links the concept of "impasse"—which connotes a forced situation—with this type of social practice in order to highlight that certain instances of identity blurring occur due to the disciplinary power held by grids of intelligibility that can only recognize certain subjects and therefore have little to do with the conscious efforts of the individual. Impassing is similar to what Nancy Arden McHugh terms "imposed passing"—moments when an identity that is created for others is imposed. This imposition is linked to a visuality of the body because "when the visible does not identify an individual self, we force them to pass as something."[20] In both contexts, passing is linked to intelligibility. When the body, or the signifier attached to that body, does not easily disclose a recognizable identity, one is chosen for that subject, and unbeknownst to them, they are read as occupying an identity to which they feel they personally do not belong. Impassing signals the overrecognition of certain identity categories with particular bodies so that an identity is imposed on certain subjects due to a broader discourse that creates such linkages. Thus impassing is about lack and excess in regard to the systems of signification through which subjects are defined and articulated. It is about reading individual bodies against cultural frames that always already link it with certain identities and almost never with others.

Central American narratives of passing encompass the full range of these forms. They have been framed as intentional (active), as imposed/impassed (nonvoluntary), as well as in terms of that ambivalent space of passive passing that requires both. This is evidenced in the epigraph from the essay "Secret Latina at Large," where the protagonist, a black Panamanian American, describes the ways her body and mannerisms are always already misrecognized as African American or Puerto Rican. However, what begins as a form of impassing changes as the protagonist becomes aware that this type of reading places her "in the closet," and she is therefore forced into a situation of either announcing the particularities of her identity and in essence "coming out" or allowing for the imposed passing to continue. But Veronica Chambers's protagonist also elucidates how seemingly "ethnic" passing is also linked with racial passing since she is not recognized as "white" but read as nonwhite. The fact that she is illegible as "Latina" also speaks to the ways in which this signifier has been racially coded as "brown"; grounded in a logic of *mestizaje*, which, as illustrated in the previous chapters, minimizes or disavows the presence of blackness. Likewise, the examples yielded from Morales's text and from the Mencia controversy also rely on impassing, insofar as, in both instances, to be read as "Latina/o" is to be (mis)read as only Mexican American. Accordingly, in the next section, I delineate the ways in which a Latina/o matrix of intelligibility has enabled these particular forms of passing to occur by rendering Central Americanness outside the realm of Latina/o recognizability.

LATINA/O GRID OF INTELLIGIBILITY

Poststructuralist theorists have asserted that our epistemological understandings are formed by "grid(s) of intelligibility." Such grids operate as conceptual frameworks for the way we come to understand subjects or recognize modes of selfhood.[21] As Ladelle McWhorter explains, such grids are more than just "a network of knowledge," since they function as "the routine exercise of social and political power. It is a network of power/knowledge."[22] Similarly, Judith Butler argues that, for gender and sexual identities, a heterosexual matrix renders some bodies intelligible, while those that do not conform "appear only as developmental failures or logical impossibilities."[23] Dominant modes of understanding then limit the kinds of bodies we see and place within a particular type of social order. Those that "fail" or are seen as unintelligible are those that fall outside the matrix of intelligibility. However, it is these "developmental failures or logical impossibilities" that can lead us to interrogate regulatory modes of legibility. If in the context of gender/sexual subjects the heterosexual matrix determines the cultural field of legibility, arguably the tripartite model of "historical minorities"—namely, Mexican American, Puerto Rican, and Cuban American—is what dominates a Latina/o grid of intelligibility.[24]

Several institutions, including census categories, state policies, academic disciplines, and the media have been pivotal in delineating what it means to be Latina/o. According to the U.S. Census Bureau, Hispanics/Latinos are not a racial group but an ethnic group. Those who classify themselves as of Hispanic/Latino ethnicity can mark themselves as being any race including "white." As an ethnic category, however, the census frames Mexican, Mexican Americans, Chicanos, Puerto Ricans, and Cubans as the national groups that define "Hispanic" and "Latino." Since 1980, when the Census Bureau first introduced the category of "Hispanic" to the questionnaire, individuals have only been given the option of checking the aforementioned national/ethnic labels; populations that do not fit this tripartite notion of Hispanidad are asked to check the box of "other Spanish/Hispanic" at the bottom and write in their national origin.[25] In this regard, what the state confers or recognizes as Latina/o is top-down and delimited to these three groups, while the other national groups are seen as more peripheral to or aberrations of a demographic norm.

Similarly, when the field of Latina/o studies emerged in the 1980s and 1990s, the focus of inquiry for this paradigm was largely centered on this Latina/o trinity. Ilan Stavans's seminal text *The Hispanic Condition,* for example, explores the conditions of possibility for the construction of Latina/o identity by showing "the multiple links between Latinos and their siblings south of the Rio Grande, a journey from Spanish to English, the northward odyssey of the omnipresent *bracero* worker, *jíbaro* immigrant, and Cuban refugee."[26] Evidenced here is that Stavans cannot think of the "Hispanic" condition outside of certain national markers. The "Hispanic" or Latina/o experience, as outlined by Stavans, is defined through very specific national, cultural, racial, gendered, and historical terms: it is the Mexican *bracero*, the Puerto Rican indigenous *jíbaro*, and the Cuban exile refugee.

Although one might be tempted to view Stavans's articulation of Latinoness as an aberration, his notion is echoed by other works in the field such as *The*

Latino Condition, The Latino Reader, Latino Cultural Citizenship, and *The Latino Body,* which conceive of "Latina/o" within these national parameters. Indeed, this notion of Latinidad is so pervasive that at the dawn of the twenty-first century, scholar Juan Flores proposed the term *pan-Latino* as a way of thinking about Latina/os as a "pan-ethnicity."[27] Interestingly, Flores's term implies that the construct of Latina/o is not already pan-ethnic but rather delimited to certain communities, hence the need to add the prefix of "pan-" to the presumably already pan-national/ethnic "Latino." Likewise, the anthology *The Other Latinos* (which indexes the literal space certain groups occupy within the census's view of Latina/o) focuses on national communities who fall outside of the purview of the Latina/o trinity, including U.S. Central Americans. As such, while the field of Latina/o studies is constantly changing, one cannot overlook that the discourse yielded from this academic space has also enabled a Latina/o matrix of intelligibility.[28]

But perhaps the most influential space for creating shared understandings and associations of what constitutes Latina/o subjects can be located in mass media forms. Media texts are critical institutional sites for producing their own epistemological ordering among social bodies, influencing "how people think and behave, how they see themselves and other people."[29] As Mary Beltrán notes, media representations of Latinoness "provide images to non-Latinos of who and what Latina/os might be"[30] and arguably prevent the broader culture from viewing certain subjects as Latina/o. Within representational practices, such as films, television, major magazines, and newspaper, unlike in the U.S. Census, "Latina/o" is viewed as both an ethnic and racial category. In these popular representations, Latina/os have been ascribed with particular phenotypical and ethnic characteristics. Clara Rodríguez contends that a dominant phenotypic face of Latinidad can be seen in the media, one embodied by a person who is "slightly tan, with dark hair and eyes."[31] Similarly, Arlene Dávila notes that a generic pan-Hispanic look has been fostered in the media by advertisers who link this perceived Hispanic phenotype "with features such as darker/olive complected skin and brown-black hair."[32] These racialized and classed visual images, which Rodríguez and Dávila refer to as "Latin looks," have influenced how many U.S. Americans and Latina/os themselves come to understand and categorize who falls within and outside a term like "Latina/o."

If the media foments the notion of Latina/os as a particular ethnoracial subject, it has also linked this construct with the same tripartite national experiences. This is in large part due to the fact that the terms *Mexican, Puerto Rican,* and *Cuban* had a well-established signifying economy of popular representation long before the categories "Hispanic" and "Latina/o" entered the lexicon of American ethnic identities. The film *West Side Story* (1961), for instance, was never meant to represent Latina/os in the United States, only a specific racialized minority group: Puerto Rican. Nevertheless, the effect is the same. Whether proliferating the notion of Puerto Ricans as racial *others* via their delinquency (as gang members in *West Side Story*) or "Mexicans" as *bandidos* (in Western films), as problematic as these representations are for positioning these populations as "exotic" and inherently racially and culturally foreign to U.S. American culture, these depictions nonetheless render them legible for audiences—that is, although clearly construed as "Latin" *others*, as a nuisance and the source of problems for Anglo-American "civility," the hypervisibility of these negative stereotypes enables legibility because being framed as second-class citizens still posits these groups within that broader U.S. national imaginary, albeit negatively. As such, while the popular television show *I Love Lucy* (1951–1957) and Ricky Ricardo was not intended to reflect a pan-ethnic form of Latino masculinity but rather a particular racialized white-yet-other, classed, and Cuban subject, due to its mass popularity, it became a formative text for current ideologies and tropes of Latinidad. Indeed, these early and often contrived media representations of "Mexicans," "Puerto Ricans," and "Cubans" enabled the conditions for conceiving of a pan-ethnic category like Latina/o; their constant positioning as racial, linguistic, cultural outsiders collectively represented them as a broader social problem that facilitated a mode of belonging. These media-based codifying practices inadvertently create and sustain a Latina/o grid of intelligibility by allowing audiences and society writ large to recognize certain bodies, geopolitical spaces, and nationalities as Latina/o, while those not represented become rendered unintelligible or "logical impossibilities." The narratives of U.S. Central Americans in the next section further reveal how this matrix of intelligibility becomes even more restricted when it congeals with geopolitical discourses that render the term *Latina/o* synonymous with Mexican and Mexican American.

(IM)PASSING IN "ALWAYS SAY YOU'RE MEXICAN" BY MORALES

The social practice of "passing" or "performing Mexicanness" is one that has been explored for the last thirty years in U.S. Central American cultural expressions. Initially, this act was often regarded as a consequence of migration, as another trial and tribulation to be endured in the transmigrant experience. The film *El Norte* (1983) and the novel *Odyssey to the North* (1998), for instance, both depict scenes that detail the need for Central American immigrants to pass as Mexican in order to cross the border.[33] *Odyssey to the North* includes several scenes that reinforce the idea that passing as Mexican is essential to one's ability to make it to "*el norte*." Repeatedly throughout the novel, Salvadoran immigrants are told by their *coyotes* that their ability to make it to the United States and avoid being deported is contingent on their ability to speak "*como un mejicano* / like a Mexican."³⁴ Passing in this context is therefore not only defined as a subdued performance where social actors only need to acquire linguistic proficiency in Mexican idioms and phrasing but also seen as a necessary evil in the process of migration.

In these early works, there was an inherent assumption that passing did not occur once one crossed the U.S.-Mexico border. This would change in 2001 with the publication of the first anthology of Salvadoran American writing, *Izote Voz*.³⁵ Comprised of several personal essays, this anthology reorientates our understanding of inter-Latina/o relations by highlighting the multiple reasons subjects born and/or raised in the United States would continue to aspire to pass as Mexican.³⁶ One of the most provocative and illustrative texts from this anthology is Marlon Morales's memoir essay "Always Say You're Mexican." In it, Morales illuminates how the demands from discourses of masculinity, heteronormativity, and Latinidad, which in Los Angeles is often conflated with "Mexican," affect the protagonist: a queer Salvadoran American. It also narrates the need and impossibility for Salvadoran Americans as a social group to (im)pass as Mexican Americans. According to Horacio Roque Ramírez, "*mexicanidad*" provides the condition of possibility for subjects like Morales to pass as Mexican, as they become in Los Angeles a "minority within a minority."³⁷

Comprised of two memorable moments of Morales's life, the first part of the essay retells his first day of the fourth grade. That day is memorable, since it is intertwined with a moment of immediate homosocial bonding with another boy named Alex. It is Alex's penetrating eyes and the way he smiles, "unlike how boys smile when they're about to size each other up,"³⁸ that distinguish him from others. Since Alex's gestures are not linked with dominant codes of violent masculinity, these welcoming mannerisms connote a different type of male fraternity, one linked with intimacy, for it is after Alex smiles and stares at Morales that he asks him, "Where are you from?"³⁹ Though seemingly trivial, Morales points out that "knowing where you are from is one of the most important things to know when you are nine years old,"⁴⁰ this type of place-based information is therefore viewed as central to one's identity in this essay. Alex's probing question about identity proves vexing for Morales, since he has been advised by his mother to say he is from Mexico but "born here." Defying convention, Morales instead reveals his "secret" and tells Alex he is from El Salvador. This is a significant revelation by Morales, who from his earliest ventures in public spaces (elementary school) has been taught to have a bifurcated identity—his Salvadoran identity needs to stay home in the private arena because "anything Salvadoran . . . was left at home, never in public."⁴¹ His Salvadoranness occupies an analogous space with his sexuality, as both are relegated to a private domain and seen as not belonging in the public sphere. Alex's response to this form of ethnonational "coming out" is by saying, "'Cool' approvingly" and asking Morales a follow-up question: "What part of Mexico is that in?"[42] Alex's positive response to Morales's disclosure is therefore contingent on the assumption that El Salvador is just another location in Mexico.

Alex's reading of Morales as first and foremost Mexican, which is based in a view of this national category as the norm within Latina/o identities, embodies what I term an OTM logic. OTM is an acronym for "Other Than Mexican," an administrative term deployed within the U.S. Border Patrol that reflects the widespread perspective within that agency that the vast majority of undocumented immigrants are Mexican nationals. Though coined with this pragmatic intent as a type of taxonomy within undocumented immigrants, what actually emerges from this U.S. biopolitical imperative is not only a totalizing discourse that yet again renders "Mexican" as a racial other within the U.S. American national imaginary but also a dichotomy from which to position immigrants and racialized bodies inhabiting the greater Southwest. Terms only gather their meaning in relation to one another, and these relations are hardly commensurate as one side of the dyad becomes viewed as the standard normative from which an *other* is defined. In this dichotomy the Mexican is legible, recognizable (albeit in highly xenophobic, racist, problematic ways), while the other remains unintelligible. There is nothing distinctive about being OTM, since that discursive space houses all subjects who are *not* Mexican. This side of the binary is defined via its relational negativity and by its vacuous empty nature. OTM as concept and way of positioning subjects discloses the problematic ways that "Mexican" in certain contexts becomes the normative way of reading not only "undocumented immigrants" but also certain ethnoracial subjects since anyone who falls outside of "Mexican" is simply positioned as "Other." Thus Mexican (and by extension, Mexican American) becomes a paradoxical normative (within Latinidad) and nonnormative (within discourses of Anglo-American citizenship and belonging) subject position within an OTM logic and gaze.

This in turn not only creates the conditions of possibility for impassing but also compounds previous discussions of how racialized politics and forms of passing operate. María Sánchez and Linda Schlossberg argue that racial readability has historically translated into social invisibility, claiming that to be "marked is to be marked out."[43] For them, only subjects who are "unmarked" occupy a type of privilege as the norm prototypically has been viewed as transparent. But in an OTM logic, which is inherently contradictory, a subject can be both marked and unmarked and can be simultaneously normative and nonnormative. Though the ethnoracial, national, and cultural features often linked to the category of Mexican and Mexican American place them as *others* within discourses of white supremacy, citizenship, and U.S. national belonging, within a Latina/o matrix, they become resituated as an ethnoracial norm. OTM signals the ways Mexicanness inadvertently enters as a type of regulatory "ideal," since this schema creates a quick shorthand for how to read racialized subjects, particularly those imbued with "Latin looks," as Mexican (or Mexican American) until proven otherwise. Though the term might be an effect of a macropower that regulates the kinds of bodies that can become citizen-subjects, it is important to note that this logic is also upheld within broader discourses of Latinidad as well as within "microphysics of power," in the everyday exchanges among individuals. In other words, the Border Patrol gaze that views ethnoracial nonwhite subjects as Mexican first until documentation or idioms prove otherwise migrates outside of that space and enters into a type of cultural practice deployed in the spheres of everyday life. In this sense, while my conceptualization of OTM parallels Frances Aparicio's term "hegemonic Mexicanization" (which refers to the ways Latina/os are assumed to be a priori Mexican by "dominant US Society or many non-Latinos") it differs insofar as Latina/os and Mexican Americans also enforce this type of impassing.[44]

This is evidenced in the scene with Alex (a Mexican American), who utilizes the normative schema of his setting (Los Angeles) and proceeds to read Morales as Mexican. When Morales attempts to assert a type of national and cultural difference, this is negated because El Salvador is an empty signifier. Alex can only think of his friend as Mexican. But when Alex's mother informs him that El Salvador is "Not Mexican" it leaves him confused. Alex begins to ask Morales if he is "Asian" or "Filipino." Since El Salvador lacks any attached significations within a Los Angeles Latina/o grid of intelligibility, Alex becomes unsure of everything including his friend's racial status. Although the narrative never provides readers with any type of racial descriptions for these two characters, what once was for Alex so recognizably Mexican, and not Asian, becomes quickly destabilized by the revelation that Morales is not Mexican, leaving Alex to think that his friend can be any other ethnoracial category but Latina/o. This moment of racial illegibility for Alex discloses how national/ethnic passing (from Salvadoran to Mexican) is contingent on broader discourses of racialization. "Mexican" in this context is predicated on the view of this ethnoracial category as nonblack and non-Asian. Alex's confusion thus underscores how regimes of recognition also delimit Mexican subjectivities as this national construct is also positioned here as a racial mestiza/o construct. Moreover, El Salvador is so far expunged from Latinidad in this narrative that both characters have a hard time conceiving of it as "real place." It is not until they look for it in an encyclopedia map—the authoritative repository of knowledge that contains all the "real" spaces/places—and locate it that they realize that a non-Mexican Latina/o permutation can exist. The idea of a Salvadoran American identity here is so unthinkable that it requires proof and confirmation of a physical place.

While the action of this scene revolves around the revelation of a covert identity—of Morales inadvertently announcing he is Salvadoran—it does not follow some of the precepts associated with "coming out" narratives. Within literary representations, "coming out" has been framed as an important moment, as an act that "signals and brings about the embracing of one's homosexual identity."[45] But in Morales's essay, this moment of consciousness and "truth" about his identity does not lead to a type of personal liberation or an embracing of his Salvadoran American identity. On the contrary, Morales's disclosure about his identity is a temporary revelation, as Alex agrees to "not tell anyone" becoming a "secret" the two friends share.[46] In doing so, the two boys engage in a clandestine friendship in which Morales's Salvadoran American self remains hidden and relegated to the private sphere.

Indeed, the first half of the essay endorses the notion that Morales is engaging in an active form of passing by both his conscious disclosure and his concealment of his Salvadoran American identity. This point is reiterated in the title, which indicates that this performance of Mexican identity is fused with a speech act—with the declaration and assertion that one is Mexican. This admonition to "always say you're Mexican" is one that appears as a refrain in a moment of stream of consciousness midway through the essay:

Always say you're Mexican
Always speak *inglish en la calle*
They'll leave you alone

Always say you're Mexican
They'll think you're from here
Mexicans have always been here

This used to be Mexico.
When you speak *inglish en la calle*
And you say you're Mexican

They'll leave you alone.[47]

There is no introductory clause that links these aforementioned lines to particular individuals within the essay, leaving readers to wonder who is uttering these words. Arguably, this polyvocality is a metaphor for the multiple forces that constrain Morales and his sense of self. For, on the one hand, this bilingual disembodied voice could emanate from his mother, who has instilled in him the importance of saying these words, or it could be a type of interior monologue for

Morales. If it is the latter, it might be that we are actually hearing two voices converge: the interior voice of the protagonist reproducing an external voice—the voice of a regime of recognition that is urging Morales to conform to the ethnoracial standard in his environment. The external voice is the call of interpellation, of being "hailed" into a particular type of ethnic subject—the voice that tells him to "always say you're Mexican" because that is the dominant script of intelligibility. The redundant and repetitive nature of some of the lines also emphasizes the inescapability of this type of logic of being "always" already Mexican. It is this exterior voice, which has been internalized, that enables self-disciplining of the subject, since it propels Morales to stay in the closet, reminding him that certain national and linguistic identities are reserved for "la calle / the streets," while others need to remain personal and private.

Also present in this passage are the contradictory ideologies and relational politics that fuel an OTM logic. The assertion that "Mexicans have always been here / This used to be Mexico," for instance, refutes the very xenophobic assumption linked with the production of the category of OTM, which within U.S. nation-state discourses views Mexican(s) as foreign. And yet, the refrain to "always say you're Mexican" underscores that to be Mexican and Mexican American occupies a type of cultural currency within the Southwest. This ironic nonnormative normativity that in one situation produces alienation in another domain allows for a type of recognizability within the realm of Latina/o subjectivity. Saying "you're Mexican" provides a type of security denied to the category of Salvadoran since it is only via (im)passing as Mexican that a Salvadoran American (and by extension U.S. Central American) can be "left alone"—or avoid a maligned social identity.

In relating how Morales is constantly being "told" to say he is Mexican, the narrative undermines the notion that he is engaged in a form of active passing. The fact that there is a voice explicitly encouraging Morales to pass as Mexican, in conjunction with an awareness that he can only be seen as Latina/o if he is read as Mexican (by Alex), suggests that passing is more an imposition than an act of volition. In fact, after this stream of consciousness moment, the essay resumes with Morales as an adult narrating his present condition and reflecting on the slippage between active and imposed passing: "I don't think my mom knew how hard it was for me to become an American. To become an American in Los Angeles, I first had to learn how to be Mexican. I think Salvadorans are all Mexican before anything else. People always call us Mexican and I'm still sure people see me and just see another Mexican. It's impossible to be anything else. I learned how to speak Mexican before English, to eat Mexican, sing Mexican, dream of Mexican men and Aztec gods."[48] Morales's declaration that he needed to learn how to speak, eat, and dream Mexican begs the question: what constitutes being

Mexican? As described, "Mexican" runs the risk of being viewed as a monolithic static ontological category. Though these are problematic assertions that need to be tempered by an understanding that all identity categories are fluid, relational, and contingent on the environmental context, this passage is nevertheless powerful for some of its other claims. One is that in Los Angeles, all Salvadoran Americans, and possibly all U.S. Central Americans, will undergo impassing. As Morales attests, passing is more of a fate than a choice, not just for him, but also for his broader social group. It is an imposition that occurs from dominant representations of Latinidad that codify brown bodies into Mexicans; for as Morales reveals, when people see him they "see another Mexican . . . It's impossible to be anything else," suggesting the inescapability of that OTM logic and gaze. Though Morales's essay is grounded in the cultural dynamics of Los Angeles, as Frances Aparicio's work on Central American immigrants in Chicago who (im)pass as Mexican, as well as Donald Trump's xenophobic rhetoric, which uses "Mexican" to index all undocumented immigrants from the U.S.-Mexico border, reveals, this logic transcends the confines of the Southwest.

Equally insightful is the notion that in Los Angeles the road to assimilation is no longer geared toward mimicking an Anglo-American norm but a Mexican American one. After all, Morales states that in order to "become an American," he first needs to be Mexican (however reified that category is presented). Contrary to popular belief, which views assimilation into an American "melting pot" as the relinquishing of all things "ethnic," Morales proclaims that one must first melt into another pot in order to enter into a broader sense of American belonging. In this regard, what we witness here is the manner in which certain ethnoracial subjects engage in what Rey Chow labels as "coercive mimeticism." According to Chow, whereas previous forms of identity mimesis were always defined by their relationship between colonizer-colonized and between nonwhite-white, in the neoliberal, postmodern moment, a third form of mimeticism has emerged for "those marginal to mainstream Western Culture" whereby mimeticism is no longer supposed to "replicate the white man or his culture but rather an image, a stereotyped view of ethnic. . . . which they are often expected to conform."[49] Similarly, within the entire essay, there is never pressure for Morales to follow and conform to some white, Western model; instead, his model is a stereotyped view of Mexican identity that constantly haunts and disciplines him into passing as a particular kind of subject.

The concluding lines of this passage demonstrate how internally colonized Morales feels by this logic and ideology. This notion of desiring to be "Mexican" becomes so embedded in his psyche and his libido—the core of his being—that he informs us that not only is his personal voice filtered through this lens ("sing Mexican"), but even in his unconscious he "dreams of Mexican men and Aztec gods."[50] The latter, a symbol of Chicano nationalism and an icon of heterosexual masculinity, illustrates the ambivalent terrain Morales negotiates. This type of impassing and coercive mimeticism then constrains not only how the self can be in the world but also who they can be with, delimiting Morales's options of same-sex desire—that is, his aspirational, sexual, and romantic yearnings are molded after what is socially desired among ethnoracial subjects. Interestingly, this second "coming out" moment in the narrative is not given much attention, perhaps revealing how his queer sexuality was viewed as less of a challenge than his national identity or, conversely, is indicative of another type of self-disciplining in which sexuality cannot find a prominent space of enunciation due to heteronormative and national narratives of identity formation.

The photo that serves as a background to the essay also thematically reinforces that this is a narrative of impassing, a by-product of an OTM logic deployed in day-to-day life. The photo is of a small child about less than a year old (presumably, since the child is shown needing assistance in standing upright). The child, who is dressed in a *traje de charro* outfit, is slightly off center frame, possibly connoting the child's peripheral social status, while the backdrop is a picture of the *Virgen de Guadalupe*. This religious image and the choice of clothing (a traditional outfit used in mariachi performance), are both iconic symbols of Mexican and Mexican American culture. The child in this photo then is literally forced to embody Mexicanness, as he or she is too young to assert any conscious preference. The photograph suggests that since their birth, this child has been surrounded and clothed by all things Mexican. In so doing, it frames becoming Mexican and/or Mexican American not as an active form of passing but as a type of socialization akin to that which occurs with gender/sexual identities. It therefore implicitly asserts that cultural/national identities are another normalizing force in the sphere of identity production, as children are encouraged to embody and mimic the normative standards of their environmental context. As the essay concludes, Morales informs his readers, "'Always say you're Mexican' were more than words . . . I felt them and became Mexican first, then American and somewhere in between I was Salvadoran."[51] This statement once again reasserts some of the thematic concerns of his essay, which illuminate how Mexican as a category and ethnoracial identity has become in certain geopolitical settings a type of normative nonnormativity in which all other Latina/o subjects first have to become Mexican on their journey to becoming an ethnoracial American.

But perhaps more important, what this statement underscores is the manner in which the text situates the production of a Salvadoran American subjectivity as analogous to Central American–American subjectivity. Salvadoran American subjectivity is delineated here as a power effect, as the residual excess that appears "in between" the construction of the other identity categories of (U.S.) American and Mexican. This is punctuated by the use of past tense from Morales who states, "I was Salvadoran," signaling that this identity is ephemeral and no longer a possibility. A Salvadoran American identity then can only exist outside of these two other categories. Ironically, Salvadoran usurps the space of the hyphen, becoming the middle point between those other identity spaces. Similar to the sign of Central American–American that uses the hyphen catachrestically, the hyphen in this context does not denote hybridity, but it marks a space of absence—the space of nonexistence for a Salvadoran American identity. In so doing, "Always Say You're Mexican" becomes a powerful vehicle that weds discourses of Latinidad, passing, and the production of Central American–American subjects. Not only does Morales's text challenge traditional accounts of passing by shifting all utterances and intentional actions of passing to a broader discussion of regimes of recognition that delimit scripts of intelligibility, but it also further discloses how narratives of Salvadoran American experiences see this subject formation as being produced from the same discursive forces that engender Central American–American subjects.

MENCIA AS A "FAKE MEXICAN" AND LATINA/O "LOGICAL IMPOSSIBILITY"

Buried within the files of YouTube is a video that illuminates how subjects who fall outside a Latina/o matrix of intelligibility can become "logical impossibilities." In the video, an Anglo-American man confronts a Honduran born immigrant over his identity. One of the accusations was that the Honduran man had created a fake identity in order to perform and keep his job. To authenticate himself to his Anglo-American accuser, the Honduran man pulls out his "green card" to verify not his citizenship but his ethnoracial ancestry. Watching the video, one witnesses an odd inversion taking place, since generally, individuals who have phenotypical brown and dark features, what Clara Rodríguez calls "Latin looks," are automatically located as racialized subjects.[52] However, in this video, it is clear that the Honduran—and by extension the Central American—body is read *outside* Latina/o and U.S. American imaginaries. This Honduran is thus confronted with Latina/o and American forms of unbelonging, departing from the myriad sociopolitical incidents in the general life of what Lázaro Lima calls the "Latino body."[53] This Central American–American marginal body politic is different, perhaps even peculiar, because the individual in the video is none other than Honduran-born comedian Carlos Mencia, who at that time was one of the most visible faces in U.S. popular culture.[54] And the YouTube video I am referring to is the notorious "Joe Rogan vs. Carlos Mencia" (2007)—a text that, for its "virality," is continually indexed in media spaces as the source of Mencia's decline into obscurity.[55]

The video captures the apex of a public controversy surrounding Mencia's artistic and ethnic credentials. It began in 2005, when comedian Joe Rogan and others accused Mencia of being a joke plagiarist and a "white" man passing as Mexican. Soon after, the blogosphere was riddled with several forums discussing both types of alleged "fraud," including a discussion thread on Yahoo, where a post asked, "Is Carlos Mencia Not Mexican?"[56] as well as an article on Snopes titled "Carlos Mencia Not Hispanic,"[57] and Reddit, which had a post titled "Carlos Mencia is Not Mexican and his first name is Ned."[58] This quirky yet highly public conversation about a Honduran American passing as Mexican American therefore offers a unique opportunity to examine how dominant scripts of Latina/o intelligibility enable not only (im)passing but also the production of Central American–American subjectivity, since both are effects of power and of discourses that locate U.S. Central American experiences as outside of the already peripheral location of Latina/o.

Though the persona "Carlos Mencia" emerged sometime in the late 1980s, the individual who brought us "Mencia"—Ned Arnel Mencía Holness—was born on October 22, 1967, in San Pedro Sula, Honduras. Like so many of his U.S. Central American compatriots, Mencia immigrated to the United States as a young child to live with extended family in Los Angeles. It seems odd that a subject with this immigrant background, and whose career firmly entrenched him as an "ethnic" comedian, would one day have to prove himself a racialized nonwhite subject. Indeed, when Mencia was able to obtain his own television show in 2005, titled *Mind of Mencia,* as program creator and producer he often fashioned himself as an ethnoracial Latino subject by utilizing Mexican and Mexican American cultural codes. The opening sequence for the pilot episode, for example, included a mariachi band playing in the background. While mariachi musical sound and the aesthetics that contribute to that style of performance are of Mexican origin, within mainstream culture, they are often viewed as iconic of Latina/o culture as well.[59] Mencia's use of mariachi music to frame his comedic show as a Latina/o cultural production invokes Morales's essay, which discloses how mariachi cultural symbols are often appropriated by non-Mexican Latina/os in order to be seen as falling in line with an ethnoracial norm. Although in Morales's essay such embodied notions of Mexicanness were imposed, in the context of *Mind of Mencia,* they are a bit more ambiguous. It remains unclear whether the inclusion of these signs were done to give the illusion to audiences that Mencia himself is Mexican, like some would later accuse, or were utilized to appeal to established culturally sanctioned norms of Latinoness, which in Los Angeles (the show's setting), tend to be synonymous with Mexican American culture.

Although at times the semiotic codes deployed in the *Mind of Mencia* rendered Mencia's national background ambiguous, it was quite explicit in its assertion that the central character was an ethnoracial subject. In the show, Mencia would commonly refer to himself as a "beaner"—a derogatory term usually ascribed to "a person of Hispanic background." Beaner symbolically connotes nonwhiteness (e.g., black beans and pinto beans) but also culturally "beans" have been viewed as a food staple within Latin American-Latino culture. Used as an alternative Latin American based identity category, Mencia's use of "beaner" reflects his own ambivalent and tenuous position within Latinidad. Its use emerges from Mencia asserting that he is an ethnoracial subject, one aligned with a broader Latin American community who has been racialized and stigmatized within Anglo-American discourse, but not always beholden or necessarily circumscribed by the category of "Latina/o." In fact, Mencia's show displayed an acute awareness of how a Latina/o matrix of intelligibility functioned and its effects on identity and (mis)recognition.

One of the show's segments, for instance, titled "Out the Beaner," was devoted to exposing individuals who should be seen as Latina/o but who are currently not recognized as such. In one segment, Mencia focused on the athlete Reggie Jackson, informing the audience that he is "actually a Puerto Rican" and concludes by telling them, "Sorry black people, he's ours."[60] At first glance, it is hard to see the humor in this segment, as it is not quite stand-up or parody nor is it a performance using hyperbolic gestures to "get a laugh." However, this segment might be more aligned with "shock humor"—often categorized by controversial or offensive observations by the comedian.[61] Presumably, the shock emerges in the "punch line," from Mencia revealing that Jackson is both black and Latino. In "outing" Reggie Jackson, Mencia brings to the forefront regimes of recognition that create this type of impassing to occur. In other words, because of Jackson's race, his last name, and the fact that he didn't frequently speak Spanish, an assumption and identity is imposed on him that views him as African American but not Latino.

Moreover, in (re)claiming Jackson as "ours," Mencia not only exposes how cultural scripts of Latinidad often exclude blackness but also squarely reclaims himself as Latino via his iteration and identification with a collective "us/ours." Though at times segments in Mencia's show cast light on the fact that Latina/os could be of any racial group, other moments stressed the notion that "beaner" was a nonwhite category. Many of Mencia's stand-up jokes involved using the second and distant pronoun "you" to refer to "white people." One joke titled "White People Camping" begins with Mencia saying, "White people, you do things I just don't understand," adding, "I'm sure you look at what some of the beaners do and say, 'What the hell are you doing?'"[62] In structuring his joke in this manner, Mencia creates an "us/them" racial binary that posits "white people" as outside of the category of "beaner"—a term he uses as a mode of self-identification.

Outside of his show, Mencia would use moments of authorized speaking, like television interviews and his stand-up comedy specials, to highlight the way dominant representations of Latinidad limit the kind of subjects and signifiers deemed recognizable as Latina/o. Mencia frequently narrated how his Honduran nationality at times makes him unintelligible to audiences, which in turn structures the conditions of possibility for impassing to occur:

> I was born in Honduras, that's where I was born. I live in California, where no matter what you say, you're Mexican. You understand that? It doesn't matter what you say . . . I'm Mexican in the Southwest, but when I go to Miami, I'm Cuban.[63]

> My birth name is Ned Arnel Mencia, but I grew up in East LA, where like everybody's Mexican . . . I was known as the "white wetback" because of my name, "Ned." And then they would call me the "wetter wetback" because I was born in Honduras . . . and my friends would say, "Ned you're the wetter wetback"! How could I be wetter? "Because you're from farther"! They didn't even know where Honduras was. My friends would come up to me and say, "Ned tell them where you were born." I was born in Honduras. "See, I told you he's Cambodian"! . . . Then when I started to do comedy, the owner of the Comedy Store [Mitzi Shore] would tell me, "you can't be an angry Mexican named Ned." First of all, I'm not Mexican, "everybody thinks you're Mexican, you're in LA"! So that's kind of weird because everybody thinks I'm Mexican when I'm in LA. And then I come here [New York], and everyone's like "Puerto Rican," no Honduran. And then when I go to Miami they're like "Cuban."[64]

Eerily reminiscent of Morales, Mencia discloses the constraining effects of the OTM gaze. His assertion that in California "no matter what you say, you're Mexican" parallels Morales who proclaims that in that setting its "impossible to be anything else." Despite one being Salvadoran American and the other being Honduran American, both are forced to contend with impassing, with having an identity they do not consider their own (in Mencia's case, Mexican, Cuban, and Puerto Rican) imposed externally. Mencia's statements also directly address the way audiences, peers, and the culture writ large render his Honduranness unrecognizable within a Latina/o matrix of intelligibility. His comments also highlight how racial ideologies and national/cultural identities like Mexican and Latina/o become defined and regulated in seemingly inconsequential cultural exchanges, often to the exclusion of U.S. Central Americans. For example, the pejorative and dehumanizing "white wetback" designation hurled at Mencia is strange—in a rich, troubling, and complicated way. As a racialized term often associated with illegal immigration, "wetbacks" have been seen as "those people" falling outside the U.S. national imaginary.[65] Since the term invariably connotes nonwhiteness, to be a "white wetback" then seems like an oxymoron, an irony that casts light on the racialization process of Latinos who can simultaneously be white and nonwhite. As a contradictory designation, "white wetback" also underscores how Mencia functions as a "logical impossibility" within Latinidad. Although Mencia himself views his identity as an ethnoracial subject ("beaner"), this type of racialized identity can only be acknowledged if he is positioned as Mexican, Puerto Rican, or Cuban.

Indeed, Mencia is not only the "white wetback" but also the "wetter wetback," a double alien, an illegible "wetback" deviating from standard LA Mexican / Mexican Americanness and recognizable Latin/Americanness. Again, the moniker of "wetter wetback" reads paradoxically, for how can some Latina/o immigrants be more "illegal" or "wetter" than others when the state views all undocumented and arguably all Latina/o immigrants as alien and foreign? More than the standard alien in the United States, Mencia is a derivative unrecognizable one, further Orientalized both geographically and phonetically through an unknown region where Honduran is not distinguished from Cambodian. The term *Honduran* in this anecdote, like Salvadoran in the Morales essay, is an empty signifier; it means nothing; it is simply read as "foreign" and not "Mexican." Honduran here is translated into a "third world" otherness, whereby a country like Honduras can be substituted for a non-Latin American country like Cambodia. Via this narration, Mencia elucidates how U.S. Central American experiences become expunged, as Honduranness is decisively viewed as *other* but not exactly a Latina/o *other.*

Mencia's testimony also illuminates how Latinidad and Latina/o subjectivity have become synonymous with localized national identities in such geographies as Los Angeles, New York, and Miami. His observation that whenever he performs in these metropolises, people readily assume that he is Mexican, Puerto Rican, or Cuban, despite his insistence that he is Honduran, suggests that audiences can only recognize or understand his body and performances within dominant articulations of Latinidad. This homologizing reading of Mencia's identity is further exemplified in his recollection of how his stage persona came into existence. According to Mencia, "Carlos" was born because the Comedy Store owner, Mitzi Shore, told him, "You can't be an angry Mexican named Ned." The authority to name, Angharad Valdivia asserts, is an "intensely political act"; it is a demonstration and an exercise of power, since historically, it was colonized peoples that were usually named by the colonizers.[66] Being able to name oneself is an assertion of autonomy, yet this act is denied to Mencia, for when he insists that he is not Mexican, Shore tells him, "Everyone thinks you're Mexican, you're in LA."

Shore's declaration is the embodied voice of interpellation telling Mencia to concede that he will always already be read as Mexican. Shore's OTM logic is one that is constantly reinforced in the physical and cultural spaces Mencia and his artistic expressions inhabit: popular culture and mass media. For instance, early mainstream films with Latina/o based characters, such as *La Bamba* (1987), *Stand and Deliver* (1987), *Born in East LA* (1987), *American Me* (1992), and *Mi Familia / My Family* (1995), focused mostly on Mexican American experiences in California. With a few exceptions, the small screen would further solidify this association as most television shows with a lead Latina/o character have taken place in California and have showcased Mexican American culture.[67] Despite having pan-Latina/o casts, popular shows like *Chico and the Man* (1974–1978) and *The George Lopez Show* (2002–2007) and not as commercially successful but nonetheless critically acclaimed dramas like *American Family* (2002–2004) and *Resurrection Blvd* (2000–2002) all had Mexican American lead characters, and all of them utilized Southern California as their setting.

Thus when Mencia parrots what Shore tells him, "Everyone thinks you're Mexican, you're in LA," he brings to bear the way media discourse taxonomizes Latina/o bodies in the Southwest and in so doing reproduces an OTM logic. His narration elucidates the ways in which U.S. society enforces homogenization and inscribes racialized bodies by insisting that his brown body is easily legible as Latina/o only if it is also labeled Mexican. Mencia's admission to Shore of being Honduran bears no signification, since it falls outside popular articulations of Latinoness. Consequently, the persona of "Carlos Mencia" needs to be read as a discursive effect of Latinidad that tries to discipline Mencia into becoming a proper, intelligible Latina/o subject. His existence is produced from the idea that one cannot have an angry Honduran named Ned perform Latina/o comedy. Latinoness and U.S. Americanness necessitate instead an angry "Mexican" named Carlos to legitimize the position of serving as a "Latino" commentator. As such, Mencia's performances disclose not only the factors that create the conditions of possibility for U.S. Central Americans to (im)pass as Mexican Americans but also the factors and the locations where Central American–Americanness is produced; it surfaces in the spaces where authority is exercised at the local level by positioning U.S. Central American culture outside of U.S. American and Latina/o imaginaries.

Shore, however, would not be the only one to find Mencia's Honduranness unintelligible. Despite Mencia's self-declaration as a "beaner," in 2005, fellow comedian Joe Rogan and others began to publicly accuse Mencia of being a joke plagiarist and an ethnic/racial imposter. One source of contention was Mencia's name change. While many actors and comedians adopt stage names for their public careers, this seemingly routine practice was read with a deeper sense of mistrust. Rather than seeing the imposition of the name "Carlos" onto the individual Ned as an effect of power, as an effect of an OTM logic whereby Mencia's body lacks the autonomy to be interpreted as anything other than Mexican,

Mencia's name change fueled a controversy surrounding his talent and ethnicity. Comedians Joe Rogan and George Lopez in particular used his name change as evidence of how Mencia was an overall fraud:

> The latest and most disgusting joke thief of all is a guy named "Carlos Mencia." The REALLY crazy thing is that's not even his real name. He sells himself as being Mexican, but the reality is his real name is Ned Holness, and he's actually half German and half Honduran. The Mexican hook is something he did to ingratiate himself with the local Mexican population of L.A.[68]

> I'd check his lineage too . . . The guy was pretty liberal with some of my [George Lopez's] material . . . the guy is like Honduran-German. . . . Why would you pretend to be [Mexican]? Why not go for Basque or Sweden . . . I think he had that intention from the beginning that he was going to play a Mexican.[69]

These accusations issued by Rogan and Lopez both reinforce and are the effect of essentialized notions of Latinoness and Mexicanness, raising a host of other questions: Why is "Carlos" thought of as a more authentically Mexican/Latina/o name than Ned? What enables Lopez and Rogan to interpret Mencia's stand-up performance and public character as an enactment of Mexicanness? Are non-Mexicans the only subjects viewed as "playing" Mexican? How, for instance, do Mexican and Mexican American subjects convey their own identities without such performative dimensions? Does engaging in "Latina/o" humor automatically suggest that the speaker has to be Mexican, lest they be accused of passing as Mexican? In addition to relying on a static notion of Mexican identity, these statements automatically assume that certain cultural markers are invariably fixed as Mexican / Mexican American, thereby denying the possibility for other Latina/o groups to employ similar types of cultural codes. Moreover, Mencia's recollection that he is read as Mexican in Los Angeles, "no matter what you say," suggests that it remains a bit unclear whether this is a case of active or imposed passing. Rogan and Lopez, for instance, only provide Mencia's name change as an example to support their claim that he is intentionally trying to pass as Mexican. However, one can see how Mencia might have created some national ambiguity via his use of cultural symbols inherently linked with Mexican culture (such as mariachi music), indicating that perhaps what started as impassing might have shifted to a form of passive passing.

These limitations notwithstanding, Rogan and Lopez's statements are insightful, since they challenge uncritical notions of an inter-Latina/o essence whereby national groups are assumed to inherently understand each other's sociopolitical location due to their marginalization from the broader U.S. American culture.

For instance, we witness more awareness for the cultural politics of Latinidad within Los Angeles emanating from Joe Rogan a supposed "external" member of the Latina/o community. Although Rogan's assumption that Mencia can only ingratiate himself into the Mexican / Mexican American community is problematic because he minimizes the city's Central American presence, he is still cognizant of the ways Mexican American experiences are culturally dominant within the Los Angeles landscape. Conversely, Lopez, who is Mexican American, seems oblivious to the predominance of Mexican American culture within the Latina/o imaginary with his inquiry, "Why would anyone pretend to be Mexican?" Lopez need only watch the Chicano written and produced film *Born in East LA* (1987) to see how even Mexican American texts acknowledge the disciplinary power of the Latina/o matrix of intelligibility by highlighting why some ethnoracial subjects have to pass as Mexicans.[70] Indeed, by claiming Mencia is European–Basque and Swedish—two countries who racially connote whiteness—Lopez disavows Mencia's embodied racism and dislocates him from Latinidad. That is, if as José Esteban Muñoz asserts, Latinidad is not just an ethnicity but an "affective difference," a "feeling brown," generated by a normalizing discourse of whiteness that marginalizes nonwhite and heteronormative subjects, Mencia is denied this form of affective belonging.[71] Nonetheless, Rogan and Lopez's public charges generated a discursive explosion concerning Mencia's talent and ethnicity. Audiences, especially those within cyberspace, became more obsessed with trying to decipher Mencia's ethnoracial status than with the accusations he was an unoriginal comic. Mencia was defamed on various websites not so much for his "joke thievery" but for his Mexican (im)passing. In fact, these two states of alleged inauthenticity dialogue with one another as they both reduce Mencia to a copy, a mere mimic of someone else's intellectual and cultural property. His nationality became the central focus for most social media spaces where online users desired to concretely situate him into one Latina/o national subgroup. Ironically, these attempts at deciphering his "true" ethnoracial national identity inadvertently ended up creating more ambiguity. Note these blog postings about Mencia:

> Last I heard he's all Honduran, but being from LA he has a lot of the Mexicanisms. Saying he's part Mexican throughout his acts would, of course, give him more credibility.[72]

> Carlos Mencia, a bad human being, a joke thief, and, even, a fake Mexican. He's half Guatemalan and half German, and all unoriginal comic. His name is only "Carlos Mencia" because his real name, Ned Holz [*sic*], didn't sound Mexican enough.[73]

OMFG! Are you all idiots.............Mencia is El Salvadorean [*sic*] he's said so himself look up his bio yes that's his birth name too MENCIA check that too.[74]

Do you think the powers of PC would allow a white guy to get away with having a show like *Mind of Mencia*? Nein mein herr! Why am I speaking German? Because Carlos aka Ned Holness is actually half German and half Central American, not Mexican.[75]

Here we see the failure to recognize certain forms of identity and the ways in which Honduran functions as a "logical impossibility" within the domain of Latinidad. Since the term lacks any dominant connotations, in these internet comments, Honduran yet again occupies a space of empty signification. It is so forgettable and amorphous that it can easily be substituted for any other Central American "third world" terrain. For these online users, Honduran does not conjure any distinct cultural references, as it becomes easily substituted by other national categories like Guatemalan and Salvadoran, which appear here as equally amorphous. Even more troubling is the implication that being Honduran is somehow less of a Latina/o experience than being Mexican American. This lack of association between Honduran and Latina/o is best exemplified in the last comment cited, where despite Mencia's phenotypical "brown Latin look" the commenter refers to Mencia as a "white guy," presumably because of his supposed half-German heritage. The history of racial passing is invoked here as a different "one-drop" rule becomes enforced. Rather than the traditional model where "one drop" of "black blood" defined an individual as nonwhite and specifically as "black," in this context "one drop" of "white blood" defines an individual as "white" regardless of phenotype. By seeing Mencia as only "white," this facile reading erases tinges of his *othered* racial cultural formations, reenacting the same form of exclusionary politics—the odd rhetoric of "white wetbackness"—that Mencia claims he faced as a child.

Although they constitute a limited sample, these blog discussions reveal how some media readers view Honduran as unintelligible and/or incommensurate with being Mexican American. This notion is reinforced by the fact that, despite questions over the veracity of Mencia's Mexican ancestry (whether or not he is indeed passing as Mexican), his Honduran national and cultural heritage has never been questioned and has remained consistent. Yet a Honduran American / U.S. Central American identity in these discussions does not provide Mencia the same "credibility" that a Mexican American experience does. The accusation that Mencia needed to "pretend" to be or pass as Mexican to obtain "credibility," as Rogan, Lopez, and this internet commentator claim, implies that to be Honduran is not to have the same type of insight into Latina/o cultures as that provided by a Mexican American experience. It also highlights how "Honduran" is not read as part of the Latina/o category. The controversy here does not emerge exclusively because of Mencia's Honduranness but is produced from the fact that Mencia might be a non-Mexican American performing Latina/o comedy, a point emphasized by the fact that most online searches regarding Mencia's ethnoracial and national identity are presented in a negative manner (e.g., "Is Carlos Mencia *Not* Mexican?"). The belief that some Latina/o subgroups are more authentic than others abounds in media culture. For example, newspaper reviews of *Mind of Mencia* often made it a point to note that Mencia was "not Mexican,"[76] which assumes an implicit OTM logic for describing Latina/os. Via constant depictions of certain racialized bodies and national experiences within Latina/o discourse an internal hierarchy (if not expectation) emerges that allows audiences to assume which national constituencies can be seen as belonging to that category. As such, this controversy about a Honduran American (im)passing as Mexican also exposes Central American–Americanness as a condition; a discursive exclusion that produces an inability to locate U.S. Central Americans in Latina/o and U.S. American imaginaries.

CONCLUSION

The narratives of U.S. Central Americans, such as Morales and Mencia (im)passing as Mexican highlight the powerful impact that regimes of recognition have on the material lives of Central American–American subjects. In disclosing the disciplinary power of an OTM logic and gaze that sees "Latin looks" as always already Mexican, both narratives also indicate that our conceptions of how passing operates need to expand. They both demonstrate not only that passing is not always linked with intentionality but also that the spatial movement within passing is not just vertical, since at times, it can be lateral or horizontal (moving from one minority position, such as Salvadoran or Honduran, to another, usually Mexican). Equally important is the way they force us to interrogate the way Latinidad operates. Though Michel Habell-Pallán and Mary Romero remind us that "as emergent signifiers 'Latina' and 'Latino' have no fixed definition; [since] historical and social location create shifting fields of meaning,"[77] Morales and Mencia's narratives suggest that, while the category of Latina/o is not static, there are some problematic limitations that are deployed in certain cultural domains. Each one magnifies the ways in which a Latina/o matrix of intelligibility structures epistemology enabling certain national identities and signifiers, such as Salvadoran American, Honduran American, and U.S. Central American, to become not only illegible but also incommensurate with other signifiers, like Mexican American. In so doing, they also illustrate the ways *completely who pride or dignity*

in which Central American–American subjectivity is produced via moments of abjection and cultural unintelligibility. These narratives and the social practice of (im)passing reveal the extent to which a Central American–American subject position interrupts and suspends Latinidad. As such, cultural expressions and the construction of a Central American–American subjectivity function as a radical form within Latinidad, one that through its persistent and pronounced exclusion from dominant imaginaries threatens the stability and ideological underpinnings of the very concept itself.

Epilogue
LA BESTIA AND BEYOND
Migration and the Politics of Mourning

It is necessary to learn a double movement: to invoke the category and, hence, provisionally to institute an identity and at the same time to open the category as a site of permanent political contest.
—Judith Butler, *Bodies That Matter: On the Discursive Limits of "Sex"*

Haunting recognition is a special way of knowing what has happened or is happening.
—Avery Gordon, *Ghostly Matters: Haunting and the Sociological Imagination*

Over the last four chapters, I have mapped the transnational circuits, governing logics, and cultural politics that produce a U.S. Central American identity. Structured in two parts and with a focus on two transnationally connected geopolitical locations, I have stressed that Central American identity is not simply the extension of a preexisting isthmian product nor, as some Central American scholars have claimed, a uniquely diasporic invention without any cultural or ideological influences stemming from the isthmus. Instead, I have aimed to show how representations of Central Americanness, both from the isthmus and the U.S. diaspora, infuse and contribute to our current understandings of what it means to be Central American within a particular translocal setting (Los Angeles). Via its several permutations (U.S.) Central American identity has revealed itself to operate not only as a cultural identity (often grounded in viewing Central America as a transnational imaginary) but also as a form of affective belonging, one generated by the multiple dislocations subjects from the isthmus are forced to occupy.

Starting in the nineteenth century on the isthmus and concluding in the late twentieth and early twenty-first century in the United States, the sites and selections of materials analyzed have emphasized that Central America(n) is not a transhistorical category. Although the *patria grande*—a Central American national imaginary—is forged in the colonial and postindependence period with the aim of defining itself in relation to other geopolitical spaces, the late twentieth century would force a revision. Migration, the racialization of immigrants in the United States, and Los Angeles–based notions of Latinidad, which render it synonymous with Mexican (American), provide the conditions of possibility for alternative iterations of Central American identity. In the United States, the idea of Central America is constantly undergoing transformation as black and indigenous communities, once expunged from this social imaginary, become symbolically incorporated within community practices such as parades, or within discourses that frame them as "Central American" (what I have labeled as Centralaméricanismo). The Central American imaginary is therefore fluid and permeable, constantly shifting to include or exclude population groups due to its own temporal, spatial, demographic, and cultural changes. The inclusion and exclusion of who or what qualifies as Central American exists within the cultural expressions emanating from geopolitical spaces like the isthmus, the United States, and Los Angeles, all of which construct distinct representations of Central Americanness. The constituents of these transnational networks continually alter what it means to be Central American from within these contexts.

I would like to conclude by returning to where we started and specifically to my assertion about the possibilities of using Central American–American as a hermeneutic to read Central American identity and texts. The antanaclastic properties of the sign Central American–American, which is also an anadiplosis, visually invoke Judith Butler's call for a "double movement," the simultaneous instance of both instituting an identity and opening it. In its analytic form, Central American–American shares this queering impetus by enabling what I have termed de-recognition—a provisional agency that underscores both the need for and limitations of recognition (both epistemologically and politically). De-recognition often transpires as a "double movement" carried out by subjects, one that reopens spaces of foreclosure within identity formations and sites of belonging. In the third chapter, for instance, we witnessed how, via their performance, local queer social actors disrupt nostalgic celebrations of Central American independence and question the identity narrative of the community (which defines itself in masculinist heteronormative terms). While this act of de-recognition does not overall improve the quotidian lives of queer Central Americans, it does however allow us to see how marginalized subjects actively contest their displacement within this social imaginary. I thus end this book by illustrating one last time how Central American–American can operate as a haunting sign that enables us to locate moments of rupture and provisional resistance within representations of Central Americanness.

THE (RE)MAKING OF *LA BESTIA* / THE BEAST

In the summer of 2014, the mass media was obsessed with what they labeled as the Central American "crisis" of Unaccompanied Alien Children (UAC). All over the internet and television were reports decrying the "surge" of undocumented immigrants, especially children, arriving at the U.S.-Mexico border. Not since the civil wars of the 1980s had Central America been in the spotlight and forefront of U.S. American popular culture. And just as it was for their 1980s compatriots, contemporary Central American immigrants were plagued by difficulties obtaining asylum or "refugee" status.[1] Despite the fact that Central America's "Northern Triangle" (composed of Guatemala, Honduras, and El Salvador) has been one of the most violent regions and is "comparable to countries engaged in civil war," undocumented immigrants from this area are not viewed as "refugees."[2] Instead, 96 percent of immigrants from this region, including "unaccompanied children," are denied U.S. asylum, and many are held for an indefinite amount of time in detention centers.[3] Not only are these detention centers structurally and spatially oppressive (crowding multiple families in one small space, depriving detainees of natural sunlight, etc.), but they also enable U.S. officials to practice or condone sexual violence on these detainees—a violence that remains unrecognized and unaccounted for.[4] This form of physical violence is complicit with an epistemic violence that emerges from the dehumanization of these detainees and the refusal to recognize them as "worthy" immigrant subjects or even humans. Fueled by a logic of xenophobia and white nationalism, conservative media outlets, the GOP, and individuals often did not view these newly arrived Central American immigrants, most of whom were minors, as "children" but instead branded them as "criminals" and "terrorists." The material repercussions of depicting immigrants in this manner were visually demonstrated in the city of Murrieta, California, when "pro-American" protestors prevented a bus transporting undocumented Central American children from stopping in the city.

But in the context of Central American immigration to the United States, xenophobia, detention centers, and asylum denial are not new phenomena. During the civil wars of the 1970s and 1980s, many Central Americans fleeing the region due to violence were classified by U.S. law and immigration criteria as "economic immigrants" rather than "refugees." The difference between both labels was a life-and-death issue for Central Americans, as the refusal to grant them asylum often led to their deportation back to their country of origin. This form of legal unrecognition enacted by the U.S. government had reverberating sociopolitical effects, some of which have been documented throughout this book. Asylum rejection, for instance, led many Central American immigrants to find creative ways to have the U.S. Border Patrol misrecognize them, including engaging in the practice of passing as Mexican and thereby avoiding deportation back to Central America. Contesting this form of legal unrecognition also politically galvanized Central American immigrants, many of who had experience as social activists in their respective countries. The formation of political organizations such as El Rescate (1981), which later proposed the creation of Plaza Morazán in 2011, and cultural practices like the Central American Independence parade (1983), emerged during this period of precarity for undocumented Central American immigrants and as a response to it.

If those political conditions generated a visible form of Central American identity politics in Los Angeles, what kind of sociocultural effects would the current era of Northern Triangle migration yield? How would representations of this particular form of migration experience expand or contract the Central American imaginary? And how would/does the local community of Central Americans in Los Angeles once again respond to a moment of isthmian hypervisibility and political unrecognition? All of these questions were on my mind in the fall of 2014 as I gathered my materials to make the annual pilgrimage to the COFECA Central American Independence parade. As part of my research for this book, I had attended this parade annually for several years. Given the incendiary political climate and the attention gravitating toward Central Americans that summer, I expected that the COFECA organizers would officially address the immigration "crisis" and its accompanying racism in some explicit statement. I was wrong. Instead, I witnessed business as usual at the parade: there were the speeches about Central American independence, the overt displays of nationalism in the form of national flags and romanticized indigenous symbols, the *misses* in their gowns waving, and the floats blasting *cumbia* music. That was my impression of the parade until I witnessed the presence of something that reaffirmed how identity-making spaces—like this parade—could be used subversively to question and critique nationalism and forms of nation-state violence. What I saw was a float that portrayed *La Bestia* / The Beast—the cargo trains migrants utilize to cross from Southern to Northern Mexico.

As a symbol, The Beast has increasingly been utilized to connote the challenges Central Americans encounter when migrating to the United States via Mexico.[5] It casts a spotlight on the perils of crossing Mexico within a distinct temporal moment: a post-9/11 neoliberal era that has altered the landscape of migration for non-Mexican immigrant subjects. While migration across Mexico has been commonplace for previous generations of Central American immigrants, the experience of crossing this terrain has profoundly changed due to economic and political processes that have developed over the last twenty-three years, and crystalize in the figure of The Beast. In 1994, Mexico agreed to "expand control of the migratory flows from various countries to the south of Mexico and other continents" in order to be in compliance with its membership in the North American Free Trade Agreement (NAFTA).[6] Since then, Mexico, at the behest of the United States, who has provided Mexico with 76 million dollars toward immigration enforcement,[7] has enacted a flurry of policies to deter undocumented immigrants, including the Plan to Seal the Southern Border (1998), the Southern Plan / *Frontera Sur* (2001), the Safe and Orderly Repatriation Plan from Mexico to Guatemala (2001), the Agreement for the Safe and Orderly Repatriation of Central American Migrants at the Mexico-Guatemala Borders (2005), and most recently the Southern Border Plan (2014). Both the Southern Plan of 2001 and 2014 are directly tied to U.S. transborder policies. After 9/11, the Southern Plan was introduced as a way to restrict migrants entering Mexico from the South in order to "synchronize its approach with United States national security concerns."[8] It became further cemented in 2014 when Mexico amended its Southern Plan. This recent border strategy oversaw a 117 percent increase in the deportations of Central Americans, as well as a rise in checkpoints and raids in spaces frequently inhabited by Central Americans.[9]

The political and material effects of these policies have been to enforce a permanent state of precarity for migrants as they are forced to find alternative dangerous routes when traversing Mexico to avoid checkpoints. Such transborder policies also discourage undocumented Central Americans from reporting crimes or from using public forms of transportation out of fear of being caught, detained, and deported by Mexican authorities. And thus, The Beast was born. The cargo trains were one of the few transportation options that allowed immigrants to cross Mexico quicker and that are not subject to the same level of surveillance by Mexican officials as other means of transportation.[10] This alternative, however, comes at a steep price. The Beast and the routes along its path are notorious for the myriad levels and types of violence migrants are made to endure at the hands of state actors like police and nonstate actors like drug cartels. Many immigrants die along the way or become mutilated or injured by the train and never make it to the U.S.-Mexico borderlands.[11]

As such, the recreation of The Beast at the COFECA parade is significant on multiple levels. Since most U.S. Central American representations of the immigrant experience and trauma have largely concentrated on the civil wars of the 1970s and 1980s, the symbolic inclusion of The Beast reveals how the archive of Central American collective memory is expanding to include new cultural traumas surrounding the experience of migration. This, in turn, marks a place of belonging for post–civil war immigrants by positioning their particular journey to the United States (one that is distinct from earlier forms of migration) as integral to a U.S. Central American identity as well as provides a counternarrative of acceptance for these immigrant subjects that is often lacking in both media and everyday social spaces. The representation of The Beast at the COFECA parade consisted of a flatbed truck lined with fabric and painted to resemble the profile image of cargo trains. In looking at the details of this text, it is clear that someone invested time and energy into making this float. Cutting out holes in the fabric ever so precisely so that it falls right above the wheels of the flatbed truck and painting each individual cloth a different color (blue, green, and grey) to resemble the multicolored boxcars. A banner with the word *La Bestia* was prominently displayed at both the front and back of the flatbed truck. And yet, unlike most popular representations of The Beast, in the COFECA parade, this train is not limited to a single geopolitical locale (Mexico) but is framed as transnational. The Beast here roams through the streets of Los Angeles, suggesting that while the "real" cargo trains are confined to specific locations across Mexico, the routes of migration and their associated dangers transcend that particular nation-state and continue to plague immigrants wherever they go. Migration is an ongoing journey for many immigrants as their undocumented status often has them constantly moving from one state to another. A point punctuated by the "Texas oil" and the "South CA" logos marked on the side of the float, which both connote that the train runs through the U.S.-Mexico borderlands. But this invocation of the Southwest also conjures the enduring legacy and

FIGURE 8. Front view of float at the 2014 COFECA parade.

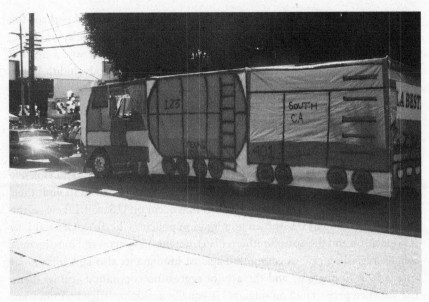

FIGURE 9. Side view of float at the 2014 COFECA parade.

violence brought forth from capitalism and U.S. state policies. One must recall that Mexican migrants were heavily utilized in the building of U.S. railroads and were probably among the first set of immigrants to think of the locomotive in a fashion similar to the way that many Central American immigrants view it: as a "wretched train of death." Mexican railroad workers often experienced the same forms of physical violence associated with The Beast, such as mutilations, injuries, and death. Recalling a broader history of migration forged via the exploitation and oppression of migrants due to U.S. state and economic projects, the float affirms the importance of interethnic solidarity among various immigrant communities.

Indeed, as I watched the float go by, I was inundated by a flurry of images and personal and political significations attached to this material text. Quiet and slow, it appeared anachronistic and displaced from within the celebratory setting of the parade. The float's grim silence was magnified by the fact that it was located between others that featured blaring loud music and young women smiling and waving. The audience's utter ambivalence vis-à-vis the text was noticeable. As I looked around, I could see that many spectators were unsure if they were supposed to cheer, clap, or remain silent. Some actually looked quite solemn as if they were holding back tears, including myself. At that moment, I realized that, contrary to the other floats in the parade that invoked nostalgia or celebration, this float connoted mourning—a type of collective mourning for migrants. It mourned for those that survived the horror and violence associated with migration to the United States, including rape, assaults, and perhaps the process of indefinite detention, as well as for those that never made it.

In that moment, The Beast float was more than a float: it was a moving memorial that allowed for the grieveability of the migrant body. Judith Butler reminds us that not all lives are grieveable, since many are denied personhood by state policies or by the "derealization of violence," which commits epistemic violence not via representation in discourse but through omission.[12] For many Central American immigrants and other non-Mexican immigrants, the violence and trauma experienced in Mexico are often unacknowledged in multiple discursive arenas. The U.S. media rarely covers stories of loss and violence experienced by immigrants crossing into Mexico, opting instead to limit their coverage to "border" or immigrant deaths that occur on U.S. soil. Likewise, the Mexican government via its own immigration policies (the 2011 General Law of Population and the 2014 Southern Plan), detention system, and bureaucratic policies regarding crimes committed against immigrants also fails to account for the lives of migrants and the acts of aggression committed against them. The violence perpetrated on migrants is equally unacknowledged within Central American countries, where current state policies like *Mano Dura* create the "push" factors for their citizens to leave their home countries.[13] Although some countries like El Salvador have created an official monument honoring their *"hermano lejano,"* they have yet to construct a government-sponsored monument recognizing those hermanos/as that never made it to the United States, nor made it back. In short, while the United States, Mexico, and Central America have all created the conditions of possibility for migrants to leave and remain politically and physically vulnerable; few have acknowledged this type of violence at the symbolic level.[14]

This is why The Beast float at the 2014 COFECA parade was so important. It demonstrated how everyday social actors use their own creative energies to generate dissonance and reorganize the context of the event (intended to promote a mythic Central American cohesion) to reflect their own concerns. It exposes the limitations of nationalism, while still showcasing how a space designed to reaffirm those categories can become a site to call them into question and elucidate their cultural and political shortcomings. The Beast float does not uncritically celebrate Central American culture, the nation-state, or nationalism. Rather, it critiques current neoliberal forces and the fervent policing of borders that go beyond just the United States and Mexico, which enable violence and death to be common experiences among migrants crossing Mexico. The Beast brings to bear all these salient issues in the most powerful of forms through silence and absence.

Not only was there no music or sound emanating from the float, but it was also missing its iconic feature: bodies. Every dominant representation of The

Beast features the train with rooftops filled with a plethora of migrants. Its human cargo is, in fact, one of The Beast's defining features, as it is rare to find an image of the train without rooftop passengers. But in the COFECA re-creation the literal lack of bodies magnified this absence, drawing the spectators' attention to that which is familiar but not the same. Here, invisibility generated a form of hypervisibility, as one could not avoid thinking about the absence of the migrant body. As Avery Gordon asserts, such texts are forms of social hauntings that allow one to paradoxically "see you are not there."[15] The float delivered a simple but powerful message, at once encouraging spectators to remember all the lives that were absent while also noting its own limitations in the act of memorialization—that is, in making absence its focal point, the float discloses how mnemonic representational practices could never name all the lives lost, nor literally quantify those lives. Its unrepresentation underscores the magnitude of migration violence and loss of life, as well as the limitations of any attempt at ever knowing all the names, number of bodies, or statistical data of Central American migrants. The float elucidates how not only the bodies that experience migrant violence are innumerable but also the flaws of even trying to quantify and use numbers to express or assert a type of recognition within political and cultural registers. The Beast therefore offers us a form of nonidentity identity politics; it proclaims that it does not matter what kinds of bodies are lost on the migrant trail, whether heteronormative families or transgendered individuals, or how many are lost (one or one hundred thousand) because they are all equally significant and worthy of being remembered.

At the time of this writing, the dawn of the Donald Trump era—characterized by a refortification of sexism, racism, classism, ableism, neoliberalism, xenophobia, Islamophobia, transphobia, and homophobia (to name a few)—has begun. For many immigrant communities, like Central Americans, the ending of Temporary Protected Status (TPS), the current proposal to build a U.S.-Mexico border wall, the rise of Immigration and Custom Enforcement (ICE) raids, privatization and proliferation of detention centers, along with the planned institutionalization of an OTM logic by deporting all undocumented immigrants (regardless of country of origin) to Mexico[16] mark the contemporary moment as a very dark time. It is precisely for this reason that I conclude this project with The Beast float. It demonstrates the ways marginalized communities navigate the tensions between repression and resistance, as they use their cultural expressions to find creative ways of addressing multiple forms of oppression enacted at the local and global level. A beacon of hope, this text not only reaffirms the important role of cultural productions as a site of contestation but also notes the perils of tactics utilized in identity politics and social movements that rely on quantification. Increasingly, in the realm of Central American identity politics, there has been a move to counter long-standing marginalization by asserting demographic presence. Currently, Central Americans are the third largest Latina/o group and many surmise that this status will soon change to second, since Salvadorans alone constitute the third largest Latina/o population in the United States. While one can understand the use of strategic demography within liberal nation-states like the United States to obtain political recognition, The Beast reminds us that there are other avenues to address sociopolitical marginalization. Rather than only relying on state notions of democratic representation, which force groups to label themselves and organize around their demographics and uphold a logic of "majority rules," the Beast provides alternative modes for political validation.[17] Serving as a material reminder of the affective power of the denumerable, the float remembers and recognizes social groups without utilizing or relying on the same techniques deployed by the nation-state—techniques that often reproduce exclusions via a binary of majority-minority. In doing so, The Beast as a COFECA float not only promotes new forms of dissent but forges new linkages between ethnoracial subjects—ones that remap strategies for the production of U.S. Central American identities and politics.

ACKNOWLEDGMENTS

Studying Central American culture has always been a deeply personal project. Over the course of my intellectual trajectory, so many of my research queries were intimately connected to questions I had about my own identity and cultural history. Being the daughter of a Salvadoran transmigrant immigrant raised in Los Angeles during the 1980s proved to be a pivotal moment in my life. During this decade, Central America was often everywhere and nowhere. Repeatedly, I struggled to come to terms with this cultural contradiction where my home was filled with Salvadoran immigrants, memories, and television news stations that reported daily about the deaths occurring on the isthmus, while in public spaces, there was often a huge void. There are two things that still strike me from those early days. The first was hearing the stories by refugees, some of whom were my family members, describing decapitated bodies on the streets of El Salvador or the lengths they would go to in order to hide and flee. The second was seeing my mother's emotive responses to anything related to Central America. My humble attempts at documenting Central American–American cultural productions are not only grounded in these personal dynamics but also a way for me to honor immigrants like my mother and countless others who due to broader socio-political and economic factors (e.g., imperialism, capitalism, etc.) were forced to leave their homelands.

Indeed, my own present geopolitical location of Tucson, Arizona, reminds me of Central American immigrants daily. Sixty miles south is the U.S.-Mexico border surrounded by the Sonoran Desert. At any given moment, I am aware that migrants are literally dying to cross into this country. Fifty-eight miles north is the Eloy Detention Center, which has been labeled as the "deadliest [detention] center" in the United States by immigration activists. I therefore think that it is only apt that an "acknowledgment" section includes a few words about the amount of privilege required to engage in these types of intellectual endeavors and the often futile nature of such projects in making a significant material difference for many Central Americans who are currently subjected to myriad forms of legal, physical, and epistemic violence. I live every day recognizing that despite my own personal struggles, which include being a first-generation college student raised in a working-class single-parent household, I am very lucky, since my mother crossed in a different historical and political moment. A few different variables and it could have been my mother, my sister, or my family crossing that Sonoran Desert or housed in those detention centers. I do not take my privilege lightly.

I am also fortunate because throughout my intellectual journey I have been supported by a number of individuals and institutions who have gone above and beyond to provide me the type of emotional and financial support I needed. I am indebted to the Ronald E. McNair Scholars program and the Mellon Mays Undergraduate Fellowship program for providing me the time and resources to imagine a career in research and academia. I am also grateful to the University of Michigan Rackham Merit Fellowship program, the Department of American Culture, and the Gayle Morris Sweetland Writing Center Dissertation Writing Institute. Research for this book was supported by the Andrew W. Mellon Foundation, the Woodrow Wilson National Fellowship Foundation, and the University of Texas Austin Center of Mexican American Studies Benson Research Fellowship.

I would also like to recognize and thank my past and present mentors and colleagues who nurtured my ideas and supported me throughout this process: Phil Deloria, Amy Carroll, Maria Cotera, Frances Aparicio, John M. González, Ernesto Martinez, Laura G. Gutiérrez, Laura Halperin, Lee Bebout, Anne Garland Mahler, Belinda Lum (especially for sharing her lovely photos with me), and Nicole Guidotti-Hernández, who constantly provided me with constructive criticism on my work and who always told me to keep my chin up even in some of my most darkest hours.

Working in the field of Central American studies can often be an isolating experience so I am grateful to a collective of scholars, colleagues, and friends who have influenced my work and life. I would like to thank Claudia Milian for her invitation to participate in the symposium *Subjects of and for Central American–American Studies* hosted by the program in Latino/a Studies in the Global South at Duke University, as well as its participants—Cary Cordova, Kirsten Silva Cruz, Kency Cornejo, and Arturo Arias—who provided me with valuable feedback on my work. Arturo Arias in particular has been a wonderful mentor to me all these years; he has inspired me with his ideas, words, and kindness for more than a decade. I can only hope that one day I am as good of a mentor to others as he has been to me. A special thanks also goes to Ana Patricia Rodríguez for her constant encouragement and thoughtful advice. In addition, I also want to express my gratitude to some Central American scholars and artists for their intellectual conviviality: Cecilia Menjívar, Maya Chinchilla, Oriel Siu, Ester Hernández, Karina Oliva Alvarado, Cecilia Rivas, Ester Trujillo, Steven Osuna, Arely Zimmerman, Leisy Abrego, and Suyapa Portillo. I would particularly like to thank Ariana Vigil, whose insightful comments on this project were instrumental in making it more cohesive and who never hesitated to provide me support when I needed it. To *mis hermanas centroamericanas*, Yajaira Padilla and Alicia Ivonne Estrada, thank you for guiding me through this journey and for creating a space for me to laugh, cry, vent, and share my troubles.

At the University of Arizona, I would first like to acknowledge and thank Sydney Rice for writing a letter of support so that I could have more time to complete this manuscript as well as Lee Medovoi, Monica Casper, John Paul Jones, and Tom Miller for supporting this request. In addition, I would also like to thank Provost Andrew Comrie for subventing this book via the Provost Author Support Fund. I would also like to extend my deepest appreciation to colleagues and staff members who have provided me with encouragement throughout the years: Javier Durán, Lyn Durán, Adam Geary, Eithne Luibhéid, Kristen Buckles, Anita Huizar-Hernandez, Lillian Gorman, Kaitlin Murphy, Ken McAllister, Anjelica Yrigoyen, Jeff Schlueter, Holly Behan, Sharonne Meyerson, Sara Vickery, Marcia Simon, Stephanie Pearmain, Meg Lota Brown, Lynda Zwinger, Allison Dushane, Susan Miller-Cochran, Manuel Muñoz, Ander Monson (for all his wonderful book cover inspirations), Paul Hurh, Stephanie Brown, and Stephanie Troutman. Although too many to mention by name here, I would also like to acknowledge all of the wonderful undergraduate and graduate students I have had the pleasure of working with; their visions of the future inspire my own. To my chosen Tucson Family—Jamie Lee, Frank Galarte, and Adela Licona—I honestly do not think this book would be a reality without any one of you. I cannot express how lucky I feel to have such wonderful people in my life, especially Adela, whom I personally want to thank for sharing her beautiful art for this book cover and for being the one person I could always count on. I love you *querida*!

They say it takes a village to raise a child, and when one is the mother of a special-needs child, it often takes more than one village to accomplish this goal. While writing this book, I had the pleasure of working with some wonderful therapists who became an extended part of our family and amplified our village. A predominately female labor force, these individuals approached my child with such care and attentiveness that it made it possible for me to spend extended periods of time at my work office writing this book. I feel it is imperative to acknowledge how my own gendered labor is tied to their efforts. I particularly want to recognize and thank Jayne Turner, Adrian Weaver, Megan Beardmore, Terre Glahn, Megan Bluemke, Jacie Larson, Lindsay Abbott, and Katherine Castro.

One of the best things about writing this book is that it allowed me to meet and work with my editor at Rutgers University Press: Leslie Mitchner. From the first day I met Leslie, I knew we were destined to collaborate and work together. Not only is she the most amazing editor a scholar could ever dream of working with, but she has become a true friend and source of inspiration. Moreover, bringing a manuscript to life takes an incredibly dedicated team, so I would like to thank the entire production team at Rutgers University Press, particularly Alissa Zarro, Kim Guinta, and Michael Miller, for their patience and hard work in seeing this book come to fruition. I am also deeply grateful to the anonymous peer reviewers from Rutgers University Press, as well as Andrew Ascherl, Isis Sadek, and Beatrice Ramírez Betances, for their keen insights and suggestions that have enabled this manuscript to improve and evolve.

So much of this project is intimately tied to my family, so I would like to begin by thanking my mother Isaura Cardenas. Her willingness to take in strangers who were fleeing the violence of El Salvador, as well as her beautiful sense of empathy and love of books, has fundamentally shaped the woman and scholar I have become. *Gracias por todo, mami!* I am also grateful for having a wonderful supportive family. My brother Steve Cardenas and his wife, Amanda, and my nephews, Junior, Nathaniel, Steven, and Jacob. My sister Jackie Galvan and her husband, Al, and my nephew and nieces, Joshua, Rachel, and Rebekah (who for years sweated it out with me at those parades). I also want to recognize my sister from another mother—Melinda Duran—who I have known for so many years and who has taught me the meaning of unconditional friendship. Closer to home, I want to thank Maureen Reid for sharing with me laughter and tears, her friendship has been such a blessing to me.

Finally, to Bram Acosta and Ellison. Bram, your unwavering support has meant the world to me. You more than anyone know how I had to write this book during some of the most painful moments of my life. Every time I would fall to pieces crying and telling you that I could not do "this" (e.g., being a woman of color in academia, a special-needs mother, etc.) you literally picked me up from the floor and reassured me that I could. When my self-confidence was low due to internal/external voices that would tell me I was not good enough, your love and words were always louder and served to drown them out. Thank you. I love you. To my Ellison, words will never be able to capture how much I love you. You have changed my life in so many ways that I cannot possibly articulate. You cast a spotlight on my intersectional politics and highlighted how it was missing some key sections. You have shown me where my new research and battles of social justice need to take place. What I want you to know is that society has always tried to marginalize and silence nonconforming subjects like us. Society will try to break you in an effort to regulate your heterogeneity. In those moments, when you begin to feel the weight of that oppression, I want you to remember two things: (1) I love you and I am proud of you for who you are; and (2) difference is beautiful.

An excerpt of chapter 1 originally appeared in *Studies in Twentieth and Twenty-First Century Literature* 37, no. 2 (2013): 111–130; it is reprinted with permission from New Prairie Press. A section of chapter 4 was previously published in the anthology *Race and Contention in Twenty-First Century U.S. Media*, ed. Jason A. Smith and Bhoomi K. Thakore (New York: Taylor and Francis,

2016), 70–84; it is reprinted with permission from Taylor and Francis Group, LLC. An earlier version of chapter 3 first appeared in the anthology *U.S. Central Americans: Reconstructing Memories, Struggles, and Communities of Resistance*, ed. Karina Oliva Alvarado, Alicia Ivonne Estrada, and Ester E. Hernández (Tucson, AZ: University of Arizona Press, 2017), 127–143; it is reprinted with permission from University of Arizona Press.

NOTES

INTRODUCTION

1. The category of Latina/o, now often referred to as Latinx, is an umbrella term that, in abstraction, is composed of pan-national (many national communities), pan-ethnic (multiple ethnicities), and pan-racial (different racial categories) subjects.

2. Oboler, *Ethnic Labels*, 150. Although Oboler's account makes it clear that Rosa rejects the category of "Hispanic," what remains a bit more ambiguous is whether her adoption of the term "Central American" is based on ideologies from the isthmus that assert that this geo-political space shares a common culture.

3. Regional spaces and identities can be either localized and internal to the nation-state (such as the Southwest in the United States) or pan-national (such as the Caribbean).

4. Basch, Schiller, and Blanc, *Nations Unbound*. In this book, the authors underscore the way migrants develop networks and sustain "multi-stranded social relations that link together their societies of origin and settlement" (8).

5. See Hamilton and Stoltz Chinchilla, *Seeking Community* (2001); and Coutin, *Legalizing Moves* (2003).

6. CASA is an acronym for the Central American Student Association, a student organization on the campus of Occidental College in Los Angeles, California.

7. Hamilton and Stoltz Chinchilla, *Seeking Community*, 56. Here the authors implicitly reinforce Arturo Arias's notion of a failed U.S. Central American sociopolitical identity. Though their work documents the social networks that created a visible diasporic community of Central American immigrants in Los Angeles, especially Guatemalans and Salvadorans, they seem to suggest that there is a tendency among American-born Central Americans to identify more as "Latino" rather than "Salvadoran," "Guatemalan," or "Central American."

8. By this, I do not mean to suggest that these categorical identities are mutually exclusive.

9. Flores, *Bomba to Hip-Hop*, 7, 197. One of the first Latino scholars to promote this dichotomy was Felix Padilla, who, in his book *Latino Ethnic Consciousness* (1985), also suggests that Latina/o as a pan-ethnicity is not a primary mode of identification. It only emerges as a strategy for political empowerment—as a "situational alliance" over particular sociocultural or political issues. In framing Latina/o as a "situational alliance" and not the categories of Mexican American and Puerto Rican (the subgroups involved in his study), Padilla implicitly suggests that a Latina/o identity is an ephemeral and therefore secondary mode of identification.

10. Flores and Benmayor, *Latino Cultural Citizenship*, 15. According to the authors, Latino cultural citizenship can be thought of "as a broad range of activities of everyday life through which Latinos and other groups claim space in society and eventually claim rights. Although it involves difference, it is not as if Latinos seek out such difference. Rather, the motivation is simply to create space where the people feel 'safe' and 'at home,' where they feel a sense of belonging and membership."

11. Oboler, *Ethnic Labels*, xix. According to Oboler, subjects born and raised in the United States after 1970 are the "first generation" who have been "specifically designated by mainstream institutions as 'Hispanics'" in the United States.

12. In Hamilton and Stoltz Chinchilla, *Seeking Community* (2001), the authors noted the trend wherein individuals of Central American descent have opted to identify simply as Latino.

13. See Menjívar, *Fragmented Ties* (2000); and Hamilton and Stoltz Chinchilla, *Seeking Community* (2001).

14. Padilla, "Central American Transnational Imaginary," 153. Similar to Padilla, throughout this book, I use the terms "Central American national imaginary" and "Central American imaginary" to refer to the ways in which discourses and representations cultivate membership and identification amongst peoples from the isthmus. However, there are some differences between these two concepts. Whereas a Central American national imaginary is often predicated on viewing this space as a national formation with common "origins," a Central American imaginary is not limited to nationalism and is more expansive since it can emerge from a shared sense of displacement and nonbelonging.

15. Hamilton and Stoltz Chinchilla, "Identity Formation," 25.

16. Hamilton and Stoltz Chinchilla, 27.

17. Laó-Montes, "Afro-Latinidades." My use of *diaspora* is derived from Agustín Laó-Montes, who views diaspora as a "multicentered historical field, a complex and fluid geocultural formation and domain of identification" (119).

18. Representations of Central America(ns) as outside the U.S. American "National Symbolic" can be found even in texts that are the most seemingly progressive. Adrienne Rich's canonical essay "Notes towards a Politics of Location" (1986) is a case in point, as she insightfully argues that feminists need to decenter their own privilege and whiteness as well as become more mindful in how these characteristics have been naturalized in the category of "woman." Rich's consciousness about feminism and her own positionality, however, is facilitated by her encounters with El Salvador on "TV" and her travels to Nicaragua, which she calls a "tiny impoverished country." It is in Nicaragua that Rich is able to feel "that [U.S.] raised boot of power" (220). That Rich's awareness of her own situatedness as a U.S. feminist emerges externally, via a trip to Central America, is temporally ironic given the fact that she is writing this essay during the 1980s—a decade that would see one of the largest migrations of Central Americans into the United States, many of whom were asylum seekers and activists testifying precisely about that "raised boot of power." And yet, Rich's U.S. gaze only allows her to see Central Americans in the "backyard." For a more detailed critique of Adrienne Rich's essay, see Kaplan, "Politics of Location" (1994).

19. Among the texts that have discussed this topic of identity and its relationship to migration, imperialism, and/or globalization are Arias and Milian, "US Central Americans" (2013); Coutin, *Legalizing Moves* (2003); García, *Seeking Refuge* (2006); Hamilton and Stoltz Chinchilla, *Seeking Community* (2001); Hamilton and Stoltz Chinchilla, "Identity Formation" (2013); Menjívar, *Fragmented Ties* (2000); Menjívar and Rodríguez, *When States Kill* (2005); and Rodríguez, *Dividing the Isthmus* (2009).

20. Alvarez et al., *Translocalities/Translocalidiades* (2014). The editors of this book state that they examine works from "Latinidad in the South, North and Caribbean 'middle' of the Americas" (2). "Central America" is notably absent here.

21. Laó-Montes, "Afro-Latinidades," 122. Laó-Montes, who coins the term "a politics of translocation," suggests that this phrase is an extension of the way women-of-color feminism has used a "politics of location" to signify the "multiple mediations (gender, class, race, etc.) that constitute the self to diverse modes of domination" (122).

22. Rodríguez, *Dividing the Isthmus*, 3.

23. Brickell and Datta, *Translocal Geographies*, 7, 2. Brickell and Datta's concept of translocality is similar to and different from Agustín Laó-Montes's use of the term in *Mambo Montage*

(2001), as he views it as not only referencing "historical/structural locations, geographic scales and subject positions" but also encompassing more than the term *transnationality*, since *translocality* is "not centered in nation-states and nationalities but articulates geographic units" (13).

24. Hall, "Who Needs 'Identity'?," 4.

25. Nagel, "Constructing Ethnicity," 156.

26. Hall, "Who Needs 'Identity'?," 6.

27. Hamilton and Stoltz Chinchilla, "Identity Formation," 1.

28. Spivak, "Subaltern Speak," 82–83.

29. Halperin, *Saint Foucault*, 62, emphasis in the original.

30. For a more detailed discussion on this particular use of Central American–American vis-à-vis Latina/o studies, see Arias, "Central American–Americans" (2003); and Milian, *Latining America* (2013), esp. 123–150.

31. Viego, *Dead Subjects*, 120.

32. Viego, 122–123.

33. For instance, generally speaking, most theorizations about the border as an analytic emerge from the groundbreaking text *Borderlands/La Frontera* (1987) by Chicana philosopher Gloria Anzaldúa. In it, Anzaldúa resignifies the border to mean a "vague and undetermined place created by the emotional residue of an unnatural boundary," one inhabited by "los atravesados"—the "squint-eyed, the perverse, the queer, the troublesome, the mongrel, the mulato, the half-breed, half dead; in short, those who cross over, pass over, or go through the confines of normal" (3). But it should be added that if the borderlands welcome basically all nonnormative subjects, then the physical borderlands of the U.S./Mexico border, which play such a prominent role in this very same text, inadvertently marginalize the experiences of non-Chicana/os. The section titled "El cruzar del mojado / Illegal crossing" describes an experience limited to crossing *one* border—a material reality that, as Oscar Martinez's searing work *The Beast* (2013) points out, eludes most Central American immigrants crossing by land. Moreover, while the borderlands may vaunt the ability to produce a type of "patois" filled with "tongues" so heterogeneous that there is "no one Chicano language" (58), the one tongue with which it does not seem to amalgamate with is often linked to Central Americans, since as Anzaldúa notes, "We don't use the word vosotros/as or its accompanying form. We don't say claro (to mean yes), imagínate, or me emociona, unless we picked up Spanish from Latinas, out of a book, or in a classroom" (57–58). Many working-class Central Americans, however, use most of these words.

34. A copy of this poem has been published on Maya Chinchilla's website, https://mayachapina.com/archives/. This poem can also be found in her book *The Cha Cha Files*, 21. However, in the book, the title has been changed to include the hyphen.

35. Arias, "Central American–Americans?," 48.

36. Arias, 48.

37. Arias, "Central American–Americans," 171.

38. Building from Arturo Arias's work, Claudia Milian in *Latining America* (2013) similarly describes Central American–American as being "in relation to—and outside the articulatory foundations of—Latinidad" and goes on to argue that Central American–Americanness should be seen as a "hermeneutic opening interrogating the presumed stability of Latinoness and Latinaness" (141). My book builds off these two important scholarly interventions but also departs by adding that Central American–American can be a hermeneutic for reading Central American textualities.

39. Arias, "Central American–Americans," 171.

40. Shankar and Srikanth, *A Part, Yet Apart*, 4.

41. Shankar and Srikanth, ix–x.

42. Hintzen and Rahier, *Problematizing Blackness*, 7.

43. Táíwò, "Prison Called My Skin," 48.

44. Cepeda, *Musical ImagiNation*, 19.

45. Mazumdar, quoted in Shankar and Srikanth, *A Part, Yet Apart*, 65.

46. Kaplan, "Identity," 125.

47. For examples of how queer women of color have theorized via literature and poetry, see Anzaldúa, *Borderlands/La Frontera* (1987); Lorde, *Sister Outsider* (1984); and Moraga, *Loving in the War Years* (1984), to name a few.

48. Hall, *Queer Theories*, 14. As explained by Hall, "queering" as a practice entails questioning systems of classification that assert a type of stability, fixity, or normative status.

49. *Oxford English Dictionary* online, s.v. "catachresis," accessed February 26, 2018, http://www.oed.com.ezproxy3.library.arizona.edu/view/Entry/28665?redirectedFrom=catachresis.

50. Freinkel, "Catachresis," 209.

51. Milian, *Latining America*, 150.

52. Arias, "Central American–Americans," 171.

53. Derrida, *Margins of Philosophy*, 255.

54. Spivak, *Teaching Machine*, 67.

55. Derrida, *Margins of Philosophy*, 255.

56. Fahnestock, *Rhetorical Style*, 134.

57. Butler, *Bodies That Matter*, 161, 167.

58. Radstone and Hodgkin, *Memory Cultures*, 2.

59. Gillis, *Commemorations*, 3.

60. Berlant, *Anatomy of National Fantasy*, 5. In this work, Berlant persuasively demonstrates the link between "affect" and "political life" by revealing how "national" culture becomes localized.

61. McQueen, *Subjectivity*, 8.

CHAPTER 1   REMEMBERING *LA PATRIA GRANDE*

1. Carpio Nicolle, *Pensamiento y acción*, 9, emphasis in the original.

2. Roberto Carpio Nicolle would become the first president of Parlamento Centroamericano (PARLACEN) and would serve from 1991 to 1992. On May 25, 1995, the Asociación Trinacional (ASIAPACTRI) decided to honor Carpio Nicolle by calling him "el padre del Parlamento Centroamericano" and stating that this recognition was being given to "un líder centroamericano cuyo pensamiento y acción se vincula en una decisión sólida de hacer de Centroamérica una sola nación." Carpio Nicolle, 192.

3. The book *Pensamiento y acción* is filled with several correspondence and announcements that celebrate Carpio Nicolle's integrationist and unionist spirit.

4. Roberto Carpio Nicolle was vice president to Vinicio Cerezo. When Cerezo was elected as president of Guatemala in 1986, he was the first democratically elected and civilian-elected president since 1966. For many, this signaled hope that the Guatemalan state would placate the years of violence. However, many organizations like Americas Watch claimed that his administration "tolerated" or condoned the violence. See Gruson, "Political Violence."

5. Hernández, "Centroamericanos Conmemoraran Independencia." Original:

Este acto es único en todos los Estados Unidos, ya que al igual que el 2012, izaremos nuevamente la bandera de Centroamérica y entonaremos el himno de Centroamérica en el corazón administrativo de la ciudad de Boston, Massachusetts (Boston City Hall). . . . Esperamos que de alguna manera el Parlamento Centroamericano se interese de estas iniciáticas y sirvan de apoyo a nuestras comunidades, ya que el proyecto de Alianza Cívica Cultural Centroamericana es una fuente de inspiración y un verdadero referente para todos aquellos que perseveran en el sueño de la construcción de la patria grande, que un día soñare [sic] Francisco Morazán.

6. Anderson, *Imagined Communities*, 6.
7. Militz and Schurr, "Affective Nationalism," 55.
8. Said, *Orientalism*, 4–5.
9. The term *Middle America* is equally nebulous. At times, the term connotes a region composed of Mexico, Central America, and the Caribbean; at other times, it is used interchangeably with Central America. Moreover, while the term *Middle America* might seem to be related to Mesoamerica, there are important distinctions. The term *Mesoamerica* is not defined geographically but culturally, since it describes an area encompassing parts of Mexico, Belize, Guatemala, Honduras, El Salvador, and Nicaragua as defined by its pre-Columbian cultures.
10. Disturnell, *Influence of Climate*, xvi. Rooted in climate theories, the distinction of zones in the process of map-making—far from being innocuous—were wedded to larger colonial, racialized discourses. As prominent cartographer of the Americas John Disturnell described, it was only within the "temperate" zones that the "full development of the human race" was possible.
11. Coined in the novel *Cabbages and Kings* (1904) by O. Henry, U.S. politicians and economists utilize the catchphrase to describe countries within Central America that are seen as being one-crop economies and politically volatile, "underdeveloped" nations largely dependent on foreign capital.
12. Aparicio and Chávez-Silverman, *Tropicalizations*, 8.
13. Berlant, *Anatomy of National Fantasy*, 5.
14. Calhoun, *Nationalism*, 5.
15. Anderson, *Imagined Communities*, 6.
16. Casaús Arzú and Giráldez, *Redes intelectuales centroamericanas*, 17. The authors argue that José Cecilio del Valle conceived of Central America as *patria grande* and considered the provinces of El Salvador, Guatemala, Costa Rica, Honduras, and Nicaragua as *patrias chicas*. In their own discussion, they too employ this distinction of Central America as a *patria grande* and the nation-states of Guatemala, El Salvador, Nicaragua, Honduras, and Costa Rica as *patrias chicas*.
17. Burke, "History as Social Memory," 191.
18. Foster, *A Brief History*, xiii, xi.
19. Brignoli-Perez, *Brief History*, xiv.
20. Brignoli-Perez, x.
21. The majority of texts, both within and outside of the field of history—such as *Central America* (1985); *Understanding Central America* (1989); *Power in the Isthmus* (1989); *Centroamérica: su historia* (1998); and *Historia de Centroamérica* (1988), to name a few—utilize a definition of Central America that sees it as a historical construct.
22. Cardenal, *Manual de historia*, 12, 15, emphasis added. Original: "Centroamérica es un istmo relativamente estrecho que conecta las areas mayores del Norte y Sudamerica. Sin embargo, pese a las apariencias, el area no tiene unidad geografica. *Tampoco tiene unidad histórica*, como iremos viendo."

23. Such as Anthony Coate's *Central America* (1997); *History of Central America* (2006); and *Brief History of Central America* (2007).

24. Sieder, "Review of Historia," 761–763.

25. It is important to mention that when not conceived as an isthmus, Central America is also referred to as a region. Here again, one should take caution, as regional geography emulated a project similar to that of the nation, which attempted to delimit and map certain spaces in a way that endowed them with unique characteristics and, at times, homogenous properties.

26. Mundy, "Mesoamerican Cartography," 184. Mundy describes the ways in which different forms of visual texts served cartographic functions. However, this type of mapping was distinct from European-based methods of documentation. Indeed, some of the Mesoamerican codices undermine this contemporary Western dyad (geography-history) about Central America, as they simultaneously map and tell the story of a space.

27. Hernández, "El nombre de Centroamérica," 3.

28. Hernández, 4. According to Hernández, "From that moment, the lands were conceived as an isthmus, as a tongue [of earth] that united two continents." Original: "A partir de ese momento, las tierras se concibieron como un istmo, es decir como una lengua de tierra que unía dos continentes."

29. For more on the export products produced in the region now known as Central America, see Patch, *Indians and the Political Economy* (2013).

30. Cole, *Geography*, 262. According to Cole, Central America was less developed and overlooked by the Spanish Empire because of "its virtual absence of precious metals." Its significance emerged only once the isthmus in Panama was discovered and goods could be transferred from the Pacific and Atlantic coasts.

31. Rodríguez, *Dividing the Isthmus*, 8.

32. Rodríguez, 2. In this sense, Rodríguez's work distinguishes itself from adhering to this position by resignifying the isthmus to be an "ever shifting discursive space" rather than a stable geophysical entity.

33. For instance, in *History of Sexuality* (1978), Foucault successfully argues that the discourse surrounding *homosexual* constituted that subject position.

34. Foucault, *Power/Knowledge*, 131.

35. Lyotard, *Postmodern Condition*, 65. While Lyotard does not use history or historians as examples, he is interested in how scientific discourses produce their own narratives of legitimacy.

36. Brignoli-Perez, *Brief History*, xv.

37. This is not to suggest that these subjects are not interpellated by other cartographic imaginaries attached to the region. Instead, it elucidates how some subjects reject a very mestiza/o, Western-based idea of Central America.

38. Gilroy, *Black Atlantic*, 4.

39. Foster, *A Brief History*, xvii–xviii.

40. Fischer, *Modernity Disavowed*, 9.

41. Fischer, 38.

42. Meléndez Obando, "Slow Ascent," 335.

43. See Minority Rights Group International, "Afro-Panamanians," and Nicole Akoukou Thompson, "UNDP Report."

44. Medina, *Negotiating Economic Development*, 49. In this book, Medina explores the tensions between Afro-Belizeans and Mestiza/o groups.

45. Herrarte, "Introducción," 7. Original: "Para reflejar de manera precisa hacia dónde apunta nuestro destino histórico, la colección comienza con nuestra fe [sic] de bautismo, el Acta de Independencia."

46. Gallardo, *Constituciones de la República*, 180, 199. Original: "Concluímos, pues, afirmando, que salvo alguna pequeña discrepancia, de escasos días, fué el 15 de septiembre de 1821 la fecha real de la independencia, de España, para todas las Provincias que en ese momento integraban la antigua Capitanía General de Guatemala . . . La nacionalidad centroamericana se originó real y efectivamente en la jornada del 15 de septiembre de 1821."

47. Las *fiestas patrias* that take place in five countries on the isthmus and in the U.S. diaspora all celebrate the date September 15, 1821, as their "official" date of independence.

48. Tuan, *Space and Place*, 6.

49. The etymology of *Guatemala* is still up for debate. In the early nineteenth century, historian James Bell, in *A System of Geography*, wrote, "The kingdom of Guatemala received its name from the word *Quauhtemali*, which, in the Mexican language, means a decayed log of wood . . . some writers, however, he tells us, have derived it from *Uhatezmalha*, which signifies, in the Tzendale dialect, a mountain that throws out water . . . another etymology is given by Francisco de Fuentes y Gusman who derives the name from Coctecmalan, signifying 'milk-wood'—a peculiar tree found only in the neighborhood of the supposed site of the original capital where now stands the village of Tzacualpa" (616). Additionally, scholar Jose Corolue claims that "Guatimala [*sic*], quiere decir árbol podrido . . . también podrá decir lugar de árboles" (qtd. in Gallardo, *Constituciones de la República*, 33). In either case, *Guatemala* links the space with attributes of the environment.

50. Throughout the provinces, there were several attempts to break from the Spanish crown. For instance, José Matías Delgado and others spearheaded a revolt on November 5, 1811, in San Salvador, while in Nicaragua, there was also a revolt against Spain on November 13, 1811.

51. Ricardo Gallardo claims that Salvadoran historian Alberto Luna begins this debate in 1920, when he asserts that it is only after July 1, 1823, when the provinces declare themselves a sovereign nation and break their ties with Spain and Mexico that they can be considered independent. In 1930, Sarbelio Navarrete would also tackle this subject matter in his book *La verdadera feche de nuestra independencia 15 de septiembre de 1821*.

52. "Acta de Independencia," 9–11. Original:

> Siendo públicos é indubables los deseos de independencia del gobierno Español, que por escrito y de palabra ha manifestado el pueblo de esta Capital[Guatemala]: recibidos por el último Correo diversos oficios de los Ayuntamientos Constitutcionales de la Ciudad Real, Comitan y Tuxtla, en que comunican haber proclamado y jurado dicha independencia, excitan á que se haga lo mismo en esta ciudad: siendo positivo que han circulado iguales oficios a otros Ayuntamientos . . . Leídos los oficios expresados: discutido y meditado detenidamente el asunto, y oido el clamor de Viva la Indpendencia, que repetía de continuó el pueblo que se veia reunido en las calles, plaza, patio, corredores y antesela de esta palacio, se acordo por esta Diputacion e individuos del Excelentisimo Ayuntamiento.

53. Bazant, "Independence to the Liberal Republic," 2.

54. Camacho, *Historia de la historiografía*, 37. Camacho argues that in an ordinance declared on September 17, 1821, by the acting captain general of Guatemala, Gabino Gaínza, he in effect banned *fiestas* and celebrations of independence in order to prevent certain populations—such as Indians, mulattos, and mestizos—from partaking in these festivities.

55. Saldaña-Portillo, *Indian Given*, 118.

56. Guzik, *Making Things Stick*, 37.

57. Twinam, *Purchasing Whiteness*, 30. In this book, Twinam explains how a *gracias al sacar* was a juridical exemption that allowed pardos and mulatos to pay a fee to "rid them of their

inferior status" in order to apply for occupations and obtain privileges reserved for colonial whites (30). Her research was able to locate forty applications in the Americas, four in Guatemala, and one in Honduras, suggesting that within the Kingdom of Guatemala, this was not a common practice.

58. Hooker, "Race and the Space," 249.

59. Komisaruk, "Becoming Free," 153.

60. Wolfe, "Cruel Whip," 178.

61. Wolfe, 179.

62. "Acta de Independencia." Original: "El senor Gefe Político, Brigadier D. Gabino Gaínza, continúe con el Gobierno Superior Político y Militar, y para que este tenga el caracter que parece propio de las circunstancias, se forme una Junta provisional consultiva, compuesta de los senores indivduos actuales de esta Diputacion Provincial."

63. Gaínza, *Bando del 17 de Septiembre 1821*. Original: "Quedan consecuentemente en su fuerza y vigor todas las leyes, ordenanzas y órdenes que antes regían" and threatened punishment by death "si alguna hubiese de cualquier clase, grado y condición que directa o indirectamente con discursos o con obras intentase trastornar, o desacreditar el gobierno español." Such people, he adds, would be labeled as "traitors" and "conspirators."

64. Bethell, *Central America*, 6.

65. Cruz, *Political Culture*, 84.

66. "Acta de los Nublados," 14. Original:

1. La absoluta y total independencia de Guatemala, que parece se ha erigido en soberana.
2. La independencia del gobierno español, hasta tanto que se aclaren los nublados del día y pueda obrar esta provincia con arreglo á lo que exigen sus empeños religiosos, y veraderos intereses.
3. Que en consequencia continúen todas la autoridades continuadas (sic) en el libre ejercicio de sus funciones con arreglo á la constitución y á las leyes.

67. "Acta de los Nublados," 14.

68. Iturbide, "Letter to Gabino Gaínza," 131. Original: "El interés actual de Mexico y Guatemala es tan idéntico, e invariable, que no pueden erigirse en naciones separadas e independientes sin aventurar su existencia y seguridad" and sees their geographical proximity "como si la Naturaleza [*sic*] hubiese destinado expresamente a ambas porciones para formar un solo y poderso Imperio."

69. Gaínza, "Letter to Agustin de Iturbide," 52. Original: "Guatemala no debia quedar independiente de Mejico, sino formar un gran imperio" because "Guatemala se hallaba todavia impotente para gobernarse por si misma . . . y que podria ser por lo mismo objeto de la ambición extranjera."

70. It is worth noting that Gaínza's gendered view of the Kingdom of Guatemala is symptomatic of the way the area was perceived by politicians and historians of the time period. Historian Matias Romero often referred to the Kingdom of Guatemala as an "accessory" to Mexico and asserts that Guatemala's independence is the result of "la consecuencia de la de Mexico." Romero, *Bosquejo histórico*, 44. Meanwhile, Historian Manuel Montúfar narrates in *Memorias para la historia* (1832) that Central America's independence occurred by chance, stating,

En 1821 todo el reino de Guatemala estaba pacíficamente sometido al gobierno español . . . En este estado se supo en Guatemala el grito de Iguala, y desde abril hasta setiembre [sic]la opinión se entendió más: los independendientes celebraban juntas en Guatemala, pero no tenían recursos ni el valor necesario para insurreccionarse contra el gobierno: todo lo esperaban de los progresos que hiciera [sic] en Mejico el plan de Iguala . . . Gaínza no tomó medidas para preservar el reino de una insurrección: tenía recursos y podía contar con todos los jefes de las provincias, tanto come el partido españolista, à cuya cabeza estaba Valle; pero cierto de que era imposible que Guatemala se conservase bajo la dependencia española siendo Mejico independiente, no oponía . . . Esta inacción animó más á los que extendían la opinion; mas á pesar de esto, todo lo que hicieron fué un escrito para pedir que Gaínza mismo proclamase la independencia. (2)

71. Cruz, *Political Culture*, 85.

72. Sommer, *Foundational Fictions*, 7.

73. Sommer, 18.

74. Although ODECA refers to this document as "Acta de La Union de Las Provincias de Centro America al Imperio Mexicano," it should be noted that in the nineteenth century, historians referred to this document as "Acta de las Provincias al Imperio Mexicano," or "Acta de las Provincias de Guatemala al Imperio Mexicano." I have therefore have opted to use the nineteenth-century title. For a more detailed example of how this moment was discussed during this period, see Romero, *Bosquejo Histórico* (1877).

75. "Acta de Union," 13–15. Original:

> Se halló: que la voluntad manifestada llanamente por la unión, exedía de la mayoría absoluta de la población reunida a este Gobierno. Y computándose la de la Intendencia de Nicaragua, que desde su declaratoria de su independencia del Gobierno español, se unió al de México, separándose absolutamente de éste; la de la Comayagua, que se haya en el mismo caso; la de la ciudad real de Chiapas, que se unió al Imperio aun antes de que se declarase la independencia de esta ciudad; la de Quezaltenango, Solola y algunos otros pueblos, que en estos últimos días se han adherido por si mismos a la unión; se encontró que la voluntad general subía a una suma casi total. Y teniendo presente la Junta que su deber, en este caso, no es otro que trasladar al Gobierno de México lo que los pueblos quieren.

76. "Acta de Union," 13–15. Original:

> Entre las varias consideraciones que ha hecho la Junta, en esta importante y grave materia, en que los pueblos se hayan amenazados en su reposo, y especialmente en la unión con sus hermanos de las otras provincias con quienes ha vivido siempre ligados por la vecindad, comercio y otros vínculos estrechos, fue una de las primeras, que por medio de la unión a México querían salvar la integridad de lo que antes se ha llamado Reino de Guatemala, y restablecer entre si la unión que ha reinado por lo pasado; no apareciendo otra para remediar la división que se experimenta.

77. Mexican merchants often bought and stocked goods from the Kingdom of Guatemala such as cacao and indigo. For more on the trade relationship between the two, see Patch, *Indians and the Political Economy* (2013).

78. Molina, *Documentos relacionados*, 91. Original: "Que siendo de necesidad su incorporación á otra nación de América conforme á lo decretado en la misma fecha . . . por el que se descretó la incorporación á los Estados Unidos de América."

79. Delgado, "Carta al General Filisola," quoted in *Nuestra patria*, 73. Original: "Estando la provincia unida a la Gran República del Norte por su espontánea voluntad, y resistiendo como parte de ella la invasión de las tropas de su mando, cuando fuése ocupada, aquélla, aún en el caso de no admitir la unión, pedirá cuenta al Gobeirno mexicano de la ocupación violenta y guerra injusta hecha a una Provincia que se habiá unida a ella, y puesto bajo su protección y amparo; y entonces San Salvador seriá libre, a pesar del Gobierno de México."

80. In *Constituciones de la República* (1958), Ricardo Gallardo views this moment as "la verdadera guerra de Independencia" (633).

81. LaFeber, *Inevitable Revolutions*, 24. According to LaFeber, these emissaries arrived in Boston but were never able to meet with the U.S. secretary of state to review it. For other references regarding Salvadoran annexation to the United States, see Brignoli-Perez, *Brief History*, 66; Buchenau, *Shadow of the Giant*, 6.

82. See Bennett, *Africans in Colonial Mexico* (2003); and Vinson and Restall, *Black Mexico* (2009).

83. Filisola, "Letter to Manuel José Arce," quoted in Benítez, *La iglesia*. Original: "Aunque ese gobierno ha declarado incorporada la Provincia a la Federación norteamericana . . . es nulo ese pronunciamiento, porque San Salvador pertenece al Imperio [Mexicano]."

84. "El Decreto," 17–20. Original:

Que la naturaleza misma resiste la dependencia de esta parte del globo separada por un Océano inmenso de la que fué so metrópoli . . .

Que la experiencia de más de trescientos años manifestó a la América que su felicidad era del todo incompatible con la nulidad a que la reduciá la triste condición de colonia de una pequeña parte de la Europa.

Que la arbitrariedad con que fue gobernada por la nación española y la conducta que ésta observó constantemente, desde la conquista, excitaron a los pueblos al más ardiente deseo de recobrar sus derechos usurpados.

Que a impulsos de tan justos sentimientos, todas la provincias de América sacudieron el yugo que las oprimió por espacio de tres siglos: que las que pueblan el antiguo reino de Guatemala proclamaron gloriosamente su indpendencia en los úlitmos meses del año de 1821; y que la resolución de conservarla y sostenerla es el voto general y uniforme de todos sus habitantes.

85. "El Decreto," 17–20. Original:

Considerando por otra parte: que la incorporación de estas provincias al extinguido imperio mexicano, verificada *sólo de hecho* en fines de 1821 y principios de 1822, fué una expresión violenta arrancada por medios viciosos e ilegales.

Que no fué acordada ni pronunciada por órgano ni por medios legitimos: que por estos principios la representacíon nacional del estado mexicano, jamás la aceptó expresamente, ni pudo con derecho aceptarla; y que las providencias que acerca de esta unión dictó y expidió D. Agustín de Iturbide, fueron nulas.

86. Sommer, *Foundational Fictions*, 31.

87. Bhabha, "Narrating the Nation," 4.

88. Bhabha, "DissemiNation," 299.

89. The area we now know as Mexico and Central America was not always divided. Pre-Columbian cultures interacted for thousands of years prior to the arrival of the Spanish. For instance, the Pipil and Nicarao cultures, which are increasingly viewed as the autochthonous segments of the current nation-states of El Salvador and Nicaragua (the state is named after this indigenous group), have Mesoamerican ties to Nahua-speaking communities from Central Mexico.

CHAPTER 2 CONSTRUCTING THE CENTRAL AMERICAN NATIONAL IMAGINARY

1. Lázaro, "Las diversas visiones," 2, 7.

2. Lázaro, 65.

3. McClintock, "Family Feuds," 1. Certainly in merely trying to describe this type of nationalist ideology we see how masculinity becomes intertwined with nationalism.

4. Lázaro, "Las diversas visiones," 64–67, emphasis added.

5. Milian, *Latining America*, 13.

6. Wald, *Constituting Americans*, 2.

7. Bhabha, "Narrating the Nation," 4.

8. Ricardo Gallardo, *Constituciones de la República*, 205.

9. vom Hau, "Nationalism and War Commemoration," 149.

10. vom Hau, 149.

11. See Pedro Jose Figuerora's oil canvas titled *Simón Bolívar, Liberator and Father of the Nation*, 1819, Quinta de Bolívar, Colombia.

12. Bulu, "Discursos inéditos," 162. Original: "Hubu un Napoleón I, un Washington, un San Martin y un Bolívar . . . Cada uno de esos hombres ha asombrado al Mundo con sus hazañas, cada uno de ellos descolló como Prócer para engrandecer á su Patria."

13. Dardón, *La cuestión de límites*, 17. Original:

> Los triunfos alcanzados en la América del Sur por el Libertador Simon Bolívar, por ese semi-dios que hacia pasear victorioso el estandarte de la República . . . y la lucha heróicamente sostenida en Nueva-España por Hidalgo que inició la gran revolucion que llevó á cabo el talento de Iturbide, eran circunstancias altamente favorables para los intereses de la América del Centro que, olvidada de sus dominadores en medio del estruendo de las harmas . . . pudo sin oposicion de ningún género y merced á los sacrificios de sus hermanos de uno y otro extremo de la América y de los suyos propios, proclamar su independencia.

14. I am not suggesting that there were no "heroes" linked to the independence movement. Several *criollos* such as José Cecilio del Valle (who I discuss in this chapter) as well as Manuel José de Arce are viewed as leaders of this movement. The difference is that unlike *criollos* from Mexico or Venezuela, *criollos* from the Kingdom of Guatemala did not engage in battles against Spain. For some countries like Nicaragua and Costa Rica, many of their war heroes would emerge from the "Guerra Nacional" against William Walker (1856–1857).

15. Castilla, *Voto particular*, 2–3. Original: "Se nos cita el ejemplo de los anglo-americanos que han justificado está feliz institución que forma de un estado grande muchas repúblicas ó pequeños estados, unidos por un solo lazo. Sin embargo, yo no lo creo aproposito en nuestras circunstancias . . . veo muy distantes nuestros estados de los del norte de América."

16. Castilla, 3–4. Original:

> Según el cálculo de Humboldt tiene lo que se llamó reyno de Guatemala 20.920 leguas cuadradas, de las de 20 al grado: poblada con mas de un millón de habitantes, deben deducirse de este número dos terceras partes de indígenas, que en la actualidad, y en mucho tiempo, son incapaces de conocer sus derechos: deben deducirse también las mugeres, los niños, y los ancianos, y otra multitud de habitantes que no se han podido reducir á poblado, cuya civilización es todabía más difícil que la de los primeros . . . Y donde encontraremos hombres para llenar tantos cuerpos legislativos como provincias, tantos directores, senadores y consejeros, tantos magistrados, y tantos otros empleados precisos para entablar el sistema.

17. Dikshit and Animesh, *Geographical Thought*, 38. Alexander von Humboldt was a German naturalist and geographer who was allowed by King Carlos IV to explore the New World Spanish colonies. During the nineteenth century, Humboldt embodied the spirit of Enlightenment and positivism, and his contemporaries often bestowed upon him such titles as "monarch of sciences" and "the new Aristotle" and viewed his taxonomies of spaces, plants, and nature as undisputed "truths."

18. Fischer, *Modernity Disavowed*, 229.

19. The fact that there is now a monument to Atanasio Tzul speaks to the ways that later nation-building elites would appropriate this figure to laud a mestiza/o nationalism within Guatemala.

20. Dym, *Sovereign Villages*, 202.

21. "Constitución de la República," 30. Original: "Art. 5 El territorio de la República es el mismo que antes comprendía el antiguo reyno de Guatemala, a excepción, por ahora, de la provincia de Chiapas. Art.6. La federación se compone actualmente de cinco estados, que son: Costa Rica, Nicaragua, Honduras, El Salvador y Guatemala. La provincia de Chiapas se tendrá por estado en la federación cuando libremente se una."

22. "Decreto sobre la abolición," 691. Original: "Desde la publicación de esta ley, en cada pueblo, son libres los esclavos de uno y otro sexo y de cualquier edad, que existan en algún punto de los Estados Federales del Centro de América; y en adelante, ninguno podrá hacer esclavo." Article 1 indicates: "As of the moment this law is publicly decreed, in all provinces, and from now on, slaves of all sexes are free, regardless of age or sex, and in none of the territories of the Federation of Central American States shall anyone be hold or made a slave."

23. This "Decreto sobre la abolición" also reminds owners that they are not to neglect feeding slaves older than sixty years old (too old for financial reimbursement) and warns them that if they continue to use their slaves, they will "perderá el derecho de ser indemnizado" (693).

24. "Constitución de la República," 30. Original:

> Art.21. Se suspenden los derechos de ciudadano:
> 1. Por proceso criminal en que se haya poveído auto de prisión por delito que según la ley merezca pena más que correccional.
> 2. Por ser deudor fraudulento declarado, o deudor a las rentas públicas y judicialmente requerido de pago.
> 3. Por conducta notoriamente viciada.
> 4. Por incapacidad física o moral, judicialmente calificada.
> 5. Por el estado de sirviente domestico cerca de la persona.
> Art.22. Solo los ciudadanos en exercicio pueden obtener servicios en la República.

25. "Orden de la Asamblea Nacional," 683. For instance, on August 4, 1823, the ANC would decree that all official memoranda from the Central American nation-state needed to contain "Dios, Union, y Libertad" instead of "Dios guarde a Ud. [*sic*] muchos años," which had been the standard form of signature during the Spanish Empire, emphasizing the importance of "union."

26. Descriptions of these events can be found in works by Briceño de Zúniga and Zúniga Reyes, *Símbolos patrios* (2003); and Ferro, *Banderas centroamericans* (1970).

27. Sörlin, "Articulation of Territory," 108.

28. Sörlin, 103.

29. Quoted in Jimenez and Acuña, "*Improbable nación*," 4.

30. Romero, "Flag of the Federal Republic."

31. Nabarz, *Mysteries of Mithras*, 55.

32. Shoat and Stam, *Unthinking Eurocentrism*, 141.

33. Martinez, "Himno a Centro America," 13–15: "Dios te puso en el centro del mundo / Y mañana su emporio serás."

34. Anderson, *Disaster Writing*, 114.

35. Anderson, 114.

36. This is not to suggest that there are no volcanoes on the Atlantic coast among those five countries, as both Honduras and Nicaragua have one volcano on that side of the isthmus.

37. Gudmundson and Wolfe, *Blacks and Blackness*, 9.

38. Brignoli-Perez, *Brief History*, 53. According to Brignoli-Perez, "The English had excellent allies in the native Miskito Indians. They intermarried quickly with the African slaves brought in for the first settlements, even including the survivors of a Portuguese slaver shipwrecked off the coast in 1641. They were therefore called zambo-mesquitos (or mosquitos, a corruption of their indigenous name already observable in the eighteenth century), and they soon shared the same hostility toward the Spanish."

39. Putnam, "Eventually Alien," 288.

40. Gudmundson, "What Difference Did Color Make?," 239.

41. Anderson, *Politics in Central America*, 3.

42. Castro, *Población de El Salvador*, 155. Castro adds, "A pesar de prohibiciones reiteradas, bien a requerimiento de las autoridades o de modo clandestino, [negros] iban incrementándose con rapidez, al grado de que en el siglo XVII llegó a considerarse peligroso su excesivo número."

43. For instance, during the colonial period, certain population-tracking documents like *Estado de las Bulas de la Santa Cruzada*, published in 1779, would act similar to the census. According to Castro, this crude form of demographic documentation "contiene en números redondos, el cálculo de bulas indispensables para cada grupo" (233). But the only groups counted were "blancos," "mestizos en general," and "indios." (234).

44. Boland, *Culture and Customs*, 15. According to Boland, "Black slaves were also brought from Africa to act as foremen over the Indians in Salvadoran cocoa and balsam plantations . . . the genes of the few thousand African slaves were spread and diluted among the mestizo population."

45. Del Valle was in contention to be the first president of the new Central American nation. He would ultimately lose that title to Manuel José Arce.

46. Del Valle, "Letter to Alexander von Humboldt," quoted in von Humboldt, "Sobre la situación actual," 21. Original:

> La naturaleza ha favorecido más a mi patria que a México. Este país, como España, sufre mucho de la aridez y la sequía en casi toda la meseta. Por el contrario, nuestra Centroamérica se encuentra abundantemente regada por magníficas corrientes fáciles de navegar. La flora con que se adorna el suelo, me parece mucho más frondosa que la de México . . . Poseemos puertos en ambos océanos, y si alguna vez dichos océanos se unen por medio de un canal en Nicaragua (sobre el cual probablemente usted ya tiene abundantes documentos), nuestra República, situada en el centro de América, deberá conectar el comercio de las Antillas al de China y al del Archipiélago Indico, con lo cual ocupará un lugar importante en el concierto de las naciones.

47. Domino, "Republic of Central America," 129, 134, 136. Political discourse from the United States during the same time period, however, would routinely view Central America and Mexico as having similar attributes. The *North American Review* claimed Central America's "Atlantic side is insalubrious, like that of Mexico" (129) and that its aboriginal inhabitants were "like that of Mexico" in obtaining "partial civilization" (134). Even political strategies are framed as similar: "Central America, it is well known, adopted like Mexico, the political system of the United States" (136).

48. Jimenez and Acuña, "Improbable nación," 8. Jimenez and Acuña include a speech delivered on April 13, 1811, by then governor of the Kingdom of Guatemala, El Capitan General José Bustamante y Guerra, which articulates how *patria* was deployed. Original: "Confunde el vulgo las palabras patria y país, patriotismo y paisanaje. Cariño merece el país en que se nace, en que se forma la razón, en que toma el espíritu las impresiones más duraderas. Pero cuan distinto es el alto y verdadero amor a la patria, que se comprende todos los pueblos unidos por los mismos vínculos sociales, todos lo que tenemos, una Religión, un Rey, una ley unas costumbres, una voluntad, y un carácter que nos distingue del resto de los pueblos."

49. Casaús Arzú and Giráldez, *Redes intelectuales*, 52. They suggest that "paso a manifestar su lealtad a la nación Americana, siempre con esa idea integredora de una sola patria / it came to pass that the same idea of having loyalty towards the fatherland was implemented in the nations of the Americas."

50. Casaús Arzú and Giráldez, 52. Original: "Lealtad a la patria centroaméricana, a una entidad grande, que cohabitaba e interactuaba con otra, la patria chica, entidida como lugar de origin."

51. Del Valle, quoted in Casaús Arzú and Giráldez, 53. Original: "Se han unido todas [las provincias] para formar una sola nación. Cada una es un estado independiente de los otros, pero todas son al mismo tiempo partes de un solo todo, fracciones de una sola unidad."

52. Del Valle, quoted in Casaús Arzú and Giráldez, 61. Original: "No dependen unos de los otros hermanos, ni hay entre ellos subordinación o superioridad de derecho; pero todos deben consideración y respeto as su padre [. . .] No depende Costa Rica de Nicaragua, ni Comayagua de San Salvador; Comayagua, Nicaragua, y Costa Rica tienen un gobierno supremo que debe extender a todos los puebles su vigilencia y protección. Este gobierno es el vínculo que los une para formar una sola nación."

53. Del Valle, "Confederación Americana," 237. Original: "Nacimos en un mismo continente; somos hijos de una misma madre; somos hermanos; hablamos un mismo idioma; defendemos una misma causa; somos llamadas a iguales destinos."

54. Alonso, "Politics of Space," 385.

55. Berlant, *Anatomy of National Fantasy*, 20.

56. Allatson, *Key Terms*, 115. Moreover, the metaphor of the family, or "*la gran familia*," as Allatson notes, was a popular trope within Latin American nationalisms.

57. Allianza Cívica Cultural Centroamericana, "Home Page," accessed November 24, 2014, http://www.acc-ca.org/?page_id=124 and Confederación Centro Americana, "Quienes somos."

58. Both Lynn Foster (2007) and Hector Brignoli-Perez (1985) have discussed the federation ending around 1838–1839. Thomas L. Karnes (1961) picks a concrete month and year, and Noé Pineda Portillo (2008) uses Morazán as a symbolic date of closure. Ironically, Morazán was killed for trying to reinstitute a Central American–based federation. By 1840, most of the individual states had ceded from the federation, and Morazán—via military force—attempted to reestablish political union. He was captured by the Costa Rican military in 1842 and executed by firing squad. The fact that he was killed by another Central American state should disclose how Central American unity is a myth, and yet, throughout the years, Morazán has been transformed into the "Central American Abraham Lincoln"—a political leader who died trying to maintain the union of the state.

59. Among the many gestures of commemoration devoted to Morazán throughout Central America are public spaces honoring him, such as Parque Morazán in Costa Rica and Guatemala (though in 2003, Guatemala would change the name of this park) and Plaza Morazán in El Salvador, Honduras, Nicaragua, and most recently Los Angeles.

60. "*Decreto lejislativo separandose Nicaragua.*" Original: "1: El Estado de Nicaragua es libre, soberano e independiente sin más restricción que la que se imponga en el Nuevo pacto que celebre con los otros Estados de Centro-América, conforme a los principios de un verdadero federalismo. 11. Promueva cada uno (estados) por su parte la formación de un Nuevo pacto federativo más análogo a las peculiares circunstancias de Centro-América."

61. This was the first of many attempts at reunification. Others that followed included

1852	La República de America Central
1889	República de América Central
1895	República Mayor de Centroamérica
1989	Los Estados Unidos de América Central
1921	La Federación Centroamericana

62. This is not to suggest that this is the first proclamation Guatemala made to assert a type of political autonomy. On April 17, 1839, the country had declared itself "independent, free, and sovereign" from the Central American federation. However, declaring itself "free" from that particular federation is not the same as announcing that the state is an independent republic, nor was that the historical moment when that territory would be represented as such.

63. "*Decreto sobre la erección.*" Original:

Considerando:

1. Que el Estado del Salvador ha hecho todo género de esfuerzos para haber de conseguir la reorganización de la Antigua Republica de Centro América, sin poder lograr aquel fin; y que antes bien por esa misma causa se ha visto envuelto en guerras y otras graves dificultades.

Decreta:

Art 1. El Estado de El Salvador reasume en lo sucesivo su soberanía externa; y se declara REPUBLICA LIBRE SOBERANA E INDEPENDIENTE.

Art 2. Esta declaratoria no obsta en manera alguna, para que El Salvador pueda concurrir a la formación de un Pacto Confederativo, en unión de los otros Estados de la América Central, siempre que asi convenga a sus intereses a juicio del Cuerpo Legislativo.

64. Juan Rafael Mora, quoted in Soto, *Guerra Nacional*, 54–55.

65. The constitution of Nicaragua (1858) states that its president needs to be "originario y vecino de la Republica . . . Pueden también ser los hijos de las otras secciones de Centroamérica que tengan quince años de vecindad y las demás cualidades referidas."

66. Article 2 of the 1879 Guatemalan constitution states, "Mantendrá y cultivará con las demás repúblicas de Centro-América intimas relaciones de familia y reciprocidad. Y siempre que se proponga la nacionalidad Centro-Americana de una manera estable, justa, popular y conveniente, la Republica de Guatemala está pronta a reincorporarse en ella." Article 151 in El Salvador's 1886 constitution proclaims, "Siendo el Salvador una parte disgregada de la Republica de Centro América, queda en capacidad de concurrir con todos, o con alguno de los Estados de ella, a la organización de un Gobierno Nacional cuando las circunstancias lo permitan y convenga asi a sus interés, lo mismo que a formar parte de la gran Confederación Latino-Americana." Whereas Article 1 of the 1888 Costa Rican constitution asserts, "Los articulos 1, 2, y 15 de la Constitución no impiden que se celebren tratados de unión política de Costa Rica con alguna o las demás Repúblicas de Centro América."

67. See the Guatemalan constitution of 1879. Original: "Cultivará con las demás republicas de Centro-América intimas relaciones de familia y reciprocidad. Y siempre que se proponga la nacionalidad Centro-Americana." It is important to note that often, these constitutions worked in tandem with the political philosophy of their given presidents. For instance, this Guatemalan constitution, both in its provisions and its rhetoric, parallels then president Justo

Rufino Barrios's (1873–1885) objective to reestablish a united Central American political entity.

68. The constitution of Guatemala (1879). Original: "Se consideran también como guatemaltecos naturales a los originarios de las otras repúblicas de Centro-América que manifiesten ante la autoridad competente el deseo de ser guatemaltecos."

69. The constitution of Costa Rica (1848). Original: "Es natural de cualquiera de las Repúblicas de Guatemala, Honduras, El Salvador y Nicaragua sera tenido como de origen costarricense."

70. This is seen in the Honduran, Guatemalan, and Salvadoran constitutions. For instance, Article 31 of the 1865 Honduran constitution states, "Para ser Presidente se requiere ser padre de familia, mayor de treinta años, del estado seglar, natural de Centroamérica, con vecindario de cinco años en Honduras," while Article 65 of the 1879 Guatemalan constitution states, "Para ser elegido Presidente se requiere: 1) ser natural de Guatemala o de cualesquiera de las otras repúblicas de Centroamérica," and Article 98 of the 1886 Salvadoran constitution claims, "Para ser Magistrado propietario o suplente, se requiere: 1) Ser natural de la República o centroamericanos naturalizado en ella."

71. The Central American Court of Justice was a product of the 1907 Conference for Central American Peace held in Washington, DC. The five countries of Guatemala, El Salvador, Nicaragua, Honduras, and Costa Rica, along with Mexico and the United States, met to strategize ways to solve internal conflicts that plagued that area. A treaty signed at the conference, "General Treaty of Peace and Amity," indicated the creation of a Central American Court of Justice.

72. Van Dyke, *Before the Central American Court*, 2.

73. Van Dyke, 23–24. The original complaint written in Spanish is stated in the following manner:

> La constitución política de El Salvador consagra el principio de que es una parte disgregada de la República de Centro América y que, como tal, queda en capacidad de concurrir con todos o algunos de los estados centroamericanos a la organización de un gobierno nacional común . . . Este mismo principio lo tienen consignado, en una forma u otra, las constituciones de los otros estados de Centro América. La de Nicaragua lo trae en el Art. 2, . . . Las enajenaciónes de territorio hechas por un estado Centroamericano a una nación extraña, resultan, por consiguiente, en mengua de los intereses trascendentales que el pueblo salvadoreño ha tenido siempre y tiene constantemente en mira, como una de sus aspiraciones más grandes y más legítimas: la de volver a formar con los pueblos hermanos la patria grande, dueña—sin merma alguna—del antiguo solar centroamericano; aspiración hacia la cual se hallan impulsados los cinco estados por su comunidad de origen, de religión y de historia. Esas enajenaciónes vendrían a herir hondamente esa aspiración y a afectar la virtualidad de los grandes intereses que el pueblo salvadoreño, como fracción del pueblo centroamericano, estima de primordial importancia para su vida nacional en el porvenir; intereses que el pueblo nicaragüense y los pueblos de los otros tres estados reconocen, sostienen y aprecian en la misma medida, según lo comprueban multitud de hechos históricos y actos políticos de su vida independiente.

74. Roniger, *Transnational Politics*, 39.

75. Embassy of Costa Rica, "Cultura." Original: "Rojo representa . . . su deramineto de sangre por la libertad."

76. For a more focused study on how the individual nations dealt with cultures and populations that went against the grain of a mestizo-based nationalist ideology, see Carmack,

Harvest of Violence (1988); Montejo, *Voices from Exile* (1999); Gordon, *Disparate Diasporas* (1998); England, *Afro Central Americans* (2006).

77. Billig, *Banal Nationalism*, 8.
78. Roniger, *Transnational Politics*, 41.
79. Billig, *Banal Nationalism*, 8.

CHAPTER 3   PERFORMING CENTRALAMÉRICANISMO

1. This poem appeared on a flyer circulated in Los Angeles in 1984 by the Clínico Msr. Romero and Santana Chirino Amaya Refugee Committee.
2. Uribe, "Inauguran en Los Ángeles."
3. More research in this area is needed. However, the work of such scholars as Carlos Cordova and Ana Patricia Rodríguez suggest that a type of Central American identity politics might also be in place in areas like the Mission district in San Francisco, California. Still one hypothesis for the emergence of this Central American identity within such a space as Los Angeles is that it is a physical space that has predominantly been associated with one particular Latino group: Mexican Americans. Perhaps in the effort to claim a form of visibility, this type of pan-ethnic identity needs to be read as a form of strategic alliance that only occurs when Central American subjects become too easily (mis)read as purely Mexican / Mexican American subjects.
4. Plaza Morazán is located on the "Valencia Triangle"—a triangular piece of land located at West Eighth Street and Valencia Street in Los Angeles. It should be noted that while Los Angeles community groups tout it as the first space devoted to Central Americans, there has been a Morazán statue in New Orleans since the 1960s. These are just but a few of the notable ways that Los Angeles is increasingly being signified to include Central American culture. For instance, in November 2013, the same year the plaza was dedicated, the city would also unveil the dedication of Plaza Monseñor Romero at MacArthur Park. Most of these highly visible manifestations of Central Americanness take place in the Westlake / Pico Union area.
5. The project was proposed in April 2011 by the immigrant advocacy organization El Rescate and was approved that July by the Board of Recreation and Park Commissioners of the city of Los Angeles.
6. Interviews that express these sentiments can be located in Uribe, "Inauguran en Los Ángeles"; Alpízar, "Plaza Morazán"; Salvadoran Power, "Vivian Painting"; and Dailymotion, "Walter Duran."
7. The Northern Triangle refers to three countries from the isthmus: Guatemala, El Salvador, and Honduras.
8. For early examples of how some Central American subjects utilized parades as a platform for identity, see Cadaval, *Creating a Latino Identity* (1998).
9. Alvarado, "Interdisciplinary Reading," 369.
10. Muñoz, "Feeling Brown," 70.
11. Following Julie Bettie, I see *performativity* as an "unconscious iteration" of discourse, while *performance* is understood as "conscious knowing display." Bettie, *Women without Class*, xix.
12. Foucault, "Of Other Spaces," 24.
13. Rodríguez, "Departamento 15," 21.
14. Rodríguez, 21.
15. Lesser and Batalova, "Central American Immigrants."
16. The Central American Common Market (Mercado Común Centroamericano) emerged in 1960, when the countries of Guatemala, El Salvador, Nicaragua, and Honduras signed the

"General Treaty on Central American Economic Integration." The treaty was an attempt to assist in developing the economic growth of the region through free trade among the countries. To facilitate this type of interaction and integration among the countries of the isthmus, certain infrastructures, like public transportation, were strengthened. This in turn created internal population shifts as more rural populations began migrating to city centers. See Brignoli-Perez, *Brief History*, 141–143.

17. Hamilton and Stoltz Chinchilla, *Seeking Community*, 29.

18. According to Durham, *Scarcity and Survival* (1979) and Homer-Dixon, *Environment, Scarcity* (1999), the war between El Salvador and Honduras had less to do with soccer and everything to do with land and employment scarcity. Homer-Dixon notes that Durham attributes the following reasons for the war: (1) the failure of the Central American Common market to be applied proportionately to the two countries, (2) tensions over a long-term border dispute, and (3) overpopulation in El Salvador, which led to an increase of Salvadoran immigration to Honduras that exacerbated tensions on the border.

19. The earthquake occurred on December 23, 1972; at the time, it was recorded at 6.2 on the Richter scale. Though the magnitude of the earthquake may not have been as high as other quakes recorded in other regions, it nonetheless greatly impacted the country of Nicaragua. According to David Alexander, 50 percent of the population lost their employment because of it, and 75 percent of the entire population of Managua was affected by this disaster. See Alexander, *Natural Disasters*, 74.

20. García, "Canada." García claims that the rise in residency applications emerged from a less stringent immigration policy by Canada, who accepted asylum petitions more readily than the United States.

21. While Nicaraguan refugees were able to receive legal entry via the Refugee Act because they were seen as political refugees, all other Central Americans, especially Salvadorans and Guatemalans, were viewed as economic refugees. As a consequence, the approval rates for asylum for Salvadorans and Guatemalans in 1984 were less than 3 percent.

22. Hamilton and Stoltz Chinchilla, *Seeking Community*, 45.

23. On November 9, 2007, this organization submitted to the City of Los Angeles a 178-page document titled "Documentation in Opposition to the Renaming of the Pico Union/ Westlake/MacArthur Park Communities."

24. Friends of Pico Union, "Documentation in Opposition," 12.

25. Friends of Pico Union, 15.

26. Friends of Pico Union, 17.

27. Padilla, *Latino Ethnic Consciousness*, 5.

28. Terrazas, "Central American Immigrants."

29. Shorris, *Latinos*, 243. It is important to note that these national assumptions and ascriptions are historically based, since up until 1848, California was Mexican territory and houses the largest Mexican population outside of Mexico to date.

30. Acuña, *Anything but Mexican*, 6.

31. Flores, *Bomba to Hip-Hop*, 198.

32. For more on how Mayas are marginalized by mestiza/o Central Americans in Los Angeles, see Estrada, "(Re)Claiming Public Space."

33. De Genova and Ramos-Zayas, *Latino Crossing*, 21. Both authors critique articulations of Latinidad that rely on "common" cultural elements.

34. Confederación Centro Americana, "Quienes somos."

35. See Bibler Coutin, *Legalizing Moves* (2003).

36. Confederación Centro Americana, "Quienes somos."

37. Confederación Centro Americana.

38. Hobsbawm and Ranger, *Invention of Tradition*, 1.

39. "¡Felices 195 años!"

40. "Centroamérica comienza conmemoración."

41. For more discussion about Central Americans forging transnational connections, see Padilla, "Central American Transnational Imaginary" (2013); Rivas, *Salvadoran Imaginaries* (2014); and Rodríguez, *Dividing the Isthmus* (2009). In this work, Rodríguez labels this process of linking the macropolitics of the isthmus with local iterations as belonging to a "transisthmus."

42. Rivas, *Salvadoran Imaginaries*, 31.

43. "COFECA Carnaval."

44. McInnes, "Guatemala Remittances."

45. Confederación Centro Americana., "Corporate Sponsorship Package 2009," 1.

46. *Tournament of Roses*, "Sponsorship Opportunities," 1.

47. Tatum, *Encyclopedia of Latino Culture*, 259.

48. Dávila, *Latinos, Inc.*, xix.

49. Confederación Centro Americana, "Corporate Sponsorship Package 2009," 4.

50. Confederación Centro Americana, "Corporate Sponsorship Package 2009," 6.

51. See Roach, *Cities of the Dead* (1996).

52. The city of Los Angeles is involved in the parade in two ways: (1) civic officials like Mayor Eric Garcetti participate in the parade and (2) city resources are used in the logistics of the parade, such as using the police to help reroute traffic. While the city of Los Angeles provides this assistance, the associated fees are paid by COFECA.

53. Previous themes include "No Human Being Is Illegal" (2008) and "United for Immigration Reform" (2010).

54. This is not to suggest that local Garifuna community organizations do not participate in the parade. For instance, in 2007, the Garifuna American Heritage Foundation United marched in the parade. The distinction I am making here is that this group was more self-contained and was not seen as a part of the Honduras constituency.

55. McClintock, "Family Feuds," 67.

56. McClintock, 66.

57. Banet-Weiser, *Most Beautiful Girl*, 6.

58. Banet-Weiser, 2.

59. Ochoa, *Queen for a Day*, 8, 208.

60. Ochoa, 8. Ochoa claims that *transformistas* utilize spectacular femininity as a means to provide "legibility, affirmation, income and other elements of survival."

61. Ochoa, 37.

62. Ochoa, 6.

63. Stanfield, *Of Beasts and Beauty* (1953).

64. In 2013, when Miss Venezuela (María Gabriela Isler) won the title of Miss Universe, the president of Venezuela Nicolás Maduro tweeted that her "triumph was the triumph of Venezuela" (translation mine).

65. Ochoa, *Queen for a Day*, 32, 36.

66. Yano, *Crowning the Nice Girl*, 14.

67. In El Salvador, for instance, women are held criminally responsible for miscarriages and can be thrown in jail for suffering one.

68. Repak, "Labor Recruitment," 65.

69. Hamilton and Stoltz Chinchilla, *Seeking Community*, 45.

70. Muñoz, "Feeling Brown," 75.

71. Roque Ramírez, "Claiming Queer Cultural Citizenship," 180.
72. Roque Ramírez, "In Transnational Distance," 7.
73. Valentine, "(Re)Negotiating the Heterosexual Street," 153.
74. "Pepe Palacios." Also see Portillo Villeda, "Respect!"
75. Valentine, "(Re)Negotiating the Heterosexual Street," 154.
76. Muñoz, *Disidentifications*, 100.
77. Subero, "Muxeninity," 178.
78. Mirandé, "Hombres Mujeres," 385.
79. Mirandé, 399.
80. Subero, "Muxeninity," 182.
81. Hames-García, *Identity Complex*, 109.
82. Fernandez de Castro, "Meet the Muxes."
83. Quoted in Mirandé, "Hombres Mujeres," 398.
84. Taylor, *Indigeneity*, 122. Taylor explains how in the 1970s, Zapotec communities actively contested Mexican state polices and the PRI in particular. Included in their political platform was a request for the restitution of peasant lands.
85. Muñoz, *Disidentifications*, 108.
86. Ochoa, *Queen for a Day*, 70.
87. Ochoa, 70.
88. In 2012, Belize was declared the "host" country and was allowed to lead the parade floats and choose the grand marshal for that year.
89. Cofeca Desfile Centroamericano, "COFECA: Entrevista."
90. Cofeca Desfile Centroamericano, "COFECA: Nestor Méndez."
91. Hooker, "Race and the Space," 248. In this essay, Hooker elaborates on how the state of Nicaragua used the Atlantic coast as a site to project blackness so that it could imagine the rest of the nation as mestiza/o.
92. Falconi and Mazzotti, *Other Latinos*, 8. Though I agree with Claudia Milian that this term overlooks the nuances within Latinidad, I think it is important to note how some manifestations of Latinidad can be homogenizing.
93. Falconi and Mazzotti, *Other Latinos*, 7.
94. On May 1, 2006, two hundred thousand protestors marched the streets to City Hall, and four hundred thousand people protested along the Wilshire Corridor during the national protest titled "A Day without an Immigrant."
95. For more information regarding Central Americans and jobs in the United States, see Hamilton and Stoltz Chinchilla, *Seeking Community* (2001).
96. Foucault, "Of Other Spaces," 24.
97. Foucault, 24.
98. Arias, "Central American–Americans," 3.

CHAPTER 4   SUBJECTS IN PASSING

1. Chambers, "Secret Latina at Large," 38.
2. Hoy, "Negotiating among Invisibilities," 426.
3. Hoy, 429.
4. Hoy, 429.
5. This tension of viewing Latinidad at times as synonymous with Mexican / Mexican American is not limited to Los Angeles, as it also occurs in Arizona and Chicago.
6. Hoy, 426.

7. Roque Ramírez, "In Transnational Distance," 8.

8. In García and Rúa, "Processing Latinidad," the authors have labeled the prominence of certain national cultures in certain locations as "geographic hegemony" (318). They cite Aparicio, who in her article "Reading the 'Latino'" (1999) also asserts this notion. Flores, in *Bomba to Hip-Hop* (2000), also suggests that some cultures monopolize certain urban spaces.

9. Scholars who study national communities outside of these three "historical minorities" have asserted the ways in which they are often not discursively configured within Latinidad. In *Borders of Dominicanidad* (2016), García-Peña asserts that "the media and advertisement industry rarely portrays Dominicans as exemplary of US Latinidad. Dominicanidad blackness does not fit the colonial fantasy that makes the light-skinned version of Latino/a mestizaje marketable in the United States" (2).

10. See Arias, "Central American–Americans?"

11. Ginsberg, *Passing*, 2.

12. Sánchez and Schlossberg, *Passing*, 3.

13. Ginsberg, *Passing*, 1.

14. Wald, *Crossing the Line*, 11.

15. African Americans during slavery often used this social practice as a means to migrate from south to north in an attempt to acquire personal freedom. Postemancipation and continuing on into the Jim Crow era, this practice would continue in an attempt to obtain economic opportunities and to ensure individuals of their physical and social well-being.

16. Ho, *Racial Ambiguity*, 118.

17. Sánchez and Schlossberg, *Passing*, 3.

18. Harrison, *Sexual Deceit*, 50.

19. Harrison, 50.

20. Chekola and McHugh, "Ontological Foundations," 22.

21. Foucault, *History of Sexuality*.

22. McWhorter, "Practicing Practicing," 153.

23. Butler, *Gender Trouble*, 17.

24. The prominence of these "historical minorities" in these different institutional spaces, however, is not arbitrary, as they operate as residual effects of sociopolitical factors and a long-standing history of U.S. colonialism and imperialism. The 1848 Treaty of Guadalupe of Hidalgo changed the landscape of the Southwest from Mexican to U.S. American. The Spanish-American war in 1898 would lead to the colonial/imperial connections between Puerto Rico, Cuba, and the United States. In the mid-twentieth century, the implementation of U.S. policies like Operation Boot Strap and the Bracero program, along with the Cuban Revolution, further impacted the sociocultural landscape of the United States. These political and historical dynamics have contributed to the predominance of particular national groups within selective geo-cultural spaces—namely, Mexican Americans in the Southwest, Puerto Ricans in New York, and Cubans in Miami.

25. This model has not changed over the years. In 2000, when the bureau added the category "Latino" to the questionnaire, it deployed the same model, requiring all other national groups to mark themselves as "Other."

26. Stavans, *Hispanic Condition*, 20.

27. See Flores, *Bomba to Hip-Hop*.

28. Perhaps another reason for the prominent location of certain national groups within this field of study is that before there was a paradigm of Latina/o studies, most scholarship was rooted in cultural nationalism, in the fields of Chicano studies and Puerto Rican studies, whose central focus was national and particular rather than comparative. Also, in

highlighting the tripartite model of Latinidad, I am not suggesting that all scholarship reproduces this configuration. Indeed, many works about Latina/os in the United States have begun to include U.S. Central American experiences, and most recently in 2013, the journal *Latino Studies* released a special issue on Central American–Americans. Moreover, in her essay "(Re)Constructing Latinidad," Frances Aparicio implores Latina/o scholars to examine interlatino relationships and complex Latino hybridities that challenge the field from merely engaging with distinct national groups.

29. Kellner, *Media Culture*, 2.

30. Beltrán, *Latina/o Stars*, 2.

31. Rodríguez, *Latin Looks*, 1.

32. Dávila, *Latinos Inc.*, 111.

33. The screenplay of *El Norte* was cowritten by Arturo Arias.

34. Bencastro, *Odyssey to the North*, 50, 51, 71.

35. Ramos, "Introduction," 3. It is notable that the title showcases the interconnections between a specific Salvadoran identity (Izote is the Salvadoran national flower) and a larger Central American collectivity, seen in the word *voz*, which references the *voseo*—a linguistic feature associated with Central American culture. Among the many objectives associated with the production of *Izote Voz* was not only to provide a discursive space to document the experiences of Salvadoran Americans but also to challenge the then "current canon of Latino identity politics."

36. Also see "Part-Time Salvi" (2000) by Raquel Gutierrez.

37. Roque Ramírez, "In Transnational Distance," 8.

38. Morales, "Always Say You're Mexican," 66.

39. Morales, 66.

40. Morales, 66.

41. Morales, 66.

42. Morales, 66.

43. Sánchez and Schlossberg, *Passing*, 5.

44. Aparicio, "Passing for Mexican." In a similar fashion, in her article "An Interdisciplinary Reading," Karina Oliva Alvarado argues that passing as Mexican might be the result of "contextual dominance" (383).

45. Bercovitch and Patell, *Cambridge History*, 561.

46. Morales, "Always Say You're Mexican," 66.

47. Morales, 66–67.

48. Morales, 67.

49. Chow, *Protestant Ethnic*, 107.

50. Morales, "Always Say You're Mexican," 67.

51. Morales, 67.

52. Rodríguez, *Latin Looks*, 1. Rodríguez describes this "look" as "slightly tan with dark hair and eyes." Similarly, in Milian, *Latining America*, 102, Milian claims, "Brownness has become a metaphoric mapping that profiles Latino and Latina migrants."

53. See Lima, *Latino Body* (2007).

54. In February 2007, Mencia was enjoying a type of cultural visibility rarely given to Latina/o performers. His *Mind of Mencia* (2005–2008; Comedy Central) comedic hybrid show, which was composed of sketches, skits, and stand-up, was averaging 2.1 million viewers, making it the highest-rated show on cable television for its time slot. Earlier that month, Bud Light had chosen him as their spokesperson when he starred in their Super Bowl commercial, and later that year, he would be featured in a minor role in a major motion picture film, *The Heartbreak Kid* (2007).

55. A year after the Youtube video "Joe Rogan vs. Carlos Mencia" (2007) went "viral," Mencia's cable television show was canceled, and according to Mencia, the backlash from the public and comedy community forced him to step away and reevaluate himself.

56. "Is Carlos Mencia Not Mexican?," Yahoo! Answers, accessed August 31, 2016, https://answers.yahoo.com/question/index?qid=20070314113003AAv49wg.

57. "Carlos Mencia Not Hispanic?," Snopes.com, accessed August 31, 2016, http://message.snopes.com/showthread.php?t=14172.

58. "TIL Carlos Mencia Is Not Mexican, and His First Name Is Ned," Reddit, accessed August 31, 2016, https://www.reddit.com/r/todayilearned/comments/14xtm2/til_carlos_mencia_is_not_mexican_and_his_first/.

59. Beebee, "Mariachi," 458.

60. Mencia, *Mind of Mencia*, episode 3, 2005.

61. Krefting, *All Joking Aside*, 4.

62. Mencia, *Mind of Mencia*, episode 2, 2007.

63. Mencia, "Carlos Mencia Jokes."

64. Mencia, interview by Conan O'Brien.

65. In 1954, the Eisenhower administration labeled their large-scale clampdown on illegal immigration "Operation Wetback."

66. Valdivia, *Latina/os in the Media*, 9.

67. Such exceptions include *I Love Lucy*, *Ugly Betty*, *Jane the Virgin*, and *Cristela*. It should be noted that out of these television shows, *I Love Lucy* and *Jane the Virgin* have a non–Mexican American lead.

68. Rogan, "Carlos Mencia."

69. Lopez, "George Lopez."

70. The film contains a scene where the Mexican American character Rudy (played by Cheech Marin) is hired to teach OTMs (Other than Mexicans) how to blend in to avoid being detected as outsiders in the United States. The film provides a quick and comedic solution: Rudy decides to teach these OTMs to "act" via bodily mannerisms, talk using linguistic idioms and intonations, and utilize material visual markers (like hair nets and bandanas) associated with Mexican American urban culture.

71. Muñoz, "Feeling Brown," 70.

72. Anonymous, "Carlos Mencia Is a Thief," weblog comment [no longer available] on carlosmencia.com, December 2, 2004, http://www.carlosmencia.com/forums/index.php?s=4d29521fa7614b45677e4022f8760ba7&act=Print&client=printer&f=2&t=95.html.

73. Anonymous, "Carlos Mencia Sucks," weblog comment [no longer available] on chucklemonkey.com, October 5, 2005, http://www.chucklemonkey.com/forums/printthread.php?t=26.html.

74. Anonymous, "Carlos Mencia," weblog comment on hedonistica.com, November 27, 2005, http://hedonistica.com/2005/09/carlos_mencia_i_locked_my_keys.php.

75. Anonymous, "Ned Holness Sucks Something Fierce," Amazon.com review, 2005, http://www.amazon.com/review/R3I2CY5EYA52ZX.

76. See Ogunnaike, "Sharpening Ethnic Barbs"; and Booth, "Mouth of Mencia."

77. Habell-Pallán and Romero, *Latino/a Popular Culture*, 2.

EPILOGUE

1. The unique status of Central American immigrants in the 1980s was marked by the ways in which the U.S. government failed to acknowledge many of these subjects, particularly

Salvadorans and Guatemalans, as "refugees," classifying them instead as economic immigrants. The U.S. government denied 97 percent of asylum applications. This led to the lawsuit and eventual settlement known as *American Baptist Churches v. Thornburgh,* where it was claimed that in the process of applying for asylum, Guatemalans and Salvadorans received discriminatory treatment from the Immigration and Naturalization Service (INS), the Executive Office for Immigration Review (EOIR), and the United States Department of State (DOS).

2. Solis, "Central American Migrants."

3. Solis, "Central American Migrants." Asylum numbers are from 2012 to 2014.

4. See Berastaín, "Sexual Assault."

5. Over the last decade, textual productions have increasingly turned The Beast into a symbol of Central American transmigrant experiences. Narrative/fiction films (Fukunaga 2009), and works of creative nonfiction (Martinez 2013; Nazario 2007) have all included the figure of The Beast in their accounts of Central American transmigration.

6. Basok et al., *Rethinking Transit Migration,* 37.

7. Solis, "Central American Migrants."

8. Basok et al., *Rethinking Transit Migration,* 37. The authors argue, "The techniques used by the US state to regulate non-citizens in the context of the United States biopolitics of citizenship have been externalized to Mexico."

9. Miller, "Mexico."

10. This would begin to change after 2014, when the Mexican government implemented a series of practices that included carrying out raids near the train tracks on which the *Bestia* travels, hiring private security to monitor the area, and constructing concrete barriers to prevent transmigrants from jumping on the train.

11. For an in-depth examination of the violence that Central American immigrants endured in Mexico, see Oscar Martínez, *The Beast* (2013).

12. Butler, *Precarious Life,* 34.

13. Mano Dura is the name given to policies enacted by nation-states in the Northern Triangle of Central America. These allow the formation of a highly militarized police force that engages in tactics that often violate the civic and human rights of Central American citizens in an effort to fight the "*mara /* gang problem."

14. It should be noted that in 2010, the state of Guatemala declared three Guatemalans whose bodies had been located in the mass grave of Tamaulipas, Mexico, as "national heroes." This has been the closest symbolic gesture to acknowledge transmigration violence.

15. Gordon, *Ghostly Matters,* 16.

16. Exec. Order 13767.

17. The realization that a minority, what the "Occupy movement" labeled as the "1%," dominates the rest of the population has done little to overturn the political system or mitigate the social and physical violence experienced by immigrants and racial, gendered, classed, and nonheteronormative subjects.

BIBLIOGRAPHY

"Acta de Independencia, 15 September 1821." In *Documentos de la unión centroamericana*, edited by Alberto Herrarte, 9–11. Guatemala: Editorial del Ministerio de Educación Pública, 1957.

"Acta de los Nublados." In *Fiesta patria centroamericana*, edited by Conny Villafranca, 12–13. Managua, Nicaragua: Editorial Hispamer, 2004.

"Acta de Union de las Provincias de Centro America al Imperio Mexicano." In *Documentos de la unión centroamericana*, edited by Alberto Herrarte, 13–15. Guatemala: Editorial del Ministerio de Educación Pública, 1957.

Acuña, Rodolfo. *Anything but Mexican: Chicanos in Contemporary Los Angeles*. London: Verso, 1996.

Alexander, David. *Natural Disasters*. New York: Routledge, 1993.

Allatson, Paul. *Key Terms in Latino/a Cultural and Literary Studies*. Malden: Blackwell, 2007.

Alonso, Ana Maria. "The Politics of Space, Time and Substance: State Formation, Nationalism and Ethnicity." *Annual Review of Anthropology* 23 (October 1994): 379–405.

Alpízar, Marvelia. "Plaza Morazán celebrará a los centroamericanos en LA." *La Opinión*, April 18, 2013. http://www.laopinion.com/2013/04/18/plaza-morazan-celebrara-a-los -centroamericanos-en-la/.

Alvarado, Karina O. "An Interdisciplinary Reading of Chicana/o and (US) Central American Cross-Cultural Narrations." *Latino Studies* 11, no. 3 (2013): 366–387.

Alvarez, Sonia E., Claudia de Lima Costa, Verónica Feliu, Rebecca J. Hester, Norma Klahn, Millie Thayer, and Cruz Caridad Bueno, eds. *Translocalities/Translocalidades: Feminist Politics of Translation in the Latin/a Americas*. Durham: Duke University Press, 2014.

American Baptist Churches v. Thornburgh. 760 F. Supp. 796 (N.D. Cal. 1991).

Anderson, Benedict. *Imagined Communities: Reflections on the Origin and Spread of Nationalism*. 2nd ed. New York: Verso, 2006.

Anderson, Mark. *Disaster Writing: The Cultural Politics of Catastrophe in Latin America*. Charlottesville: University of Virginia Press, 2011.

Anderson, Thomas. *Politics in Central America: Guatemala, El Salvador, Honduras, and Nicaragua*. New York: Praeger, 1982.

Anonymous. "Angelino Landscape." In *Flight to Freedom: The Story of Central American Refugees in California*, edited by Rossana Pérez and Henry A.J. Ramos, 80. Houston, Tex.: Arte Público Press, 2007.

Anzaldúa, Gloria. *Borderlands/La Frontera: The New Mestiza*. San Francisco: Spinsters/Aunt Lute, 1987.

Aparicio, Frances. "Passing for Mexican: Relational Identities in Latino Chicago." Paper presented at the Latina/o Studies Association Conference, "Deliberating Latina/o Studies: Promiscuity, Incivility, and (Un)Disciplinarity," Los Angeles, 2016.

———. "Reading the 'Latino' in Latino Studies: Towards Reimagining Our Academic Location." *Discourse* 21, no. 3 (1999): 3–18.

———. "(Re)Constructing Latinidad: The Challenge of Latina/o Studies." In *A Companion to Latina/o Studies*, edited by Juan Flores and Renato Rosaldo, 39–48. Malden: Blackwell Publishing, 2007.

Aparicio, Frances, and Susana Chávez-Silverman, eds. *Tropicalizations: Transcultural Representations of Latinidad*. Hanover, N.H.: University Press of New England, 1997.

Arias, Arturo. "Central American–Americans: Invisibility, Power and Representation in the US Latino World." *Latino Studies* 1, no. 1 (2003): 168–187.

———. "Central American–Americans? Re-mapping Latino/Latin American Subjectivities on Both Sides of the Great Divide." *Explicación de Textos Literarios* 28, no 1–2 (1999): 47–63.

Arias, Arturo, and Claudia Milian. "US Central Americans: Representations, Agency and Communities." Special issue, *Latino Studies* 11, no. 2 (2013): 131–266.

Arnaz, Desi, Jess Openheimer, and Jack Aldworth, prods. *I Love Lucy*. CBS Television Broadcasting Company (1951–1957).

Augenbraum, Harold, and Margarite Fernández Olmos, eds. *The Latino Reader: An American Literary Tradition from 1542 to the Present*. Boston: Houghton Mifflin, 1997.

Banet-Weiser, Sarah, *The Most Beautiful Girl in the World: Beauty Pageants and National Identity*. Berkeley: University of California Press, 1999.

Basch, Linda, Nina Glick Schiller, and Cristina Szanton Blanc. *Nations Unbound: Transnational Projects, Postcolonial Predicaments and Deterritorialized Nation-States*. London: Routledge, 1994.

Basok, Tanya, Danièle Bélanger, Martha Luz Rojas Wiesner, and Guillermo Candiz. *Rethinking Transit Migration: Precarity, Mobility, and Self-Making in Mexico*. New York: Palgrave Macmillan, 2015.

Bazant, Jan. "From Independence to the Liberal Republic, 1821–1867." In *Mexico since Independence*, edited by Leslie Bethell, 1–48. Cambridge: Cambridge University Press, 1991.

Beebee, Thomas. "Mariachi." In *Latin Music: Musicians, Genres and Themes*, edited by Ilan Stavans, 459–468. Santa Barbara, Calif.: Greenwood, 2014.

Bell, James. *A System of Geography, Popular and Scientific: Or a Physical, and Statistical Account of the World and Its Various Divisions*. Glasgow: Archibald Fullerton, 1832.

Beltrán, Mary. *Latina/o Stars in U.S. Eyes: The Making and Meanings of Film and TV Stardom*. Urbana: University of Illinois Press, 2009.

Bencastro, Mario. *Odyssey to the North*. Translated by Susan Giersbach Rascón. Houston, Tex.: Arte Público Press, 1998.

Bennett, Herman. *Africans in Colonial Mexico: Absolutism, Christianity and Afro-Creole Consciousness 1570–1640*. Bloomington: Indiana University Press, 2003.

Berastaín, Pierre. "Sexual Assault: From Central America to the Halls of Family Detention Centers." *Huffington Post*, June 26, 2015. http://www.huffingtonpost.com/pierre-r-berastain/sexual-assault-from-centr_b_7670780.html.

Bercovitch, Sacvan, and Cyrus R. K. Patell, eds. *The Cambridge History of American Literature*. Cambridge: Cambridge University Press, 1999.

Berlant, Lauren. *The Anatomy of National Fantasy: Hawthorne, Utopia, and Everyday Life*. Chicago: University of Chicago Press, 1991.

Bethell, Leslie. *Central America since Independence*. New York: Cambridge University Press, 1991.

Bettie, Julie. *Women without Class: Girls, Race and Identity*. Oakland: University of California Press, 2014.

Bhabha, Homi. "DissemiNation: Time, Narrative and the Margins of the Modern Nation." In *Nation and Narration*, edited by Homi Bhabha, 291–322. New York: Routledge, 2000.

———. "Narrating the Nation." In *Nation and Narration*, edited by Hommi Bhabha, 1–7. New York: Routledge, 2000.

Billig, Michael. *Banal Nationalism*. London: Sage, 1995.

Boland, Roy. *Culture and Customs of El Salvador*. Westport, Conn.: Greenwood, 2001.

Booth, John A., Christine J. Wade, and Thomas W. Walker. *Understanding Central America*. Oxford: Westview Press, 1989.

Booth, William. "The Mouth of Mencia." *Washington Post*, September 28, 2005. http://www .washingtonpost.com/wp-dyn/content/article/2005/09/27/AR2005092701875.html.

Briceño de Zúniga, Alma Nubia, and Hernán Zúniga Reyes. *Símbolos patrios centroamericanos: historia y decretos*. Tegucigalpa: Imprimatur, 2003.

Brickell, Katherine, and Ayona Datta, eds. *Translocal Geographies: Spaces, Places and Connections*. London: Routledge, 2016.

Brignoli-Perez, Hector. *A Brief History of Central America*. Translated by Ricardo B. Sawrey and Susana Stettri de Sawrey. Berkeley: University of California Press, 1989.

Buchenau, Jürgen. *In the Shadow of the Giant: The Making of Mexico's Central America Policy 1876–1930*. Tuscaloosa: University of Alabama Press, 1996.

Bulu, Antonio J. "Discursos Inéditos." In *Homenaje de Colombia al libertador Simon Bolívar en su primer centenario*, edited by Manuel Ezequiel Corrales, 162–163. Bogota: Imprenta de Medardo Rivas, 1884.

Burke, Peter. "History as Social Memory." In *The Collective Memory Reader*, edited by Jeffrey Olick, Vered Vinitzky-Seroussi, and Daniel Levy, 188–192. New York: Oxford University Press, 2011.

Butler, Judith. *Bodies That Matter: On the Discursive Limits of "Sex."* New York: Routledge, 1993.

———. *Gender Trouble: Feminism and the Subversion of Identity*. New York: Routledge, 1990.

———. *Precarious Life: The Powers of Mourning and Violence*. London: Verso, 2006.

Cadaval, Olivia. *Creating a Latino Identity in the Nation's Capital: The Latino Festival*. New York: Garland, 1998.

Calhoun, Craig. *Nationalism*. Minneapolis: University of Minnesota Press, 1997.

Camacho, Juan Rafael Quesada. *Historia de la historiografía costarricense, 1821–1940*. Vol. 9. San José: Editorial de la Universidad de Costa Rica, 2003.

Cardenal, Rodolfo. *Manual de historia de Centroamérica*. San Salvador: Talleres Gráficos UCA, 1996.

Carmack, Robert M. *Harvest of Violence: The Maya Indians and the Guatemalan Crisis*. Oklahoma City: University of Oklahoma Press, 1988.

Carpio Nicolle, Roberto. *Pensamiento y acción*. 2nd ed., vol. 1. Guatemala: Ediciones Internacionales, 1998.

Casaús Arzú, Marta, and Teresa García Giráldez. *Las redes intelectuales centroaméricanas: un siglo de imaginarios nacionales*. Guatemala: F&G Editors, 2005.

Castilla, José María. *Voto particular del ciudadano José María Castilla, diputado á la Asamblea Constituyente de las Provincias Unidas del Centro de América por el partido de Verapaz, dado en la misma asamblea con ocasión de discutirse las bases para la constitución de dichas provincias*. Guatemala: Beteta, 1823.

Castro, Rodolfo Barón. *La población de El Salvador*. Madrid: Instituto Gonzalo Fernández de Oviedo, 1942. Central America (Federal Republic, 1823–1840). *Proyecto de bases constitucionales para las Provincias Unidas del Centro de América*. Guatemala: Beteta, 1824.

"Centroamérica comienza conmemoración de su independencia." *Prensa Libre*. September 1, 2016. http://www.prensalibre.com/internacional/honduras-comienza-fiestas -conmemorativas-de-195-aos-de-independencia-de-espaa.

Cepeda, María Elena. *Musical ImagiNation: U.S.-Colombian Identity and the Latin Music Boom.* New York: New York University Press, 2010.

Chambers, Veronica. "Secret Latina at Large." In *U.S. Latino Literature Today*, edited by Gabriela Baeza Ventura, 38–43. New York: Pearson, 2005.

Chekola, Mark, and Nancy Arden McHugh. "The Ontological Foundations of Passing." In *Passing/Out: Sexual Identity Veiled and Revealed*, edited by Dennis R. Cooley and Kelby Harrison, 13–40. Surrey: Ashgate, 2012.

Chinchilla, Maya. *The Cha Cha Files: A Chapina Poética*. San Francisco: Kórima Press, 2014.

———. "Welcome to Epicentroamerica: An Anthology." *Welcome to EpiCentroAmerica* (blog), 2010. http://epicentroamerica.blogspot.com/.

Chow, Rey. *The Protestant Ethnic and the Spirit of Capitalism*. New York: Columbia University Press, 2002.

City of Los Angeles Board of Recreation and Park Commissioners. "Valencia Triangle Conceptual Approval for the Creation of the Francisco Morazán Central Community Square and Placement of a Map and Bust." July 13, 2011. https://www.laparks.org/sites/default/files/pdf/commissioner/2011/jul13/spPack1.pdf.

City of Los Angeles Office of the City Clerk. "Application to Name or Rename Communities." May 7, 2007. http://clkrep.lacity.org/onlinedocs/2007/07-1971_app_6-18-07.pdf.

Coates, Anthony G. *Central America: A Natural and Cultural History*. New Haven: Yale University Press, 1997.

"COFECA Carnaval y Desfile por Independencia." *Día a Día*. September 13, 2013. https://issuu.com/diaadianews/docs/1209/17.

Cofeca Desfile Centroamericano. "COFECA: Entrevista a la reina de Belize Cofeca, 2014, Desfile Centroamericano." YouTube video, July 21, 2016. https://www.youtube.com/watch?v=_y6VIAGUnpw.

———. "COFECA: Nestor Méndez, Embajador de Belize en el Desfile Centroamericano 2012." YouTube video, July 21, 2016. https://www.youtube.com/watch?v=vVd34wzLn-0.

Cole, John Peter. *Geography of the World's Major Regions*. New York: Routledge, 1996.

Confederación Centro Americana. *Central American Independence Festival & Parade Corporate Sponsorship Package*. Los Angeles, CA: Community Consulting Services, 2009. Accessed May 11, 2015. http://wilfredolinks.com/DOC/COFECA2009.pdf.

———. "Quienes somos." Accessed April 16, 2016. http://www.cofeca.org/quienos-somos.html.

"Constitución de la República Federal de Centroamérica, dada por la Asamblea Nacional Constituyente en 22 de noviembre de 1824." In *Documentos de la unión centroamericana*, edited by Alberto Herrarte, 29–58. Guatemala: Editorial del Ministerio de Educación Pública, 1957.

Coutin, Susan Bibler. *Legalizing Moves: Salvadoran Immigrants' Struggle for U.S. Residency*. Ann Arbor: University of Michigan Press, 2003.

Cruz, Consuelo. *Political Culture and Institutional Development in Costa Rica and Nicaragua*. New York: Cambridge University Press, 2005.

DailyMotion. "Walter Duran Consul de El Salvador en Los Angeles." January 28, 2015. http://www.dailymotion.com/video/x2zis2u.

Dardón, Andres. *La cuestión de límites entre México y Guatemala*. Mexico: Imprenta de Ignacio Escalante, 1875.

Dávila, Arlene. *Latinos, Inc.: The Marketing and Making of a People*. Berkeley: University of California Press, 2001.

"Decreto lejislativo separandose Nicaragua de la Federacion de Centro-America, 30 abril 1838." In *Símbolos patrios centroamericanos: historia y decretos*, edited by Alma Nubia Briceño de Zúniga and Hernán Zúniga Reyes, 194. Tegucigalpa: Imprimatur, 2003.

"Decreto sobre la abolición de la esclavitud, de 17 de Abril de 1824." In *Las constituciones de la República Federal de Centroamérica*, edited by Ricardo Gallardo, 691–694. Madrid: Instituto de Estudios Políticos, 1958.

"Decreto sobre la ereccíon de la República de El Salvador, 18 febrero 1859." In *Símbolos patrios centroamericanos: historia y decretos*, edited by Alma Nubia Briceño de Zúniga and Hernán Zúniga Reyes, 94. Tegucigalpa: Imprimatur, 2003.

De Genova, Nicholas., and Ana Y. Ramos-Zayas. *Latino Crossings: Mexicans, Puerto Ricans, and the Politics of Race and Citizenship*. New York: Routledge, 2003.

Delgado, José Matías. "Carta al General Filisola." In *Nuestra patria centroamericana*, 72–75. San Salvador: Secretaría de Información y Relaciones Públicas de Casa Presidencial, 1968.

Delgado, Richard, and Jean Stefancic, eds. *The Latino/a Condition: A Critical Reader*. New York: New York University Press, 1998.

Del Valle, José Cecilio. "Confederación Americana." In *Obra escogida*, 237. Caracas: Biblioteca Ayacucho, 1982.

Derrida, Jacques. *Margins of Philosophy*. Chicago: University of Chicago Press, 1982.

———. *Positions*. Chicago: University of Chicago Press, 1981.

Dikshit, R. D., and Das Animesh. *Geographical Thought: A Contextual History of Ideas*. Delhi: Prentice Hall India, 2004.

Disturnell, John. *Influence of Climate in North and South America*. New York: D. Van Norstrand Press, 1867.

Domino, D. "Republic of Central America." In *North American Review*, vol. 26, translated by J. Baily, 127–145. Boston: Hilliard Metcalf, 1828.

Dunkerley, James. *Power in the Isthmus: A Political History of Modern Central America*. New York: Verso, 1989.

Durham, William H. *Scarcity and Survival in Central America: Ecological Origins of the Soccer War*. Stanford: Stanford University Press, 1979.

Dym, Jordana. *From Sovereign Villages to National States: City, State, and Federation in Central America, 1759–1839*. Albuquerque: University of New Mexico Press, 2006.

"El Decreto de Independencia Absoluta de las Provincias del Centro de América." In *Documentos de la unión centroamericana*, edited by Alberto Herrarte, 17–20. Guatemala: Editorial del Ministerio de Educación Pública, 1957.

Embassy of Costa Rica. "Cultura: Símbolos Nacionales." Embajada de Costa Rica. Accessed February 7, 2018. http://www.costarica-embassy.org/index.php?q=node/30.

England, Sarah. *Afro Central Americans in New York City: Garifuna Tales of Transnational Movement in Racialized Space*. Gainesville: University Press of Florida, 2006.

Estrada, Alicia Ivonne. "(Re)Claiming Public Space and Place: Maya Community in Westlake/MacArthur Park." In *U.S. Central Americans Reconstructing Memories, Struggles, and Communities of Resistance*, edited by Karina O. Alvarado, Alicia Ivonne Estrada, and Ester E. Hernández, 166–187. Tucson: University of Arizona Press, 2017.

Exec. Order 13767, 82 Fed. Reg. 8793 (Jan. 25, 2017).

Fahnestock, Jeanne. *Rhetorical Style: The Uses of Language in Persuasion*. New York: Oxford University Press, 2011.

Falconi, José Luis, and José Antonio Mazzotti, eds. *The Other Latinos: Central and South Americans in the United States*. Cambridge: Harvard University Press, 2007.

"¡Felices 195 años de independencia patria!" *El Heraldo.* September 9, 2016. http://www
.elheraldo.hn/pais/1000083-466/felices-195-a%C3%B1os-de-independencia-patria.

Fernandez de Castro, Rafa. "Meet the Muxes: How a Remote Town in Southern Mexico Rein-
vented Sex and Gender." Fusion. Accessed August 16, 2016. http://interactive.fusion.net/
meet-the-muxes/.

Ferro, Carlos. *Las banderas centroamericans: su inspiración en el pabellón argentine.* San José:
Editorial Centroamericana, 1970.

Filisola, Vicente. "Letter to Manuel José Arce, January 1823." In *La iglesia y la independencia
política de Centro América: el caso de el estado de El Salvador 1808–1833,* by Luis Ernesto
Ayala Benítez, 151–152. Rome: Gregorian University Press, 2007.

Firmat, Gustavo Pérez. *Life on the Hyphen: The Cuban-American Way.* Austin: University of
Texas Press, 1994.

Fischer, Sibylle. *Modernity Disavowed: Haiti and the Cultures of Slavery in the Age of Revolution.*
Durham: Duke University Press, 2004.

Flores, Juan. *From Bomba to Hip-Hop: Puerto Rican Culture and Latino Identity.* New York:
Columbia University Press, 2000.

Flores, William Vincent, and Rina Benmayor, eds. *Latino Cultural Citizenship: Claiming Identity, Space, and Rights.* Boston: Beacon Press, 1997.

Fonseca, Elizabeth. *Centroamérica: su historia.* San José, Costa Rica: FLACSO, 1998.

Foster, Lynn. *A Brief History of Central America.* New York: Facts on File Press, 2007.

Foucault, Michel. *The History of Sexuality.* New York: Pantheon Books, 1978.

———. "Of Other Spaces." *Diacritics* 16, no. 1 (1986): 22–27.

———. *Power/Knowledge: Selected Interviews and Other Writings, 1972–1977.* New York: Pantheon Books, 1980.

Freinkel, Lisa. "Catachresis." In *The Princeton Encyclopedia of Poetry and Poetics,* edited by
Roland Greene, Stephen Cushman, Clare Cavanagh, Jahan Ramazani, Paul F. Rouzer,
Harris Feinsod, David Marno, and Alexandra Slessarev, 209–211. Princeton: Princeton
University Press, 2012.

Friends of Pico-Union. "Documentation in Opposition to the Renaming of the Pico Union/
Westlake/MacArthur Park Communities." Office of the City Clerk of Los Angeles.
November 9, 2007. http://clkrep.lacity.org/onlinedocs/2007/07-1971_misc_11-09-07
.pdf.

Fukunaga, Cary Joji, dir. *Sin Nombre.* 2009; Madrid, Universal Studios. DVD.

Gaínza, Gabino. *Bando del 17 de Septiembre de 1,821.* Orgullo Guatemalteco. August 5, 2013.
http://orgulloguatemalteco.blogspot.com/2013/08/bando-del-17-de-septiembre-de
-1821.html.

———. "Letter to Augustin de Iturbide." 1821. Quoted in *History of Central America, Vol. III,
1801–1887,* by Hubert Howe Bancroft, 42–59. San Francisco: History Company, 1887.

Gallardo, Ricardo. *Las constituciones de la República Federal de Centroamérica.* Vol. 10. Madrid:
Instituto de Estudios Políticos, 1958.

García, Lorena, and Mérida Rúa. "Processing Latinidad: Mapping Latino Urban Landscapes
through Chicago Ethnic Festivals." *Latino Studies* 5 (2007): 317–339.

García, María Cristina. "Canada: A Northern Refuge for Central Americans." Migration Policy Institute. April 1, 2006. https://www.migrationpolicy.org/article/canada-northern
-refuge-central-americans.

———. *Seeking Refuge: Central American Migration to Mexico, the United States, and Canada.*
Berkeley: University of California Press, 2006.

García-Peña, Lorgia. *The Borders of Dominicanidad: Race, Nation and Archives of Contradiction.* Durham: Duke University Press, 2016.

Gillis, John. *Commemorations: The Politics of National Identity.* Princeton: Princeton University Press, 1994.

Gilroy, Paul. *The Black Atlantic: Modernity and Double Consciousness.* Cambridge: Harvard University Press, 1995.

Ginsberg, Elaine K. *Passing and the Fictions of Identity.* Durham: Duke University Press, 1996.

Gordon, Avery. *Ghostly Matters: Haunting and the Sociological Imagination.* Minneapolis: University of Minnesota Press, 1997.

Gordon, Edmund T. *Disparate Diasporas: Identity and Politics in an African Nicaraguan Community.* Austin: University of Texas Press, 1998.

Gruson, Lindsey. "Political Violence on the Rise Again in Guatemala, Tarnishing Civilian Rule." *New York Times*, June 28, 1990.

Gudmundson, Lowell. "What Difference Did Color Make?" In *Blacks and Blackness in Central America: Between Race and Place*, edited by Lowell Gudmundson and Justin Wolfe, 209–245. Durham: Duke University Press, 2010.

Gudmundson, Lowell, and Justin Wolfe, eds. *Blacks and Blackness in Central America between Race and Place.* Durham: Duke University Press, 2010.

Gutierrez, Raquel. "Part-Time Salvi." In *Izote Voz: A Collection of Salvadoran American Writing and Visual Art*, edited by Katherine Cowy Kim, 28–29. San Francisco: Pacific News Service, 2000.

Guzik, Keith. *Making Things Stick: Surveillance Technologies and Mexico's War on Crime.* Oakland: University of California Press, 2016.

Habell-Pallán, Michelle, and Mary Romero, eds. *Latino/a Popular Culture.* New York: New York University Press, 2002.

Hall, Donald E. *Queer Theories.* New York: Palgrave Macmillan, 2003.

Hall, Stuart. "Who Needs 'Identity'?" In *Questions of Cultural Identity*, edited by Stuart Hall and Paul Du Gay, 1–17. London: Sage, 1996.

Halperin, David. *Saint Foucault: Towards a Gay Hagiography.* New York: Oxford University Press, 1995.

Halter, Marilyn, and Violet Showers Johnson. *African and American: West Africans in Post-civil Rights America.* New York: New York University Press, 2014.

Hames-García, Michael. *Identity Complex: Making the Case for Multiplicity.* Minneapolis: University of Minnesota Press, 2011.

Hamilton, Nora, and Norma Stoltz Chinchilla. "Identity Formation among Central American Americans." USC Dornlife Center for the Study of Immigrant Integration. November 2013. http://dornsife.usc.edu/assets/sites/731/docs/identity_central_american_americans_web.pdf.

———. *Seeking Community in a Global City: Guatemalans and Salvadorans in Los Angeles.* Philadelphia: Temple University Press, 2001.

Harrison, Kelby. *Sexual Deceit: The Ethics of Passing.* Lanham, Md.: Lexington Books, 2013.

Henry, O. *Cabbages and Kings.* Garden City: Doubleday, Page & Company, 1904.

Hernández, Alfonso. "Centroamericanos Conmemoraran Independencia en la Ciudad de Boston. Invitan al Presidente del PARLACEN." *Parlamento Centroamericano.* December 9, 2013. http://www.parlacen.int/Prensa/Prensa/tabid/145/EntryId/698/Centroamericanos-conmemoraran-independencia-en-la-ciudad-de-Boston-Invitan-al-presidente-del-PARLACEN.aspx.

Hernández, Silva Margarita. "El nombre de Centroamérica y la invención de la identidad regional." Paper presented at the Coloquio Internacional, "Creando la nación," Mexico, June 28–30, 2006. http://shial.colmex.mx/textos/MargaritaSilva.pdf.

Herrarte, Alberto. "Introducción." In *Documentos de la unión centroamericana*, edited by Alberto Herrarte, 7–8. Guatemala: Editorial del Ministerio de Educación Pública, 1957.

Hintzen, Percy C., and Jean Muteba Rahier, eds. *Problematizing Blackness: Self-Ethnographies by Black Immigrants to the United States.* New York: Routledge, 2003.

Ho, Jennifer Ann. *Racial Ambiguity in Asian American Culture.* New Brunswick: Rutgers University Press, 2015.

Hobsbawm, Eric, and T. O. Ranger. *The Invention of Tradition.* Cambridge: Cambridge University Press, 1983.

Homer-Dixon, Thomas F. *Environment, Scarcity, and Violence.* Princeton: Princeton University Press, 1999.

Hooker, Juliet. "Race and the Space of Citizenship: The Mosquito Coast and the Place of Blackness and Indigeneity in Nicaragua." In *Blacks and Blackness in Central America: Between Race and Place*, edited by Lowell Gudmundson and Justin Wolfe, 246–277. Durham: Duke University Press, 2010.

Hoy, Vielka Cecilia. "Negotiating among Invisibilities: Tales of Afro-Latinidades in the United States." In *The Afro-Latin@ Reader: History and Culture in the United States*, edited by Mirian Jimenez Roman, 426–430. Durham: Duke University Press, 2010.

Humboldt, Alexander von. "Sobre la situación actual de la República de Centroamérica o Guatemala." *Anuario de estudios centroamericanos* 1 (1974): 9–32.

Iturbide, Agustin de. "Letter to Gabino Gaínza." October 19, 1821. In *Nuestra patria centroamericana*, 131–132. San Salvador: Secretaría de Información y Relaciones Públicas de Casa Presidencial, 1968.

Jimenez, Alexander, and Victor Acuña. "La improbable nación de Centroamérica." *Biblioteca Valenciana.* Accessed July 12, 2008. http:/bv.gva.es/documenos/Jimenez.doc.

Kaplan, Caren. "The Politics of Location as Transnational Feminist Critical Practice." In *Scattered Hegemonies: Postmodernity and Transnational Feminist Practices*, edited by Inderpal Grewal and Caren Kaplan, 137–152. Minneapolis: University of Minnesota Press, 2002.

Kaplan, Carla. "Identity." In *Keywords for American Cultural Studies*, edited by Bruce Burgett and Glenn Hendler, 123–126. New York: New York University Press, 2007.

Karnes, Thomas. *The Failure of Union: Central America, 1824–1960.* Chapel Hill: University of North Carolina Press, 1961.

Kellner, Douglas. *Media Culture: Cultural Studies, Identity, and Politics between the Modern and the Postmodern.* New York: Routledge, 1995.

Komisaruk, Catherine. "Becoming Free, Becoming Ladino: Slave Emancipation and Mestizaje in Colonial Guatemala." In *Blacks and Blackness in Central America: Between Race and Place*, edited by Lowell Gudmundson and Justin Wolfe, 150–176. Durham: Duke University Press, 2010.

Krefting, Rebecca, *All Joking Aside: American Humor and its Discontents.* Baltimore: Johns Hopkins University Press, 2014.

LaFeber, Walter. *Inevitable Revolutions: The United States in Central America.* New York: W. W. Norton, 1993.

Laó-Montes, Agustin. "Afro-Latinidades Bridging Blackness in Latinidad." In *Technofutures: Critical Interventions in Latina/o Studies*, edited by Nancy Raquel Mirabal and Agustin Laó-Montes, 117–140. Lanham, Md.: Lexington Books, 2007.

———. "Mambo Montage: The Latinization of New York City." In *Mambo Montage: The Latinization of New York City*, edited by Agustin Laó-Montes and Arlene Dávila, 1–54. New York: Columbia University Press, 2001.

Lázaro, Luis Armando. "Las diversas visiones sobre la región." In *Estado de la región: un informe desde Centroamérica y para Centroamérica*, edited by Miguel Gutiérrez Saxe and Jorge Vargas Cullell, 63–75. San José: Editorama S. A., 1999.

Lesser, Gabriel, and Jeanne Batalova. "Central American Immigrants in the United States." Migration Policy Institute, April 5, 2017. https://www.migrationpolicy.org/article/central-american-immigrants-united-states.

Lima, Lázaro. *The Latino Body: Crisis Identities in American Literary and Cultural Memory*. New York: New York University Press, 2007.

Lopez, George. "George Lopez on Howard Stern Show." KROCK, September 26, 2005. Radio.

Lorde, Audre. *Sister Outsider: Essays and Speeches*. New York: Crossing Press, 1984.

Lyotard, Jean-François. *The Postmodern Condition: A Report on Knowledge*. Minneapolis: University of Minnesota Press, 1984.

Marin, Cheech, dir. *Born in East LA*. 1987; Clear Type.

Martínez, Oscar. *The Beast: Riding the Rails and Dodging Narcos on the Migrant Trail*. London: Verso, 2013.

Martinez, Rafael. "Himno a Centro America." In *El lector centroamericano*, edited by Victor Recalde and Carmen Huembes de Recalde, 13–15. Managua: Editorial Recalde, 1900.

McClintock, Anne. "Family Feuds: Gender, Nationalism and the Family." *Feminist Review* 44 (1993): 61–80.

McInnes, Christopher. "Guatemala Remittances January 2017." Focus Economics, January 2017. https://www.focus-economics.com/countries/guatemala/news/remittances/growth-in-remittances-gains-momentum-in-january.

McQueen, Paddy. *Subjectivity, Gender and the Struggle for Recognition*. New York: Palgrave Macmillan, 2015.

McWhorter, Ladelle. "Practicing Practicing." In *Feminism and the Final Foucault*, edited by Diana Taylor and Karen Vintges, 143–162. Urbana: University of Illinois Press, 2004.

Medina, Laurie. *Negotiating Economic Development: Identity Formation and Collective Action in Belize*. Tucson: University of Arizona Press, 2004.

Megill, Allan. "History, Memory, Identity." In *The Collective Memory Reader*, edited by Jeffrey Olick, Vered Vinitzky-Seroussi, and Daniel Levy, 193–197. New York: Oxford University Press, 2011.

Meléndez Obando, Mauricio. "The Slow Ascent of the Marginalized." In *Blacks and Blackness in Central America*, edited by Lowell Gudmundson and Justin Wolfe, 344–352. Durham: Duke University Press, 2010.

Mencia, Carlos. "Carlos Mencia Jokes | Comedy Central Stand-Up | Carlos Mencia: Mexican in the Southwest." Comedy Central. Accessed September 3, 2016. http://www.cc.com/jokes/37bslu/stand-up-carlos-mencia-carlos-mencia-mexican-in-the-southwest.

———. Interview by Conan O' Brien, *Late Night with Conan O'Brien*, NBC, July 13, 2006.

———, prod. *The Mind of Mencia*. 2005; Comedy Central.

———, prod. *The Mind of Mencia*. 2007; Comedy Central.

Menjívar, Cecilia. *Fragmented Ties: Salvadoran Immigrant Networks in America*. Berkeley: University of California Press, 2000.

Menjívar, Cecilia, and Néstor Rodríguez. *When States Kill: Latin America, the U.S., and Technologies of Terror*. Austin: University of Texas Press, 2005.

Mignolo, Walter. *The Idea of Latin America*. Oxford: Blackwell, 2005.

Milian, Claudia. *Latining America: Black-Brown Passages and the Coloring of Latino/a Studies*. Athens: University of Georgia Press, 2013.

Militz, Elizabeth, and Carolin Schurr. "Affective Nationalism: Banalities of Belonging in Azerbaijan." *Political Geography* 54 (2016): 54–63.

Miller, Todd. "Mexico: The US Border Patrol's Newest Hire." *Aljazeera America*. October 4, 2014. http://america.aljazeera.com/opinions/2014/10/mexico-us-borderpatrolsecurity immigrants.html.

Minority Rights Group International. "Afro-Panamanians." Minority Rights Group International. December 2008. http://minorityrights.org/minorities/afro-panamanians/.

Mirandé, Alfredo. "Hombres Mujeres: An Indigenous Third Gender." *Men and Masculinities* 19, no. 4 (2016): 384–409.

Molina, Pedro. *Documentos relacionados con la historia de Centro-America año 1822*. Guatemala: La República de Guatemala, 1896.

Montejo, Victor. *Voices from Exile: Violence and Survival in Modern Maya History*. Oklahoma City: University of Oklahoma Press, 1999.

Montúfar, Manuel. *Memorias para la historia de la revolución de Centro-América*. Jalapa: Aburto y Blanco, 1832.

Moraga, Cherríe. *Loving in the War Years: Lo Que Nunca Pasó por Sus Labios*. Boston: South End Press, 1983.

Morales, Marlon. "Always Say You're Mexican." Edited by Alfonso Serrano. In *Izote Voz: A Collection of Salvadoran American Writing and Visual Art*, edited by Katherine Cowy Kim, 66–67. San Francisco: Pacific News Service, 2000.

Mundy, Barbara. "Mesoamerican Cartography." In *The History of Cartography Volume Two Book Three*, edited by David Woodward and G. Malcolm Lewis, 183–256. Chicago: University of Chicago Press, 1998.

Muñoz, José Esteban. *Disidentifications: Queers of Color and the Performance of Politics*. Minneapolis: University of Minnesota Press, 1999.

———. "Feeling Brown: Ethnicity and Affect in Ricardo Bracho's 'The Sweetest Hangover (and Other STDs)." *Theatre Journal* 52, no. 1 (2000): 67–79.

Nabarz, Payam. *The Mysteries of Mithras: The Pagan Belief That Shaped the Christian World*. Rochester, Vt.: Inner Traditions, 2005.

Nagel, Joane. "Constructing Ethnicity: Creating and Recreating Ethnic Identity and Culture." *Social Problems* 41, no. 1 (1994): 152–176. doi:10.1525/sp.1994.41.1.03x0430n.

Nava, Gregory, dir. *El Norte*. 1983; American Playhouse.

Navarrete, Sorbelio. *La verdadera fecha de nuestra independencia 15 de septiembre de 1821*. San Salvador: Talleres Tipográficos del Ministerio de Educación, 1930.

Nazario, Sonia. *Enrique's Journey*. New York: Random House, 2007.

Oboler, Suzanne. *Ethnic Labels, Latino Lives: Identity and the Politics of (Re)presentation in the United States*. Minneapolis: University of Minnesota Press, 1995.

Ochoa, Marcia. *Queen for a Day: Transformistas, Beauty Queens, and the Performance of Femininity in Venezuela*. Durham: Duke University Press, 2014.

Ogunnaike, Lola. "Sharpening Ethnic Barbs and Hoping for a Hit." *New York Times*, July 6, 2005. http://www.nytimes.com/2005/07/06/arts/television/sharpening-ethnic-barbs -and-hoping-for-a-hit.html?_r=0.

"Orden de la Asamblea Nacional Constituyente, de 4 de Agosto de 1823." In *Las constituciones de la República Federal de Centroamérica*, edited by Ricardo Gallardo, 683. Madrid: Instituto de Estudios Políticos, 1958.

Padilla, Felix M. *Latino Ethnic Consciousness: The Case of Mexican Americans and Puerto Ricans in Chicago*. Notre Dame: University of Notre Dame Press, 1985.

Padilla, Yajaira M. "The Central American Transnational Imaginary: Defining the Transnational and Gendered Contours of Central American Immigrant Experience." *Latino Studies* 11, no. 2 (2013): 150–166.

———. *Changing Women, Changing Nation: Female Agency, Nationhood, and Identity in Trans-Salvadoran Narratives*. New York: SUNY Press, 2012.

Pastor, Rodolfo. *Historia de Centroamérica*. Ciudad de México: Colegio de México, 1988.

Patch, Robert. *Indians and the Political Economy of Colonial Central America, 1670–1810*. Norman: University of Oklahoma Press, 2013.

Pearcy, Thomas. *The History of Central America*. Westport, Conn.: Greenwood Press, 2006.

"Pepe Palacios, LGBT Activist in Honduras, Talks about Crimes against the Community." *Queer Voice* (blog). *Huffpost*, February 19, 2003, updated February 2, 2016. https://www.huffingtonpost.com/2013/02/19/honduras-lgbt-violence-pepe-palacios_n_2672205.html.

Pérez, Rossana, and Henry A. J. Ramos, eds. *Flight to Freedom: The Story of Central American Refugees in California*. Houston, Tex.: Arte Público Press, 2006.

Portillo, Noé Pineda. *Identidad y apodos colectivos en Centroamérica: por qué chapines? Por qué guanacos? Por qué catrachos? Por qué nicas? Por qué ticos?* Tegucigalpa: Impresión Offset, 2008.

Portillo Villeda, Suyapa. "Respect! The Hemispheric Fight for Trans and Queer People of Color." *Latino Rebels*, July 11, 2015. http://www.latinorebels.com/2015/07/11/respect-the-hemispheric-fight-for-trans-and-queer-people-of-color/.

Putnam, Lara. "Eventually Alien: The Multigenerational Saga of British West Indians in Central America, 1870–1940." In *Blacks and Blackness in Central America: Between Race and Place*, edited by Lowell Gudmundson and Justin Wolfe, 278–306. Durham: Duke University Press, 2010.

Radstone, Susannah, and Katharine Hodgkin, eds. *Memory Cultures: Memory, Subjectivity and Recognition*. New York: Routledge, 2009.

Ramos, Leda. "Introduction." In *Izote Voz: A Collection of Salvadoran American Writing and Visual Art*, edited by Katherine Cowy Kim, 2–3. San Francisco: Pacific News Service, 2000.

Repak, Terry A. "Labor Recruitment and the Lure of The Capital: Central American Migrants in Washington, DC." In *Global Dimensions of Gender and Carework*, edited by Mary Zimmerman, Jacquelyn Litt, and Christine Bose, 65–74. Palo Alto: Stanford University Press, 2006.

———. *Waiting on Washington: Central American Workers in the Nation's Capital*. Philadelphia: Temple University Press, 1995.

Rich, Adrienne. *Blood Bread and Poetry: Selected Prose 1979–1985*. New York: Norton, 1986.

Rivas, Cecilia. *Salvadoran Imaginaries: Mediated Identities and Cultures of Consumption*. New Brunswick: Rutgers University Press, 2014.

Roach, Joseph R. *Cities of the Dead: Circum-Atlantic Performance*. New York: Columbia University Press, 1996.

Rodríguez, Ana Patricia. "'Departamento 15': Cultural Narratives of Salvadoran Transnational Migration." *Latino Studies* 3, no. 1 (April 2005): 21.

———. *Dividing the Isthmus: Central American Transnational Histories Literatures, and Cultures*. Austin: University of Texas Press, 2009.

Rodríguez, Clara. *Latin Looks: Images of Latinas and Latinos in the U.S. Media*. Boulder, Colo.: Westview Press, 1997.

Rogan, Joe. "Carlos Mencia Is a Weak Minded Joke Thief." *Joe Rogan* (blog), 2005, accessed September 9, 2015. http://joerogan.net/blog/carlos-mencia-is-a-weak-minded-joke-thief.

———. "Joe Rogan vs. Carlos Mencia," YouTube video, 10:24, February 13, 2007, updated July 23, 2013. https://www.youtube.com/watch?v=gdugSUFbzws.

Romero, Guillermo. "Flag of the Federal Republic of Central America." Wikimedia Commons, March 31, 2006, last updated October 7, 2016. https://commons.wikimedia.org/wiki/File:Flag_of_the_Federal_Republic_of_Central_America.svg.

Romero, Matias. *Bosquejo histórico de la agregación a México de Chiapas y Soconusco*. Mexico: Imprenta del Gobierno en Palacio, 1877.

Roniger, Luis. *Transnational Politics in Central America*. Gainesville: University Press of Florida, 2011.

Roque Ramírez, Horacio N. "Claiming Queer Cultural Citizenship: Gay Latino (Im)migrant Acts in San Francsico." In *Queer Migrations: Sexuality, U.S. Citizenship, and Border Crossings*, edited by Eithne Luibhéid and Lionel Cantú, 161–188. Minneapolis: University of Minnesota Press, 2005.

———. "In Transnational Distance: Translocal Gay Immigrant Salvadoran Lives in Los Angeles." *Diálogo* 12 (2009): 6–12.

Said, Edward. *Orientalism*. New York: Random House, 1979.

Saldaña-Portillo, María Josefina. *Indian Given: Racial Geographies Across Mexico and the United States*. Durham: Duke University Press, 2016.

Salvadoran Power. "Vivian Painting Ex-consul de Honduras en Los Angeles, Plaza Morazán." YouTube video, April 20, 2013. https://www.youtube.com/watch?v=iH65pZAgwWo.

Sánchez, María Carla, and Linda Schlossberg, eds. *Passing: Identity and Interpretation in Sexuality, Race, and Religion*. New York: New York University Press, 2001.

Shankar, Lavina Dhingra, and Rajini Srikanth, eds. *A Part, Yet Apart: South Asians in Asian America*. Philadelphia: Temple University Press, 1998.

Shaw-Taylor, Yoku, and Steven A. Tuch, eds. *The Other African Americans: Contemporary African and Caribbean Immigrants in the United States*. Lanham, Md.: Rowman & Littlefield, 2007.

Shohat, Ella, and Robert Stam. *Unthinking Eurocentrism: Multiculturalism and the Media*. New York: Routledge, 1994.

Shorris, Earl. *Latinos: A Biography of the People*. New York: W. W. Norton, 1992.

Sieder, Rachel. "Review of Historia General de Centroamérica." *Latin American Studies* 26, no. 3 (1994): 761–763.

Solis, Gustavo. "Do Central American Migrants Have Legal Claim to Asylum?" *USA Today*, September 27, 2016. https://www.usatoday.com/story/news/2016/09/27/do-central-american-migrants-have-legal-claim-asylum/90519522/.

Sommer, Doris. *Foundational Fictions: The National Romances of Latin America*. Berkeley: University of California Press, 1991.

Sörlin, Sverker. "The Articulation of Territory: Landscape and the Constitution of Regional and National Identity." *Norwegian Journal of Geography* 53, no. 2–3 (1999): 103–112.

Soto, Marco. *Guerra Nacional de Centroamérica*. Guatemala: Editorial del Ministerio de Educación Pública, 1957.

Spivak, Gayatri Chakravorty. "Can the Subaltern Speak?" In *Colonial Discourse and Postcolonial Theory: A Reader*, edited by Patrick Williams and Laura Christman, 66–111. New York: Columbia University Press, 1994.

———. *Outside in the Teaching Machine*. New York: Routledge, 1993.

Stanfield, Michael Edward. *Of Beasts and Beauty: Gender, Race, and Identity in Colombia*. Austin: University of Texas Press, 2014.

Stavans, Ilan. *The Hispanic Condition: Reflections on Culture and Identity in America*. New York: Harper Collins, 1995.

Subero, Gustavo. "Muxeninity and the Institutionalization of a Third Gender Identity in Alejandra Islas's Muxes: Auténticas, Intrépidas, Buscadoras De Peligro." *Hispanic Research Journal* 14, no. 2 (2013): 175–193.

Táíwò, Olúfémi. "This Prison Called My Skin: On Being Black in America." In *Problematizing Blackness: Self-Ethnographies by Black Immigrants to the United States*, edited by Percy Hintzen and Jean Rahier, 35–52. New York: Routledge, 2003.

Tatum, Charles, ed. *Encyclopedia of Latino Culture*. Santa Barbara, Calif.: Greenwood, 2014.

Taylor, Analisa. *Indigeneity in the Mexican Cultural Imagination: Thresholds of Belonging*. Tucson: University of Arizona Press, 2009.

Terrazas, Aaron. "Central American Immigrants in the United States." Migrationpolicy.org. January 10, 2011. https://www.migrationpolicy.org/article/central-american-immigrants-united-states-0.

Thompson, Nicole Akoukou. "UNDP Report: Afro-Panamanians Suffer Discrimination at Every Level in Panama." Latin Post. December 19, 2013. http://www.latinpost.com/articles/4981/20131219/undp-report-afro-panamanians-discrimination-panama.html.

Tournament of Roses. "Sponsorship Opportunteis." Accessed March 5, 2018. https://www.tournamentofroses.com/sites/default/files/TOR_Sponsorship_Opportunities.pdf.

Tuan, Yi-Fu. *Space and Place: The Perspective of Experience*. Minneapolis: University of Minnesota Press, 1997.

Twinam, Ann. *Purchasing Whiteness: Pardos, Mulattos, and the Quest for Social Mobility in the Spanish Indies*. Palo Alto: Stanford University Press, 2015.

Uribe, Luis. "Inauguran en Los Ángeles la primera plaza Centroamericana de Estados Unidos." *Impacto Latino*, April 21, 2013. http://www.impactony.com/inauguran-en-los-angeles-la-primera-plaza-centroamericana-de-estados-unidos/#sthash.FBn10TSf.dpbs.

Valdivia, Angharad N. *Latina/os and the Media*. Cambridge: Polity Press, 2010.

Valentine, Gill. "(Re)Negotiating the Heterosexual Street: Lesbian Productions of Space." In *Bodyspace: Destabilizing Geographies of Gender and Sexuality*, edited by Nancy Duncan, 146–155. New York: Routledge, 1996.

Van Dyke, Harry Weston. *Before the Central American Court of Justice: The Republic of El Salvador against the Republic of Nicaragua: Opinion and Decision of the Court*. Washington, D.C.: Gibson Bros, 1917.

Viego, Antonio. *Dead Subjects: Toward a Politics of Loss in Latino Studies*. Durham: Duke University Press, 2007.

Vigil, Ariana. *War Echoes: Gender and Militarization in U.S. Latina/o Cultural Production*. New Brunswick: Rutgers University Press, 2014.

Vinson, Ben, and Matthew Restall. *Black Mexico Race and Society from Colonial to Modern times*. Albuquerque: University of New Mexico Press, 2009.

vom Hau, Matthias. "Nationalism and War Commemoration—a Latin American Exceptionalism?" *Nations and Nationalism* 19 (2013): 146–166.

Wald, Gayle. *Crossing the Line: Racial Passing in Twentieth-Century U.S. Literature and Culture*. Durham: Duke University Press, 2000.

Wald, Priscilla. *Constituting Americans: Cultural Anxiety and Narrative Form*. Durham: Duke University Press, 1995.

Wise, Robert, and Jerome Robbins, dirs. *West Side Story*. 1961; Mirisch Corporation.

Wolfe, Justin. "The Cruel Whip: Race and Place in Nineteenth-Century Nicaragua." In *Blacks and Blackness in Central America: Between Race and Place,* edited by Lowell Gudmundson and Justin Wolfe, 177–208. Durham: Duke University Press, 2010.

Woodward, Ralph Lee. *Central America: A Nation Divided*. 2nd ed. New York: Oxford University Press, 1985.

Yano, Christine R. *Crowning the Nice Girl*. Honolulu: University of Hawai'i Press, 2006.

INDEX

ABOUT THE AUTHOR

MARITZA E. CÁRDENAS is an assistant professor in the Department of English at the University of Arizona. She is affiliated with the Institute of LGBTQ Studies and the Program in Social Cultural Critical Theory.

Available Titles in the Latinidad:
Transnational Cultures in the United States Series

Cecilia M. Rivas, *Salvadoran Imaginaries: Mediated Identities and Cultures of Consumption*

Jayson Gonzales Sae-Saue, *Southwest Asia: The Transpacific Geographies of Chicana/o Literature*

Mario Jimenez Sifuentez, *Of Forest and Fields: Mexican Labor in the Pacific Northwest*

Maya Socolovsky, *Troubling Nationhood in U.S. Latina Literature: Explorations of Place and Belonging*

Susan Thananopavarn, *LatinAsian Cartographies*

Printed in the United States
By Bookmasters

Printed in the United States
By Bookmasters